Buying In

A Complete Guide
to Acquiring a Business
or Professional Practice

Lawrence W. Tuller

LIBERTY HALL
PRESS™

This publication is designed to provide accurate and authoritative information in regard to the subject matter covered. It is sold with the understanding that the publisher is not engaged in rendering legal, accounting or other professional service. If legal advice or other expert assistance is required, the services of a competent professional person should be sought.
—*from a declaration of principles jointly adopted by a committee of the American Bar Association and a committee of publishers.*

LIBERTY HALL PRESS books are published by LIBERTY HALL PRESS, an imprint of TAB BOOKS. Its trademark, consisting of the words "LIBERTY HALL PRESS" and the portrayal of Benjamin Franklin, is registered in the United States Patent and Trademark Office.

First Edition
First Printing

Library of Congress Cataloging-in-Publication Data

Tuller, Lawrence W.
Buying in : a complete guide to acquiring a business or
professional practice / by Lawrence W. Tuller.
p.   cm.
ISBN 0-8306-7061-0
1. Business enterprises—Purchasing. 2. Professions. I. Title.
HD1393.25.T83   1990
658.1'6—dc20   90-36725
                                                            CIP

TAB BOOKS offers software for sale.
For information and a catalog, please contact:

TAB Software Department
Blue Ridge Summit, PA 17294-0850

Questions regarding the content of this book
should be addressed to:

Reader Inquiry Branch
TAB BOOKS
Blue Ridge Summit, PA 17294-0214

Acquisitions Editor: David J. Conti
Book Editor: Shelly Chevalier
Production: Katherine G. Brown
Book Design: Jaclyn J. Boone
Cover Photography by Brent Blair, Harrisburg, PA

Contents

Dedication

THIS BOOK, WHICH STRESSES THE VALUE OF HUMAN CARING, DETERMINATION and faith, is dedicated with love to my dear departed mother, Marie. Without her love, determination and unyielding faith, I could not have mustered the courage to risk—the basic thesis upon which this book is based.

This book is also dedicated to the late C.S. Broadston, my mentor and dearest friend for many years, who taught me the values of honesty, integrity, and a moral code of ethics without which life has no meaning.

A special dedication and gratitude goes to my wife, Barbara, who never fully understood why this book had to be written nor why I have been driven to do so many things which seemed irrelevant at the time, yet stood by me with support and assistance when it appeared that all would be lost.

Acknowledgments

I BEGAN WRITING THIS BOOK AS AN ACCOUNT OF MY EXPERIENCES OVER THE past 30 years in the hope that one day it might be of some use in studying the pros and cons of entrepreneurship. Initially I had no thought of publication and intended to donate the work to a small business school. Judy White convinced me a wider audience of business managers, dreaming of becoming entrepreneurs, could be helped by having it published, and for this advice I am indebted.

Over fifty would-be and actual entrepreneurs have contributed material to this book taken from their own experiences. It would be impossible to acknowledge them all. Several people have offered invaluable help along the way, however, who should be recognized as being major contributors both to my knowledge and to the writing of this book. John Irwin and Roman Fedirka for their critiques of some of the technical sections; Ernest H. Perreault for teaching me the M&A game in the first place; Donald A. Bordlemay for basic training in forecasting and planning; my son Charles for giving me courage to continue when I was ready to quit; David J. Conti for editorial critique and assistance; and finally, my agent, Michael Snell, for his more than patient guidance and helpful suggestions, particularly when the book was in its infancy. Without Michael, this book would never have been published.

Introduction

ENTREPRENEURS FORM THE FOUNDATION OF OUR FREE ENTERPRISE SYSTEM. While daily newspapers recount the antics of Wall Street tycoons and greedy maneuvers conducted in corporate board rooms, millions of small business owners and professionals quietly support the pyramid of American business. Fortunately, the number of men and women forsaking the corporate umbrella for a chance to make it on their own has been increasing for the past 40 years. In addition, the number of people who, out of work and on the street as a result of corporate mergers, cost reductions, and bankruptcies, turn to self-employment rather than relying on another employer multiplies every year. No golden parachutes for these folks should they err in business judgment. No million dollar retirement programs for them to fall back on in middle age. No fat bank accounts built from million dollar salaries and fortuitous stock options to cushion their fall. They live or die by their own wits.

Some try to start a business or professional practice from scratch, and there are certainly advantages in doing so. A faster, and in many cases, easier way to get started, however, is to buy an existing business with customers, employees, products, and cash flow already in place.

The purpose of this book is to help those business and professional men and women who, for one reason or another, elect to follow the acquisition road to achieve their dream. The road is bumpy and full of potholes. Buying a business requires a huge amount of effort, time, and perseverance. Each milestone begets another—the next more hazardous than the last. Buying a business can also be very costly. It takes time and money to locate the right business, investigate it, arrange financing, and perform audits, appraisals, and legal work before a deal can ever close. This book provides a road map to make the journey as easy, rapid, and cost-effective as possible.

Previous books on this subject have tried to simplify the acquisition process by encouraging the would-be entrepreneur to follow a few mechanical rules and procedures that, presumably, will result in the achievement of his goals. But there is nothing simple about buying a business or a professional practice. Each case has different characteristics. Each financing package requires special arrangements to make it fly. Each negotiation results in special purchase terms and conditions. Acquiring a small business requires a different emphasis than larger companies—and buying a professional practice is different from both. Furthermore, valuation techniques, financing methods, and funding sources keep changing. New approaches to financing through equity sources such as investment banks, limited partnerships, and initial public debt and equity issues have sprung up in recent years. Changing tax laws encourage creative variations in structuring the buying entity. The list of new methods and procedures seems endless. There is no simple way to buy a business or professional practice.

This book is founded on the principle that success in buying a business is predicated on the ability of the entrepreneur to effectively utilize the human approach in every step along the way. It encourages the use of caring human relations not only in implementing current, state-of-the-art acquisition techniques, but also in utilizing proven methods for transition management after the deal closes, and in making subsequent acquisitions from an established business base.

Few business situations, if any, are so unique that someone hasn't already been there at least once. There's no sense reinventing the wheel if another entrepreneur has already wrestled with and resolved the issue. For this reason, the format of the book is fashioned around the experiences of more than 50 entrepreneurs who have traversed the acquisition trail. Of these, 28 are still in business; the others have either sold, filed bankruptcy, liquidated, died, or never closed their deals. Many of these men and women have been clients of mine. Others are friends and business associates. A few were clients of other management consultants in a consortium to which I belonged. Although real names have been used whenever appropriate, most have elected to retain their anonymity. In those cases, I have respected their wishes for confidentiality and privacy by using only first names, or none at all, and merely referring to them as clients.

These anecdotes and case studies illustrate proven methods for coping with each of the steps in buying a business or professional practice for the first time, handling transition management, and structuring a second or subsequent acquisition. Those who have followed these guidelines and practiced caring and compassionate human relations have succeeded. Many of those who didn't, failed.

Buying a business or professional practice covers a host of complex actions and evaluations. Focusing on the overall objective of making the best acquisition at the lowest price, the book segregates the process into six sections. The first four chapters identify preliminary procedures: clarifying major risks, evaluating economic conditions and timing, selecting the right type and size of business, structuring the buying entity, and investigating tax implications.

Chapters 5 through 13 point the way through the maze of acquisition steps from locating and valuing a target, to financing the deal, to the preparation of closing documents. Chapter 14 offers suggestions for the first day, week, and month of transition management after the deal closes. Though many techniques are common regardless of the size of the acquisition target, Chapter 15 delineates those specific variances applicable to buying a very small retail or service business.

Chapter 16, specifically focused on buying a professional practice either in its entirety or a partnership share, provides unique guidelines for lawyers, doctors, accountants, consultants, and other personal service professionals. Locating a practice, tax implications, valuations, financing, and succession partnerships are all explained in detail.

The final chapter offers recommendations and guidelines for those entrepreneurs already owning a company and ready to expand through additional acquisitions.

Over a lifetime of buying and selling companies for my own account and working as a consultant helping others achieve their dreams, I have developed the following 12 rules for making a successful acquisition. They won't guarantee success, but they're a good starting point.

1. Buy for the right reasons.
2. Buy only what you can afford.
3. Buy only in a market in which you have experience and understand.
4. Buy only when the timing is right.
5. Buy only with family support.
6. Choose a location compatible with family requirements.
7. Seek and listen to competent professional advice.
8. Practice caring and compassion at every turn.
9. Be honest and above board.
10. Plan tax strategy well in advance.
11. After the close, ask employees for help and advice—and then follow it.
12. Keep your eyes on the stars and your dream alive—regardless how tough the going may be.

Good luck in achieving your dream. Godspeed.

1

A New Beginning
Deciding to Buy

"Buying a business is like playing the casinos—you can make a fortune or lose your shirt."

BEING HIS OWN BOSS WAS A FANTASY JIM OFTEN PLAYED OUT. AS DIVISION SALES manager for a large paint manufacturer, Jim was sure he could make a lot more money by starting up his own business than by annual merit increases and an occasional incentive bonus. With a family of four kids, however, he couldn't bring himself to risk little or no income while starting a business from scratch. The answer was to buy one already operating with an existing cash flow.

Hal had just been given his walking papers. After 18 years of dedication to IBM, Big Blue had no further use for him. He was out of a job and frustrated. All those years of struggling to climb the corporate ladder were wasted. And he was now 58 years old—not an attractive commodity on the job market. But why not buy a business of his own? Nobody could fire him then. Hal figured he could run a business as well or better than most people. Besides, he had always dreamed of being his own boss. Every week the Wall Street Journal listed hundreds of "businesses for sale" ads. He'd just pick out an interesting one, write a letter, talk to his friendly banker, and be in his own business in no time—probably even make enough money to take that vacation in Europe this winter.

Jim was dissatisfied with his corporate life-style. Hal was on the street. Both were bitten by the acquisition bug. And both believed those articles and books they had read about "How to Buy a Business" with little or no money down, something called leveraged buyouts. What could be easier—buy a business with someone else's money and become independently wealthy.

Unfortunately, buying a business isn't that simple. If it was there would be far more buyers than sellers, rather than the other way around.

Literally thousands of people dream of owning their own business. Many actually try it—some fail. But most only dream. An employee's security blanket is too comfortable and the perceived risk of starting on his own too great to voluntarily make the jump. Some external event usually pushes a person into taking that first step toward entrepreneurship. Being laid off, missing a promotion, having a fight with the boss, or other conflagration often provides the stimulus to end the dreaming and take the plunge. Too often, however, a tidal wave of hazards swamps a person trying to buy a business without adequate preparation and tools to finish the job.

This books lays out in clearly defined terms the steps and sequences mandatory to fulfilling that lifelong dream of buying a business. It succinctly details a four-step program used by many others successfully completing the journey. It highlights both the secrets and mistakes they have made along the way. The program consists of four broad segments:

1. Defining major risks in taking the plunge.
2. Learning the basic elements involved in locating, valuing, negotiating, and financing the deal.
3. Hiring the right lawyers, accountants, and consultants.
4. Constructing a plan for the transition period after closing.

These segments are detailed in the following chapters to forge a path through the maze of steps and procedures for buying that first company—whether a corner video store, a $50 million manufacturer, or a professional practice—and define a workable plan for transition management after the close. The final chapter establishes guidelines for making the second or subsequent acquisition.

WHY BUY A BUSINESS

Before getting started, however, there are a few housekeeping matters to attend to. First and foremost is to clearly define why you want to buy a business. Without a precise definition it is too easy to go off on a tangent wasting time, effort, and money, and ending up with something you really don't want. What are you trying to accomplish? To make a million? To be your own boss? Provide retirement income? Build an estate? To provide a decent living for you and your family without worrying about getting fired? Or perhaps to experience some of that power and prestige other entrepreneurs enjoy?

These are all valid reasons. Nothing wrong with making a million or building a power base. Retirement income, security, freedom of choice are each achievable from buying a business—but they might not all come together. If you're trying to make a million, don't waste effort searching for a small retail or service business. However, if you're interested in steady income with minimal risk, one of these might be just the ticket. On the other hand, trying to build a retirement nest egg in five or six years probably points toward a larger manufacturing or distribution business with opportunities for substantial cash accumulation. An egotist should stay away from mundane businesses and go after one of the high-flyers, tempting speculative investment from Wall Street. Whatever your objective, try to define exactly what you want before spending a lot of time and money shotgunning the market.

The idea of buying a business seems almost magical, an illusion, especially for a person who has spent his entire career working for someone else. There's an indescribable excitement about having your own company. To be able to make your own decisions, call your own shots, succeed or fail on your abilities alone without interference from a boss or established corporate policy. For many, this will be the first time they have been totally responsible for everything—selling, producing, financing, human relations, engineering, planning, research and development. Quite naturally, this approaches the realm of fantasy. Something dreamed about for years but something you never thought could be accomplished. It's a feeling of unabashed enthusiasm. A sense of adventure. A chance to be someone, to make a contribution, to be self-sufficient. It's the epitome of the American dream.

The Down Side

There's also something frightening about being out there by yourself with nobody to lean on when things go wrong. No safety net. No large company with unlimited resources to pick up the slack in a recession. No stock options, retirement programs, or Golden Parachute to cash in if the company falters. No one from whom to get advice or to learn the tricks of the trade. No organization hierarchy to share responsibility with. No boss to pass the buck to. True, an operating business brings money and power, but it also demands sacrifice and involves obligations—financial and otherwise.

It's nervewracking being stuck out on a limb all by yourself knowing full well that a wrong step can mean catastrophic failure for both the business and yourself. When the cash gets tight and the banker won't increase your operating line. When customers clamor for better deliveries and lower prices and your marketing manager quits. When the EPA or OSHA inspector announces he'll close the place down if new pollution control equipment isn't installed this month—but there's no cash to buy it with. Or when the Union goes on strike demanding a

12% wage increase but the company is so highly leveraged, current payrolls are difficult to meet. When that friendly banker asks you to lunch only to drop the bombshell that they don't want your account anymore and you have 60 days to find a new bank to take over the revolving credit line.

Problems similar to these, and many more, will begin surfacing the day you take over your new company. And that's frightening—especially with personal guarantees warranting payment of huge amounts of debt.

I certainly don't mean to dissuade potential entrepreneurs from experiencing the euphoria of business ownership for the sake of a few problems. Having acquired and operated six companies myself, I know that no potential adversity can discourage anyone determined to take the plunge. Nevertheless, the severity of potential calamities facing a new entrepreneur dictates that you clearly assess your reason for buying the company in the first place—and that it is the right reason. Because on top of all the problems you certainly don't want to wake up one morning and ask, "Now why did I ever buy this company? What a dumb thing to do." If you do, the bankruptcy courts won't be far away. There's no need to bore you with all the grandiose reasons people have for buying a company. If you haven't already decided to do it, you wouldn't be reading this book. And if you have already decided, such a discussion is a waste of time. Just be certain to clearly define your own reason. Write it down and refer to it periodically when the going gets tough. Keep it for ready reference if you ever doubt your ability to succeed. And we all do—sooner or later.

There are also some very real personal hazards to venturing into uncharted waters and it might prove fruitful to explore at least some of the major ones—assuming there's still time to sound a note of caution. Three of the heaviest are:

1. The high level of personal commitment.
2. Personal financial risk.
3. Stress encountered during the acquisition process and for the first two years after the close.

One of the dangers present in all books describing methods or procedures for taking action is the tendency to be overly optimistic about the subject. While many topics carry little risk, buying a business for the wrong reasons, using inappropriate techniques, or being unaware of the difficulties and costs associated with the process can bring immeasurable psychological and financial harm to the first time buyer. For this reason, the promulgation of procedures and techniques included herein, without at least a minimum commentary on downside risks, would be irresponsible. Enumeration of the following hazards is not meant to frighten off a legitimate business buyer, but merely to point out that the acquisition process and subsequent entrepreneurial efforts are not beds of roses.

Personal Commitment. Three levels of personal commitment face the potential business buyer:

1. Commitment of time and energy.
2. Commitment from family.
3. Commitment of financial resources.

When trying to buy a business a person must be prepared to make a full commitment of his time, energy, and resources. Probably no other endeavor demands such total dedication. Be it large or small, manufacturing, services, retailing, or distribution, the time and energy required usually exceed all expectations. Everything else gets shunted aside in favor of working on the problem. Searching out the right target might literally take months of research, letter writing, phone calls, and meetings. Investigating accounting books and records through the due diligence process might require six, seven, or eight trips to the target's location. Negotiating a favorable deal with the seller usually involves several knock-down, drag-out, gut-wrenching sessions with lawyers, accountants, and the seller himself. Sourcing a financing package can be frustrating and demeaning. Just putting the business plan together very often takes weeks of bone-crunching labor and complex calculations. And the final negotiation of contract language usually occurs when all parties are bone-tired and bedraggled. It's about this time a buyer wishes he had never started the process.

Buying a business is a full time job. Those who try it while holding down another job nearly always fail. There can be no deterrents once started down the trail. No time off for that vacation in the mountains—you might miss an important phone call. No long weekends at the shore—you'll need to get ready for next week's onslaught. Long days and nights figuring, calculating, strategizing, arguing with yourself, or just thinking and hoping. There's little time now for even a part time job to provide much needed income to keep going. There just aren't enough hours in the day.

This level of personal commitment not only requires the potential buyer to be in excellent health and fully motivated but also places substantial demands on his spouse and family members. Missed dinners and school meetings, unweeded gardens and unmowed lawns, irritable and reclusive around the house, and generally unresponsive to family needs and desires are common maladies experienced more or less by everyone trying to buy a business. It takes strong family ties to weather this storm and without full family support, an acquisition bid generally fails.

Conversely, a loving spouse and understanding kids willing to sacrifice along with the dreamer, can, and most certainly will, tip the scales toward a successful acquisition. Clients, friends, and business associates have repeatedly admitted that without a full commitment from their spouses and families they could never have closed the deal. A cliche? Perhaps. Overstating the difficulties in making an acquisition? Maybe. Glamorizing the role of others in contributing to your success? It's possible. But hundreds of successful buyers vouch for the profundity of family support.

And even with active family support, relationships during the acquisition process inevitably become strained, as my friend Perry learned the hard way.

Martha was seriously considering divorce toward the end of Perry's acquisition search. He had been at it for over a year. The severance pay from Boeing Corp. had run out several months ago and their savings were being depleted at an alarming rate. When Perry told her another $20,000 would be needed for appraisal fees and a legal retainer, Martha blew her top. ''Not out of our savings! You've been trying to find a company for over a year with nothing to show for it. Our bank account is at rock bottom and I'm not going to squander the last $20,000 on your wild schemes! Go sell your car, or borrow from your mother, or find a partner. I don't care what you do, but you're not taking any more from our savings!''

Perry finally did close the deal and their marriage was saved. But it was nip and tuck for a while. He told me later that had he known how much the acquisition search was going to cost and what it would do to his marriage—not to mention how long it would take to find a company and close the deal—he never would have started. As it was, by the time he did close, Perry's blood pressure was way up, his nerves shot, and stress had all but done him in.

Nearly everyone starting down the acquisition trail underestimates the costs involved in locating, financing, and closing a deal. In the beginning, a person visualizes letterhead, telephone bills, and perhaps a few plane fares as the major expenses. Once making the decision to buy, most expect to close a deal in a matter of weeks—or perhaps a few months at the outside. But nothing could be further from the truth. The average time to make an acquisition of any size ranges from six to twelve months. There are exceptions, of course.

A friend or relative knows a business owner anxious to sell and willing to finance the deal himself. Or a local retail or service business advertised in the paper meets all your criteria and there's enough money in the bank to do the deal. Or perhaps your employer wishes to divest a division or plant and is willing to bankroll the sale for you. Sometimes an accounting, legal, or medical practice down the street comes up for sale and you have the inside track through a mutual acquaintance. But these are the exceptions. In most acquisitions, the search alone consumes three or four months. Putting together a financing package involves another nine to twelve weeks. And negotiations and due diligence seem to take forever.

During this period, not only must a person provide for his normal living expenses—food, mortgage payments, utilities, college bills, taxes, and so on—

he must also spend money on travel, telephone, office supplies, professional fees, appraisal costs, and other expenses of the acquisition process. For the average buyer, these expenditures can add up to a bundle. Twelve months' living expenses for the average family of four can easily total $30,000. Expenses and fees in making the acquisition often exceed $25,000—not including the buyer's equity contribution to the deal. Such a financial commitment is not easy to come by. Yet, before starting the acquisition process, the neophyte buyer should understand that buying a company is costly and planning for six to twelve months living expenses and acquisition costs of $20,000 to $40,000 is just prudent personal financial management.

In addition to personal commitments, the novitiate should fully comprehend and accept the financial risk of going into business for himself.

Financial Risk. If not willing to risk everything he owns, now and in the future, no one should attempt to buy a business. As the sayings go: "Don't play poker unless you can afford to lose your stake," and, "Don't invest in speculative stock issues unless you can afford to lose your investment." The same principle holds true in acquisitions: don't buy a business without recognizing the possibility of losing everything.

The use of debt—either as acquisition funding or to provide working capital—will probably require personal guarantees. This means that personal assets such as a home, car, and investments, as well as all business assets, will be pledged as loan collateral. Clearly, if the business fails, there's a real possibility of losing everything. Even in death, most personal guarantees pass to the estate: now a spouse, children, or other beneficiaries must settle the loans.

Financial risk is probably the single greatest disadvantage in buying a business. If unwilling or unable to risk everything, find some other way to earn a living. Don't buy a business. Thousands of businesses file bankruptcy each year and the number is growing. In the past three years alone, business bankruptcies have tripled, so the possibility of failure is very real.

Bankers, consultants, and yes, even authors, who advocate buying a business with extraordinarily high levels of borrowed money are doing the entrepreneur a disservice. Seldom do these advisors consider the risk to personal assets pledged to secure this debt. And even more infrequently, do these "experts" recognize and explain the agonizing, soul-wrenching experience inevitably befalling the entrepreneur if, and when, the business fails.

Chapters 11 and 12 deal with alternate ways of financing a business to reduce the financial burden of acquisition debt; however, even under the most favorable financing terms, the risk of financial loss remains very real.

Stress. In addition to total personal and family commitment and recognition of the financial risk in making an acquisition, a person's health must enter the equation. Money and power are great but without good health, is any of it worth the price?

Like failure, stress is an unpopular subject and often ignored by authorities in the business acquisition field. This is a shame, because hypertension, anxiety, and a variety of other maladies have been and continue to be directly attributable to entrepreneurial stress. Stressful situations occur time and again during the acquisition process and for the first two years after closing. If anything can go wrong, it will go wrong. It seems obvious that an individual easily flustered and upset by conflict, confrontation, and pressure should never undertake either an acquisition or a business start-up, no matter what the potential material benefits.

As a typical example of the type of stress engendered by high leverage buy-outs and what it can do to both the business and an individual's health, the following events occurred to three ex-executives of ITT who decided to become entrepreneurs. Although they managed the acquisition process without mishap, once they started running the company, all hell broke loose.

Morgan Lathrop and his two friends, Clayton and Larry, acquired a mid-sized manufacturing company. Together with several friends as passive investors, the group raised $1 million and leveraged the balance of the purchase price of $15 million with debt.

About three months after the close, the partners realized their new company was more than they had bargained for. The industry business cycle began a devastating drop and customer orders practically dried up. A Union petitioned for an election, won, and immediately demanded higher wages. With the spring rains came the first flood in the history of the town, and the entire first floor manufacturing area was under three feet of water.

With all these problems, the new entrepreneurs pleaded with their friendly banker for an addition to the working capital line. Seeing they were floundering, of course he refused. Bills mounted, orders continued to drop, and soon layoffs became a reality. Before the year ended the asset-based lender became nervous and started dictating operating policy. Additional debt service payments were missed and soon the banks threatened foreclosure.

Meanwhile, the new venture was taking its toll on the partners. Stress wreaked havoc with Larry's health. His doctor told him to take a six-month vacation or he would likely have a stroke—but of course that was impossible. Within a few months Larry entered the hospital. Clayton was no better off. His wife, hospitalized with malignant cancer, was given three months to live. This, coupled with pressures from the business, contributed to a mild heart attack and took Clayton out of action.

Morgan's health didn't go, but his emotions sure did. A near breakdown lead him to two, then three, then six-martini dinners. Then an additional three for lunch. It wasn't long before he was a confirmed alcoholic.

The following year the asset-based lender threatened foreclosure again if the group did not sell the company. Rather than selling, with Larry and Clayton incapacitated, Morgan took the company into Chapter XI bankruptcy to prevent foreclosure. Their shares were eventually sold for $1.00 and the entrepreneurial saga ended for all three.

The stress of getting caught in a deep recession soon after acquiring the company was bad enough, but it was the added pressures from the financial community—which almost always result from high leverage deals—that pushed the three partners over the edge.

The acquisition process and the first two years' operations are fraught with stressful situations. Because an acquisition takes so long and because one never really knows if the deal will close until it actually does, financial worries, exhaustion, financing problems, negotiating difficulties, and a myriad of other stressful activities create a pressure cooker for the buyer. After watching so many buyers suffer stress and anxiety, and going through it myself a few times, I came up with the following list of ten helpful hints to keep these pressures under control, not only through the acquisition process, but in managing the new company as well:

1. Don't take problems to bed with you. They'll still be there in the morning and your spouse is a much better campanion.

2. Don't try to do everything yourself. Hire professionals, ask help from friends, and rely on your family.

3. Don't be discouraged. The odds are against closing the first deal you look at.

4. Don't try to be Godlike. Only God can do that successfully.

5. Don't try to do more than you are financially capable of handling. Running out of money can kill even the best deal and the best company.

6. Don't attempt something that isn't doable. It's a lost cause before you begin.

7. Don't hitch your star to power addicts. Lawyers, accountants, consultants, bankers, partners, sellers, general managers, and department managers addicted to power will get you every time.

8. Don't forget your instincts. Intuitive judgment is usually reliable.

9. Don't ignore your conscience—listen to it. Learn to do and say those things which you know are right regardless of the opinions of others.

10. Don't be a dictator. Practice merciful management techniques with employees, customers, and suppliers as well as professional advisors and sellers along the acquisition trail.

So those are some of the risks of buying a company and becoming an entrepreneur. Why do so many people venture down the acquisition trail even though they recognize the deck may be stacked against them? Why do they risk the hardship and sacrifice when it's so much easier working for someone else? Because the American entrepreneurial dream promises excitement, challenge, and the opportunity for enormous financial and other rewards. Because the desire for power, money, and the freedom to run their own show outweigh all the risks. And because, in the end, the entrepreneurial spirit cannot be extinguished.

Entrepreneurs are a tough breed. They are risk takers, determined to meet their goals no matter what obstacles might be cast in their path. Every entrepreneur I have ever known, whether starting a business from scratch or buying a going business has been unequivocally creative and optimistic, mentally tough, and emotionally stable, with an overwhelming ambition to do things his way. And above all, he cares about other people. It's probably possible to make it in the highly competitive, risk oriented world of private business enterprise without one or more of these traits, but I have never seen it happen.

Now let's get moving along the acquisition trail.

GETTING STARTED

There are nine steps to any business acquisition, regardless of its size or industry:

1. The search—locating businesses available for sale.
2. Identifying alternative candidates.
3. Valuing the business.
4. Negotiating a price and terms.
5. Investigating the company.
6. Preparing the business plan.
7. Sourcing the financing.
8. Preparing the closing documents.
9. Managing the transition period.

These acquisition steps are not new. Successful entrepreneurs have proven them workable, over and over again. No procedural definitions will guarantee success, but adhering to these basic tenets will certainly reduce the likelihood of failure.

Whether the business happens to be a $50 million manufacturing company, a small retail or service establishment, or a professional practice, these same steps are followed. Some may be shortened under specific circumstances. You might already know of the company you want. Personal financial resources could be used to finance the deal. A professional partnership might already exist that you're buying into. The seller's financial records may be limited to tax returns.

Any number of conditions might arise to abbreviate one or more of the steps. Nevertheless, even when the detailed process is shortened, none of the steps can be overlooked. They must be followed for every acquisition and performed in the stated sequence. Any other route leads to chaos.

Chapters 5 through 14 examine each of these acquisition steps and point out tips and variations to improve the overall process. Specific differences and emphasis when buying a small retail or service business will be covered in Chapter 15 and unique variations in acquiring a professional practice are explored in Chapter 16. Even if you're specifically interested in one of these versions, I strongly suggest reading Chapters 5 through 14 for a full explanation of detailed steps.

For those already owning a business and considering a second acquisition, the final chapter elaborates on some special steps involved in this expansion process. But here again, conditions may have changed in the financial markets, valuation procedures, or search techniques since the first acquisition, and it certainly wouldn't hurt to review the full process.

PRELIMINARY CONSIDERATIONS

Before actually starting the acquisition process, however, there are several preliminary matters to be disposed of. Among the most important are:

- Evaluate economic timing factors.
- Consider alternate locations.
- Define most likely industries and markets.
- Structure the buying entity.
- Develop a tax strategy.

Most of us are not professional economists. We read with interest about fluctuations in the stock markets and government statistics showing trends in unemployment and inflation. A bit confused, we hear about leading and trailing indicators as a reflection of economic trends. Headlines flash across our morning newspapers proclaiming this or that bank has raised or lowered its prime rate. Politicians from right and left debate the niceties (or destructive nature) of the national debt and deficit spending. We hear about the steel industry, autos, semiconductors, or machine tools suffering economic repression because of foreign imports. Corporate and financial icons call for protectionist legislation and lower tax rates to save America from certain economic disaster. But what do all these statistics, opinions and prognostications have to do with the private business buyer? And how can he minimize their negative impacts and take advantage of favorable influences on his acquisition?

Though many would-be business buyers ignore the role economics plays in the success or failure of closing a deal at the best price and terms, smart buyers are fully cognizant of the importance of economic timing. As with any major business transaction, the current and anticipated state of the economy and the optimism or pessimism prevalent in the market place play a significant role in determining price, market acceptance, and payment conditions. A thorough understanding of the nuances of the interaction of economic and market forces on today's pricing and tomorrow's opportunities requires study in greater depth than possible in this book. All we can hope to accomplish here is an examination of some of the key elements to consider before embarking on an acquisition search.

Alternate Locations

The location of the target can also be a major determinate in both the financing of the deal and probable success in managing the business after closing. Competitive constrictions in small retail or service businesses dependent upon an immediate locale for customers preclude buying in an overbuilt area. Opportunities for growing a professional practice in a rural setting might overshadow advantages of a metropolis. A business requiring an available skilled labor supply would probably face difficulties if located in an area of low unemployment or suffering a dearth of technical or skilled labor.

A major concern for the buyer of a larger manufacturing or distribution business requiring capable and diverse management talent is the distance of the facility from his home. Can he commute comfortably? How much added expense must be included in the business plan for traveling to and from the location? Will his family relocate if the distance precludes commuting? Or will the new owner try to manage the business in absentia? And if so, what provisions and expenses need to be built into his financial projections and financing schemes to compensate for not being on the premises? Of equal importance, will the location attract qualified talent for the management team?

These and other questions should be examined and dealt with long before beginning the search process. There's no sense spending time, effort, and money on a target located in the wrong place.

The Right Market

The potential entrepreneur must also decide in what industry and market to search for his target. One of the greatest mistakes is to buy a company producing a product or providing a service about which you have little or no knowledge. Time and again, businesses fail, not because of undercapitalization—although financing remains a major cause of business failures—but because the new owner doesn't understand how to make or sell the product. Most people are wise enough not to buy a car if they can't drive. They won't purchase an airplane without a pilot's license. And they certainly wouldn't buy a bookkeeping practice without a thorough knowledge of debits and credits. Or would they? It's truly amazing how many eager business buyers plunge ahead with only the barest knowledge of a target's technology, production requirements or markets. Once the acquisition bug has bitten, it's difficult to hold back and wait for a target in an industry or market you know. Yet, by not doing so, the odds of failure escalate geometrically.

The Right Structure

The final preliminary steps—structuring the buying entity and developing a relevant tax strategy—take considerably more time and effort than the first three. Appraising economic timing, deciding on location criteria, and waiting for opportunities in a business you understand, are steps which can be taken by the individual alone without a great deal of research, consultation, or technical advice. But structuring and tax implications are different. They require time, effort, and in many cases the expenditure of money for competent professional advice.

In some instances, decisions for structuring a buying entity rest on tax strategy. Current tax regulations might very well determine whether you should incorporate or not, or whether it would be beneficial to form a partnership— either with family members or outsiders. A corporation certainly provides greater personal protection from legal liability than either a proprietorship or a partnership. On the other hand, without careful tax planning, double taxation can easily arise through the corporate form.

Anticipated financing requirements can also impact on structuring decisions. Banks look more favorably on loaning to a corporation than to an individual. Outside investors might require the corporate form or perhaps a limited partnership. Maybe you don't have enough personal equity to swing the right deal and decide to bring in one or more partners—either as working partners or through a limited partnership. If the deal dictates the use of a venture capitalist or investment banker, it might be better to form a partnership with the financier than to borrow the money. And some enterprising entrepreneurs find that multiple corporations building a hierarchy to a holding company bring the greatest advantage.

Structuring the buying entity is a complex and intricate undertaking. Yet, structuring decisions very often influence whether a deal can be financed or even if the deal will ever close. Obviously, most of us don't have the legal, tax and financing expertise to weigh all the consequences of alternative structures. Outside professional advisors, well versed in such matters, must be consulted. This requires money as well as time and effort to search out the right professional.

Taxes

In addition to impacting the structure of the buying entity, current and anticipated tax laws play a major role in negotiating and financing a deal, as well as influencing language in the closing documents. Deferred payments or cash at closing, interest versus dividends, capital gains or ordinary income, deductible expenses or personal expenditures, all exert major influences on how to structure a deal. The type of financing package, classification of acquisition costs, and negotiated contract clauses are all influenced by the tax code.

But even people who spend their entire careers working with the tax code and providing advice to clients can't keep up with the onslaught of new tax court decisions, IRS regulations, and Congressional revisions flowing from taxing bureaucracies. And if these professionals can't keep up, what chance does the average entrepreneur have for planning his own tax strategy? None.

Regardless of complexities and changes, without competent professional tax advice before and during the acquisition process, costly errors and omissions are inevitable. One of the first steps a potential buyer should take is to locate and retain a competent tax professional who will remain available for consultation throughout the entire process.

Timing, location, industry, structure, and taxes are all critical topics to investigate before starting out. Resolution of these issues will save an enormous amount of time and energy later on. There's nothing more frustrating than realizing half way through the acquisition process that the timing is all wrong, or you've structured a corporation when it should be a limited partnership, or you forgot to consider the tax consequences of future cash distributions. Slipping, sliding, and backtracking once started can be extremely costly. The cost of buying a business can bring even affluent entrepreneurs to their knees. To backtrack and do something over again for the second or third time can escalate the cost to stratospheric proportions.

The two biggest mistakes made by inexperienced buyers are ignoring the necessity for planning the steps of the process and then following that plan, and, underestimating the time it takes from start to finish. Time is money. When there's little or no income coming in, when your spouse begins to lose faith in your ability to close a deal, when cash outflow is more than expected, the temptation to try to cut corners is great.

Of the more than 50 entrepreneurs and would-be entrepreneurs contributing personal experiences to this book, not one has successfully closed an acquisition without first resolving the preliminary issues and then religiously adhering to the prescribed acquisition steps. Some have tried to shortcut the process—and failed. Some ignored competent professional advice—and failed. Some underbudgeted their acquisition costs or the time it takes to finish the process—and failed. And some realized part way through that the stress, commitment and risk were too much to bear—and failed.

The next three chapters examine ways to resolve the preliminary issues of timing, location, industry choice, structure, and tax implications. I urge you not to skip over these important areas. I also urge you not to begin the acquisition process without a full and clear understanding of the risks involved.

Although each acquisition deal is unique unto itself, there are common threads. Where someone else has encountered and resolved a specific problem, try his approach first. Don't re-invent the wheel if it isn't necessary.

2

Where to Start
Choosing the Right Time,
Place and Type of Business

"Timing is to business acquisitions what food is to good health."

"IF YOU DON'T PRACTICE THE RIGHT DIET, YOU MAY STILL LIVE, BUT YOU WON'T be healthy for very long. If you acquire a business at the wrong time, the business may survive, but it won't be very strong in the competitive market place."

I've been credited with this admonition more than once. In fact, my business friends are tired of my preaching about the timing principle; but I find it so crucial to a successful acquisition—or sale—and so often overlooked by both buyer and seller, that I keep warning the unwary.

Most authors as well as many business consultants tend to relegate timing to the bottom of the priority list. There seems to be a prevalent opinion among these expert advisors that an acquisition can be made at any time as long as the buyer is ready, willing, and able. I strongly disagree with this philosophy. The buyer is only one part of the acquisition equation. Other people and factors such as the seller, bankers, the industry, and conditions in the national and regional economies may not be ready for the buyer. If you attempt to make an acquisition at the wrong time you either will fail in your efforts or pay the consequences after the deal closes.

What do I mean by timing and why is it so important? There are three external factors which have a direct bearing on the growth, stagnation, or decline of an operating entity:

1. Macro economic conditions reflected in the stock market and in Government fiscal and monetary policies.
2. Industry business cycles and product maturation in the target candidate's market.
3. Banking regulations (or deregulation) and the bankers' perceived state of the economy in his region and/or in the target company's market.

Making an acquisition at the wrong time will inevitably result in destroying the health or hampering the growth of the business because:

- If the price paid for the business is too high relative to the company's capacity to earn profits, the cash paid to satisfy investor return—whether it be debt service or dividends—will strangle business growth.
- Earnings of a company acquired on the down side of the business cycle will be driven further down by competitive factors during the same period the buyer needs to demonstrate increasing profitability.

THE STOCK MARKET AND PUBLIC COMPANIES

Several years ago I performed an acquisition search in the water products industry. Examples of such products include valves, pipe fittings, filters, electronic measuring devices, monitoring instruments, drilling rigs, pumps, screens, transportation equipment, tanks, softeners, electronic flow control devices, packing materials, and so on. The search criteria specified a manufacturer or distributor of products with sales in the $10 million to $50 million range. Location was open—any part of the Western world was satisfactory.

My client could invest up to $1.5 million of his own equity and was willing to pay a fair, but not exorbitant price relative to historical earnings. Ideally, the target would have a commanding position in its market niches or unique products permitting my client to take the company public within four years—assuming the earnings record justified such a move.

It turned out that most of the candidates meeting this criteria were divisions or subsidiaries of listed corporations. This presented a peculiar problem because large public corporations tend to overprice divestitures and be inflexible in negotiating price and terms. Divisions or subsidiaries of public companies are generally valued by the parent in one of two ways:

1. At the same, or greater, multiple of earnings as the parent company.
2. At book value plus a premium for goodwill.

If the parent's stock trades for 20 times earnings and the operating unit plays a minor role in profit contribution, the parent will upgrade its value to that of the consolidated parent. After all, they argue, the division isn't producing greater profits because the parent diverts some of its resources to augment other operating units.

On the other hand, many public companies point to a subsidiary out-performing the parent and claim that if consolidated earnings bring a multiple of 20, then certainly the star of the group should be valued at more.

The second method—book value plus premium—is usually defended by, "if we can't get at least book value (so the corporation will not have to report a loss on the sale) then we won't sell." What corporate officials really mean is that if the unit were to sell at a loss, someone will be held accountable by the Board of Directors—and no one wants that responsibility. Therefore, the path of least resistance leads them to keep the operating unit, even if it drags down the earnings of the corporation as a whole.

I encountered both of these arguments during my search for the water products target. But my client was insistent that he wanted to acquire now, not when the stock market turned down in a few years; so, undaunted, I continued to search the ranks of public companies, even though the market controlled the price. The few unrelated private companies we looked at also insisted that since the big boys were selling at those ratios then they should be also.

Fortunately, my client finally realized that prevailing P/E ratios of 20 to 30 times earnings were just too high for a company with stable earnings in a mature market. The timing was all wrong. It became very clear that the bull market had driven prices up past a reasonable level and the only logical thing to do was wait for prices to retreat during the next downturn.

THE INDUSTRY CURVE

Industry economic cycles do not always coincide with stock market cycles. For many years, segments of the aerospace industry were on a seven year business cycle that only coincidentally might fit with sporadic stock market swings. Department of Defense budget allocations control the industry cycle and the national political climate establishes the level of Defense expenditures. In the late sixties and early seventies with a bull market on Wall Street, the aerospace industry floundered. In the later seventies, as the stock market first rose and then declined, the aerospace industry maintained a steady ascent buoyed by the introduction of new technologies and favorable support in Washington.

Segments of the water products industry—pumps, valves, pipe—also exhibit counter-cyclical movement. These products have been in a mature state for several years, with severe price competition from both domestic and foreign sources. Changing fortunes in the stock market have very little effect on companies producing these products.

The business cycle for agricultural products, specifically farm equipment, also moves independently of the stock market. The industry responds somewhat to changes in interest rates—the lower the rate the more attractive to buy heavy equipment with borrowed money—but government subsidy programs, worldwide weather conditions and Federal export policy have a greater effect. Foreign competition also impacts on several agriculture products. But the stock market? Very little effect over the past 30 years.

These examples illustrate that for many companies, the industry economic cycle reflects a far more relevant picture of economic health or disorder than the stock market. If the business cycle just begins an upward climb on its normal curve, chances are the target will have relatively poor profitability for the recent preceding years which in turn helps the buyer negotiate a fair price. Additionally, post closing operating results should be enhanced as the growth cycle accentuates, thus giving the new owner a better chance of succeeding. The worst possible case arises when buying a company at the peak of a business cycle. Abnormally high recent earnings records drive the price of an acquisition up, yet with a downturn on the horizon, a buyer can expect lower earnings after he closes.

The entrepreneur venturing forth on his first journey into the world of business acquisitions must spend enough time and effort up front learning as much about the economics of his chosen industry as he possibly can. If the pricing appears to be unreasonably high, withdraw immediately. National economic factors and industry cycles strongly influence the price of the company as well as the new owner's success in running the business after closing. To make a deal there must be a willing buyer and a willing seller. If the seller demands a price far out of line with his company's performance, or inconsistent with expected near term potential, the deal will never close. Skyrocketing prices recently affected the market for many small and mid-sized companies in basic capital goods and certain consumer industries. Buyers decided to wait it out for prices to reasonably approximate value, and many businesses remained unsold.

The bottom of the economic cycle foreshadows the best time to make an acquisition—immediately after the industry curve starts back up but before quarterly operating results indicate the bottom has been reached. If a buyer can pick a target and close the deal at this point in time he will pay the least price and have the highest probability of achieving success after the takeover. Don't be impatient. Learn the economics of your industry and watch the timing carefully.

A Checklist of Economic Factors

The following checklist ensures the inclusion of all relevant external and internal factors in weighing the timing of an acquisition. It's helpful to use this checklist when you first begin to think about buying a business. Economics are dynamic, however. Just because conditions seem favorable when you make your first survey don't assume they will stay that way. You'll need to update this checklist right up to the time you negotiate a deal.

CHECKLIST OF ECONOMIC FACTORS

National

- Current trend in the stock market.
- Average P/E ratios for similar companies.
- Current interest rates.
- Forecast of interest rates next year.
- Inflation rate—last year, this year, forecast for next year.
- National unemployment rate last year; forecast for this year.
- Local unemployment rate—last year, this year.
- Foreign exchange rates against free world currencies.
- Oil price per barrel—current, projected next year.
- National indicators:
  - Capital appropriations.
  - Inventory/sales ratios.
  - Housing starts/building permits—last year, this year, next year.
  - Other relevant indicators.

Industry

- Industry growth rate last three years.
- Industry growth rate forecast for next year.
- Major changes in industry technology.
- Business failures last year.
- Major changes in market position of competitors.
- Recent major acquisitions.

Company

- Sales and profits last three years.
- Sales forecast next three years.
- Debt to equity ratio last three years, this year.
- Major workforce additions/reductions anticipated next year.
- Inventory growth rate versus sales growth rate—last year.
- Capital expenditures last year, this year, next year.
- New product introductions last year, this year, next year.
- Changes in competitive position/market share last year, this year.

TIMING FROM THE BANKERS' PERSPECTIVE

Chapters 11 and 12 examine various methods of financing an acquisition and the effect different methods have on the operations of the business after closing. But before worrying about financing a deal, an understanding of the effect of timing from the perspective of the financial institution would be helpful.

The term "banker" as used in this book, refers both to the financial institution itself—banks, investment banks, finance companies, venture capital firms, and so on—and to the people representing these institutions.

A banker worries about two timing factors in his loan activities:

1. Factors influenced by current monetary policy of the Federal Reserve Board, such as interest rates, discount rates, and reserve requirements.

2. The current status of the bank's investment portfolio in mortgage loans, installment loans, asset based loans, or foreign loans.

Be aware that the composition of the portfolio in a given financial institution has a major impact on whether or not they will seriously consider your loan application, but there's nothing you can do about it so don't lose sleep: just prepare to make several simultaneous submissions.

You can't control Federal monetary policy either. But an understanding of the current trend in interest rates and discount factors, within which a bank must operate, and how this trend affects the receptivity of a given type of financial institution will be helpful in formulating alternative sourcing strategies when it's time to raise debt or equity capital. Clearly, with a plentiful supply of money, a commercial bank or finance company looks more favorably on a loan request—everything else being equal—than when funds are tight. If interest rates are declining a bank might very well look favorably on a fixed rate loan now. Conversely, if rates are rising, a bank will be less receptive to a long term loan with a fixed rate but might negotiate for a variable rate tied to prime.

A good friend was going down the acquisition trail eagerly trying to close a deal for a target in the industrial gas distribution industry. Barry identified the appropriate candidate and performed all the proper acquisition steps, until it came time to arrange for financing. It was very evident that he had negotiated a bargain price for a $12 million candidate with a good earnings record and plenty of assets for debt collateral. Barry's business plan was well constructed and there should have been no difficulty in locating a lender, but there was.

Barry contacted over 13 commercial banks and finance companies and although he was well received by several of them, could not bring the financing to conclusion. "What am I doing wrong?" he asked me one night.

"Nothing, as far as I can see," was my response. "I couldn't have done the job better myself, up to now. I am concerned about the outlook for interest rates, however. It seems that the downward trend we've been seeing for the past four months will continue, at least for a while yet."

"So how should that affect my ability to get financing? This is obviously a very good deal for a lender—the right price and terms, a growing industry, lots of collateral—why should they worry about long term interest rates? All I want is a seven year loan for $8 million. It's not that big a deal."

I suggested he ask one of the bankers with whom he had established a good rapport if they would be interested in a fixed rate now but tied to prime as rates turned upward. I also cautioned him not to accept an offer on that basis but to come back and talk to me about it.

The answer Barry received was predictable. The bank would love to make a deal with him on that basis and would have a Level of Interest letter in the mail tomorrow.

The timing was all wrong. From the bank's viewpoint, the only way they would lend long-term money under current monetary conditions was with a no-lose interest rate. From my friend's perspective, such an arrangement would put him at an extreme disadvantage if rates should ever hit high double digits (which they did). He decided to stall the seller and nine months later, when the financial markets stabilized, negotiated a more favorable financing arrangement and closed the deal.

Once again, timing was crucial to success.

The same conditions hold true for investment bankers and venture capitalists—although projected movements in the stock market and alternate investment opportunities affect willingness to invest more than do interest rates. These institutions look at long-term return on invested dollar either through asset appreciation, new stock issues or dividend distributions. When macro economic curves and industry business cycles both spiral upward, they eagerly look for equity deals offering a hefty return. On the other hand, in a downward cycle, they become much more choosy about investment criteria.

THE THIRTEEN STEPS

If the economics look about right, then it's time to move forward with the acquisition process. Although not foolproof, there is a logical path to follow through the acquisition labyrinth. Professionals in the mergers and acquisitions game work by a set of 13 basic steps which, if adhered to, minimize the possibility of failing.

An acquisition normally takes between six and twelve months to close. During that period there will be expenditures for legal fees, accounting fees, appraisals, travel, financing fees, and telephone expense. It's not unusual to invest $30,000 or more in an acquisition search for a mid-sized company without any firm assurance that the deal will close. By knowing precisely what steps to take in the proper sequence and working against a predetermined budget, this time and money can be more productively utilized. The same steps hold true whether you're buying a small retail business or a mid-sized manufacturing or distribution company. The following 13 steps will help to locate a target and close the deal in the shortest possible time—and when buying a company, time is money.

1. Define realistic parameters.
2. Prepare a reasonable Acquisition Plan.
3. Review current tax laws for structuring the deal.
4. Develop a detailed plan for sourcing potential targets.
5. Perform a preliminary due diligence investigation.
6. Negotiate price and terms based on a realistic valuation.
7. Perform a thorough due diligence investigation.
8. Prepare a complete business plan.
9. Develop sources for at least three alternative financing structures.
10. Arrange for the final updated due diligence investigation.
11. Write the Buy/Sell Agreement and negotiate the final contract language.
12. Plan how you will operate the company after closing.
13. Attend the closing.

Long-term entrepreneurial goals of creating a power base, making money, and achieving freedom of action are valid objectives and certainly worth striving for. The trick is to achieve these objectives within your own capabilities and resources. Specific parameters delineating these limitations must be clearly established before the target search can begin.

HOW MUCH INCOME DO YOU NEED?

One of the most obvious questions, and yet the one seldom asked until near completion of the acquisition process is, "How much income do I need to survive for at least a few years?" Do you really need $100,000 a year or can you get by with $30,000? If you need $100,000, then don't look at smaller companies which can only yield $30,000. You'll only waste your time as well as that of many others. Conversely, if you can get by on $30,000 it makes no sense to go after a bigger target that might yield $100,000. The bigger the target, the greater the financial risk, and why take on more risk than absolutely necessary? You might want more than $30,000 eventually, and with the right company, increased growth and profitability should be achievable. But don't get greedy in the beginning. Remember, the bigger the deal, the bigger the risk. So figure out what that minimum number really is. It determines how big the acquisition must be, whether it must be profitable now or in a turnaround situation, and how much debt service you can afford.

Try completing the following form to determine what your financial needs really are.

PERSONAL STATEMENT OF LIVING INCOME AND EXPENSES

Prepared_____   Updated_____

Annual Income
    Dividends   _____
    Interest   _____
    Annuities   _____
    Rent   _____
    Company pension   _____
    Government pension   _____
    Alimony   _____
    Income from spouse   _____
    Other regular income (list)   _____

       Total Annual Income   _____

Annual Expenses
Household:
    Heating oil, Gas   _____
    Electricity   _____
    Water   _____
    Telephone   _____
    Mortgage payment or rent _____
    Real estate taxes   _____
    Repairs and maintenance   _____
    Redecorating   _____

Insurance:
    House   _____
    Auto   _____
    Life   _____
    Health   _____
    Other   _____

Auto:
    Gas and oil   _____
    Repairs and maintenance   _____
    Tires   _____

Dues and subscriptions   _____

Clothes:
    Yourself   _____
    Spouse   _____
    Children _____
Medical, including eye glasses _____
Dental _____
Contributions and gifts, total _____
Legal and accounting fees _____
Travel expenses for vacations/trips _____
Entertainment _____
College and other educational expenses _____
Alimony _____
Other expenses (list) _____

                                               _____

    Total Annual Expenses _____

Excess Expenses Over Income _____

Obviously, the excess of expenses over income must be the salary from your new company. If your expenses vary quite a bit month to month, try laying this form out on a fourteen-column spreadsheet and budget both income and expenses each month.

Ernie, an IBMer for 10 years, worked as a department manager at an assembly facility in Florida. Disillusioned with promises made but not kept by Big Blue, and seemingly stuck in his $65,000 a year job, he bit the bullet. Leaving the company, he purchased a small engineering testing lab in Virginia. With little capital, Ernie leveraged the deal to the hilt. He wasn't about to take a cut from his salary at IBM. He convinced the asset-based lender that he could double the lab's volume over the next two years and that this would easily support a $65,000 draw.

It became clear in short order that this growth just wasn't going to happen. A born optimist, Ernie refused to recognize his limitations and continued to draw his salary. Because the company was generating profits of only $32,000, Ernie used borrowed money to pay himself. It took about two years of milking the company before he ran out of operating cash. Still refusing to take a cut in salary, Ernie took the company into a Chapter XI bankruptcy, at which time the finance company forced him to reduce his salary to $10,000.

So don't get greedy. Use the above forms to establish the rock bottom minimum you can live on and then go after a target to support that criteria.

Do You Want a Partner?

Income requirements also influence the decision about bringing in a partner or two. Do you want to go it alone or would you be more comfortable operating a business with partners? Will the acquisition be a one-family business, a two-family business or more? Do you have enough equity yourself to make a deal? If electing the partnership route, should they be active partners or passive investors? There are some definite advantages to having partners:

- Additional equity funding would lower the debt load.
- Continuity of the business is ensured in the event of illness, disability, or death.
- Varied backgrounds provide a much broader and sounder management base.
- It's always better to review important decisions with someone who has a stake in the business.

But be sure the business is big enough to support these other equity owners. That's what I mean by a one-family, two-family or three-family business. With one partner the business must be a two family business—with enough income to support two families; two partners require enough income for three families and so on. Chapter 3 examines unique ways of structuring deals with one or more partners.

The biggest risk in having partners centers around decision making. Unless you are the majority equity holder—which most active partners won't agree to—resolving differences of opinion about how to solve a problem or make a decision will be a continuous headache. It's hard enough to make a successful acquisition on your own; the difficulty doubles when criteria must meet goals of two or more owners. Additionally, after the deal closes, trying to run the business with more than one boss can be a nightmare. Chapter 14 illustrates this problem of "two bosses—no decisions" and how it reduces the probability of running a business effectively. Nevertheless, partnerships are popular and there are ways around decision-making standoffs.

Where Should the Business be Located?

What about location? Unfortunately, a target matching your capabilities and resources might not be in your home town. Auto parts manufacturers are difficult to locate in mid-town Manhattan and publishers in Key West are rare. Or perhaps there are so many video stores in the neighborhood that none are making money: you certainly wouldn't want to get into that kind of competition. On the other hand there might be very real reasons to insist the business be in close proximity to your home:

- Relocation is out of the question because your spouse has a career she won't leave, or the kids don't want to change schools, or you like your house so much you wouldn't leave for anything.
- Long-distance commuting won't work because you don't like to fly, or it's too expensive, or you don't want to be away from home.
- Perhaps you are physically handicapped and it's difficult to get around.

Any number of reasons might preclude the possibility of buying a company any place other than in the immediate locale. With this limitation, don't bother looking at targets in some other location. You'll just waste a lot of time and money. And by limiting location criteria, the sourcing task actually becomes easier:

- You eliminate a great many variables.
- You reduce your search data base.
- You might even redirect your choice of industry.

If a location close to home is not of primary importance, then you must decide whether to move to a new location or operate the company with absentee management—which involves a fair amount of commuting. Some companies can be effectively managed by absentee management—but not many. To do so requires an effective, honest management team capable of operating with little supervision, a profitable company, and a good financial reporting system.

An exceptionally strong management team must be in place to make absentee management work. They must be able to operate as a homogeneous unit without an in-place leader and with no weak link in the team. The production manager must be able to handle all the daily crises of running a shop. The marketing manager must have an excellent rapport with all customers to solve their pricing, delivery, and quality problems. The financial manager must be exemplary in his management of cash and other assets. The personnel director must be respected by all employees and willing and able to make decisions involving human relations problems. The engineering manager must be creative, a leader in new product development, and able to resolve application engineering problems. And above all, the entire management team must be trustworthy and honest. That's a tall order for a group who are strangers when you first take over.

Additionally, the company must be profitable and able to sustain this profitability without major personnel or operating changes after closing. It's extremely difficult, if not impossible, to implement significant operating changes such as revisions to systems, recruiting management personnel, major cost cutting moves, or changes in pricing procedures, in absentia.

An absentee manager must also have an effective system of operating and financial reports. How else will you know what's going on? Many of these reports should be issued daily, such as orders received, delivery promises kept, cash collections and expenditures, and this necessitates some type of electronic information transfer—perhaps computer telecommunications or facsimile transfer.

Finally, but most important of all, the banker handling the financing must be in agreement that you can manage the company in absentia. It's because of a buyer's management capabilities that a banker is willing to loan the money in the first place. If your absence from the premises on a daily basis makes him uncomfortable, then don't plan on absentee ownership. In countless cases entrepreneurs have tried to manage a remote location without banker concurrence and have failed miserably.

So choosing the right location becomes a crucial decision. It must be weighed not only in light of what you want, but also in terms of the practicalities of operating the company after closing, and from the viewpoint of the banker—however irrational he may seem. If you buy a company beyond commuting distance, plan to relocate as soon after closing as possible: don't try absentee management.

What Markets Do You Know?

Dale, a young attorney, stopped in one day grinning like the Cheshire Cat. "What's up?" I questioned.

"Last week I heard about this terrific little company for sale in Miami. They make sporting equipment like fishing poles, tennis rackets, and so on. Cash flow looks great, the price is right, and I've always wanted to live in Florida. Will you take a look at the projections for me?"

"Sure, Dale. But what do you know about manufacturing—and sporting goods at that?"

"Don't know anything, but if I could get through law school I can sure as hell learn the sporting goods business!"

"But why?" I was aghast that this promising young lawyer, with an outstanding future ahead of him in the legal profession, was actually considering throwing it all away on something he knew nothing about.

Against my advice he closed the deal and moved to Miami. About two years later I ran into Dale one Saturday afternoon at a Penn football game. "How's the fishing rod business?" I queried.

"Not good." Dale looked morose. He related that it was far more complicated than he ever imagined. He had made the deal with 95 percent leverage financing but could never increase the volume fast enough to meet the debt payments. "Two months ago I filed bankruptcy under Chapter VII, the company has now been liquidated, and I'm trying to find a job here in Philadelphia. Know anyone looking for a good lawyer but a lousy businessman?"

Even though the deal seemed like a great idea at the time and matched his goals fairly well, Dale missed a crucial point: he tried to step into a business he knew nothing about—without adequate training or education. This cannot be done. So many would-be entrepreneurs buying their first company make the decision based on what they see as available—not on what they know how to do. Invariably this leads to disaster. So don't, under any circumstance, incur the substantial risk of doing something you know nothing about. This would be as silly as me trying to repair car engines—I can't even change a spark plug.

How Much Can You Afford?

These parameters are all important: How much income do you need? Should you go it alone or bring in a partner? What location makes the most sense? What businesses do you know something about? But the most important question of all is: How much of your own money can you afford to put up as equity in a deal? The other goals may be just a wish list if the acquisition strategy evolving from them does not match your financial capabilities. In determining how much you can afford to put into a business, bear in mind that a financial institution making a long-term loan will expect you to be fully committed financially and any personal assets will probably be pledged to the bank to secure the loan.

The following format of a personal financial statement offers some guidelines for calculating how much you already own and therefore how much equity you can raise.

PERSONAL STATEMENT OF FINANCIAL CONDITION

Prepared (date)_____   Updated_____

Cash in bank: Amount

    List bank account numbers   _____
                                 _____
                                 _____
                                 _____
                                 _____

Stocks, Bonds, Investment Funds
    (including stock options)
    Broker Company   # of shares   Value Last Statement
                                   _____
                                   _____
                                   _____
                                   _____
                                   _____

IRAs, Company Pension, Trusts
   Custodian   Value Last Statement
                                                          _____
                                                          _____
                                                          _____
                                                          _____
                                                          _____

Life insurance and annuities
   Company   Face Value   Cash Value Last Statement
                                                          _____
                                                          _____
                                                          _____
                                                          _____
                                                          _____

Personal Assets Which Can Be Converted to Cash: Current Market Value
   House   _____
   Second/third cars   _____
   Household items not needed (furniture,
      lawn equipment, office equipment, etc.)   _____
   Jewelry   _____
   Antiques   _____
   Collections (stamps, coins, etc.)   _____
   Boat/airplane   _____
   Motorcycle   _____
   Other assets not included above (list)   _____

Other Investment Assets with Market Value: Current Market Value
   Vacation home   _____
   Land   _____
   Trusts   _____
   Rental property   _____
   Other assets   _____

      Total Cash Value of Assets   _____

Debts Which Must Be Paid: Current Balance
   House mortgage   _____
   Life insurance loans   _____
   Loans from credit union   _____
   Loans from banks (list)   _____

                                                          _____
                                                          _____
   All credit card balances   _____

Other debts   _____
    Total Debts Which Must Be Paid   _____

Equity, or Net Worth
    (Subtract total Debts from total Assets)   _____

The more equity contribution, the larger the target can be, and the easier it is to raise debt capital (more on this in Chapter 11). A good rule of thumb in the current financial markets is a ratio of at least 25%. This means for every dollar of equity, a financial institution should be willing to put in three. If the acquisition price is $100,000, a buyer should put up $25,000 of his own money; at a $1,000,000 price, he should be willing to put up $250,000.

Although there have been a number of acquisitions made over the past 10 years using all or nearly all borrowed funds, many of these highly leveraged deals have failed because the cash flow was not sufficient to support debt service. Even if failure is not imminent, the amount of error allowed in a high leverage deal is so small that the risk becomes exorbitant. Stress and anxiety engendered by such a large risk can, in and of themselves, cause an entrepreneur to fail. Many a stroke or heart attack has stopped an otherwise successful business and I cannot in good conscience recommend a highly leveraged acquisition. And why make the bankers rich while you suffer?

Therefore, determine the maximum amount of equity and go after a target with a price not in excess of four times this amount. With $50,000 to invest, you will be far better off—and probably make a lot more money—making an acquisition for $200,000 than leveraging up and buying a company for $1,000,000.

If you are still determined to join the ranks of entrepreneurs, and assuming the timing looks right, the next step is to begin the planning process. First, an outline of the activities to follow in the acquisition process to show how much each step will cost and how long it should take. This is called the Acquisition Plan.

But before getting into the preparation of the formal Acquisition Plan, let's take a look in the next chapter at some of the advantages and pitfalls of buying a company with partners—either individuals or an investment group.

3

Too Big for One
Partners and Investor Groups

"The more the merrier. There's safety in numbers."

"I'VE JUST LOCATED THE BEST DEAL OF THE CENTURY. IT'S DOING ABOUT $20 million in sales and throwing off over $250,000 a year in cash after taxes. And best of all, it's right down the street from where I live. There's only one problem: the real estate is leased and there are hardly any hard assets in a computer repair business so I can't figure out how to finance the deal. Any ideas?"

"Probably the best way is to find a partner or partners to kick in some equity. Do you know anybody who might be interested in going in with you?" I asked Josh.

"No! That's the problem. None of my friends have that kind of money."

Josh was serious about this so I put on my thinking cap, made some phone calls and within a few weeks we put together a group of five equity investors, one of which wanted to participate in the management of the company—much to Josh's delight.

PROS AND CONS OF ACQUISITION PARTNERSHIPS

Although most small retail or service businesses are acquired by individuals, the bigger the company, or the more complex the financing, the more beneficial it is to form a partnership or an investor group to make the purchase. The most obvious reasons for going this way are:

- Raise additional equity.
- Cross-fertilization of backgrounds.
- Easier to raise outside financing.
- Succession is not a problem.
- Share the risk of failure.

Most acquisition partnerships are formed to raise additional equity capital. As long as you're interested in buying a service station, or fast food franchise, or hardware store, or other small retail businesses, you can usually do it on your own. And of course, professional practices are nearly always acquired by individuals. Some buyer might have $1 million or more of savings to invest in a deal, but few individuals have much more than $25,000 to $100,000. That's why small retail or service businesses are the most popular size of businesses to buy. Acquisitions requiring more than $50,000 in equity contributions are normally acquired by groups of two or more entrepreneurs.

Varied backgrounds can also be beneficial both during the acquisition process and later on in running the company. If a buyer with expertise in marketing buys a manufacturing company, partners with production and engineering experience can be invaluable. If the objective is to bring the company public in a few years, a partner with financial experience can be most helpful. If you have a legal background, partners with almost any hard core business experience should be welcome.

For some obvious reasons, and some not so obvious, financial institutions prefer to finance acquisitions made by a group of partners rather than an individual. With three active partners the bank has three times the amount of personal assets to secure personal guarantees. If one of the partners turns out to be a poor manager, the others can carry him through. If one should die or become disabled, the bank's investment remains secure through automatic succession provisions made in the Partnership Agreement. And psychologically, a bank finds security in numbers. Most bankers believe the risk of default is substantially higher with one person as the business owner than with a group of managers. This is another reason why management buyouts are so popular with financial institutions as a vehicle for selling a company, as pointed out in my companion book, *Getting Out: A Step-by-Step Guide to Selling a Business or Professional Practice*, (Liberty No. 30063).

So multiple ownership makes sense in larger acquisitions both for acquiring the company and in operating it after the takeover. But there are some strong disadvantages as well that create higher risks and less freedom for the individual entrepreneur:

- The more people, the more difficult to make decisions.
- Disagreements about acquisition or operating criteria.
- Personality clashes.
- Political in-fighting might develop.
- Predetermined payoffs through dividends or distributions can fracture the company's cash flow.
- Sharing the profits means less for you.
- Liquidating partners' shares can be a problem.

We all know how difficult it is to reach any kind of decision in a group. Committees are fine as a vehicle for debate, and many times such debate can clear the air of misgivings and erroneous opinions. Committees can be extremely helpful in ascertaining compromises for unpopular or complex issues. But seldom, if ever, can a committee make a definitive decision and then implement such action. This must be done by individuals. Yet, a partnership of two or more investors becomes a committee and multiple ownership demands that the active partners, at least, act together as a homogeneous unit to make and implement decisions.

Disagreements, personality clashes, and eventually, group politics will inevitably be present in any partnership. These conditions further complicate the decision-making process. That's why a partnership with equal ownership shares rarely works in practice. In theory it sounds magnanimous to share and share alike, but when it comes to actually running a company, equal authority among partners spells defeat. So if you form a partnership, be sure that one person, preferably yourself, either has a larger share of equity than anyone else, or is designated the boss of the group. This designation should be in contractual form so there won't be any misunderstanding later on when conflicts arise.

When a partnership consists of both active and passive partners, the latter usually get predetermined annual dividends or other cash distributions in return for their equity investment. Except in cash-cow acquisitions, such fixed cash distributions can cripple the business—particularly in the first few years of ownership. More than one newly acquired company has faltered because investors have demanded their cash returns regardless of company performance.

The most obvious drawback to any partnership arrangement is that with more than one finger in the pot, less cash will be available for you. If the business is large enough—and that's why it's crucial to structure the number of partners and their cash payouts on the size of the business—there should be sufficient income for everyone. But if it's really a one-family business and you acquire it through a partnership, somebody, and that means you, will be shortchanged.

Finally, raising cash to liquidate a partner's interest can be a huge problem. As will be seen a little later, the Partnership Agreement must have provisions for buying out a partner's share should he die, become disabled, or just want to get out. This usually means a huge outlay of cash and if the timing is wrong it can cripple the company just as easily as predetermined distributions to passive investors.

So multiple ownership is not for everyone. A true entrepreneur can find acquiescing to his partner's or partners' wishes onerous and not much better than being an employee. The individualism characteristic of most entrepreneurs makes it a risky alternative over the long term. Two or more people can be great friends as long as they don't do business together, but too often the old maxim, "never mix business and pleasure" holds true, and a partnership becomes a disaster. If it appears that some form of partnership might be for you, however, following ten rules of partnership will help to avoid many of the pitfalls encountered by others trying this route.

1. Price—Agree to a fixed price in the beginning for each partnership share. If there are only two or three partners and you don't intend to bring anyone else in later on, this is an easy step—the price of each partner's share equals the amount of his contribution. If you do plan to admit additional partners later on, however, a fixed price for their shares should be established in the beginning and reviewed every year for changes in the value of the business.

2. Share—Determine what percentage of the assets and what percentage of the profits and losses each partner shall have. They may or may not be the same and the shares may or may not be proportionate to cash contributions.

3. Terms—Determine specific terms of distribution for profits—cash or otherwise—and when such distributions will be made.

4. Cash Contribution—Except in rare cases, each partner should be required to make his cash contribution in the beginning. Promises to pay in the future won't do much good when financing the deal.

5. Escape Clause—Leave the door open for any partner to back out if he becomes dissatisfied with the arrangement. If he backs out before the first deal closes, he should forfeit at least half his investment. After the takeover, the value of a partner's share for purposes of getting out can be established by a qualified and previously named independent business appraiser, or it can be fixed in the Partnership Agreement.

6. Early Buyout—Have a buyout clause in the agreement to ensure that the remaining partners will buy the share of any partner who dies or becomes disabled. An estate buyout can be funded with "key man" life insurance. Disability presents a different problem.

7. Background—Choose partners with diverse backgrounds. You'll need all the variety of experience you can get when it comes time to run a new company.

8. Honesty—If you don't know him personally, check character references—bank, neighbors, prior employers, school, family, church, and so on. Any blemish on his honesty disqualifies him.

9. Financial Integrity—If you don't know him personally, check credit references, personal financial statements, police records—even tax returns if you have suspicions. Look for bankruptcy history.

10. Authority—Right in the beginning, establish written descriptions of the responsibilities and authority of each partner.

One word of caution. A multiple partner group by necessity requires written agreements covering every phase of the partnership. With only two people the tendency is to do things informally. Don't succumb to this temptation. When two people, usually long-term friends, decide to join forces to make an acquisition they almost always ignore the importance of written agreements. They trust each other to do what's best for both. Nothing will change once they make the acquisition. They will remain good friends forever. Baloney. There is a 100 percent probability that someplace along the line they will disagree vehemently, and without a contractual agreement to use in mediation, fast friends can easily become bitter enemies.

Bob and Mike were long-term friends and business associates. For over 10 years they had worked together and socialized with their families. They combined forces to make an acquisition with each owning 50 percent. No contractual partnership agreement was ever drafted because they felt it unnecessary and a waste of time and money. Plus they really didn't want to think of the possibility of anything ever going wrong with the business or with their relationship.

Two years after their first acquisition, Bob and Mike were at each other's throats. Though risky, Bob wanted to expand the business. Mike being more conservative, wanted to cut back to something they could afford. Finally Mike wanted out of the deal and Bob said no, he needed Mike's financial expertise. Quarreling became commonplace and soon the effect on the business became severe. So severe, in fact, that the partners drove their company into the bankruptcy courts.

If Bob and Mike had foreseen the trouble they would have agreeing on crucial operating issues, they certainly would have drawn a definitive partnership agreement in the beginning. But neither did—and now they are out of business.

WHEN MULTIPLE OWNERSHIP MAKES SENSE

Although there are no hard and fast rules in the acquisition game specifying when multiple ownership is preferable to buying on your own, the following guidelines generally hold in practice. Though they are not sacrosanct and exceptions always arise, these guidelines form a cauldron of conditions which most entrepreneurs have found accurately reflect the need for acquisition partnerships. It's important to remember, however, that the type of business you go after can have a significant influence on any one of these criteria.

GUIDELINES FOR MULTIPLE OWNERSHIP

- If the annual sales exceed $5 million.
- If the company is engaged in manufacturing or distribution.
- If there are more than 50 employees.
- If the purchase price exceeds $1 million.
- If you are required to put in more than 75 percent of your savings and liquid investments as equity to meet the financing requirements.
- If you must run the business as an absentee owner.
- If there are critical technical parts of the business in which you have no background and are unlikely or unable to learn quickly.
- If you intend to buy more than one operating company.

There are a host of different ways to structure a buying group, ranging from two individuals on one end of the spectrum to complicated multiple investor limited partnerships on the other. The number of people involved and the complexity of the structure is largely determined by the size of the deal. Though it's not practical to examine all possible combinations, let's take a look at three of the most popular partnerships:

1. A small group of individuals.
2. An investor group and an investment banker.
3. A limited partnership.

A Partnership

A partnership is a very simple legal form of doing business. All you need, in addition to a partner, is a Partnership Agreement spelling out the rights and responsibilities of each partner, procedures for distributing profits, cash, and other assets of the business, and a mechanism to dissolve the partnership. Because of potential legal liability problems, however, most acquisitions are not made through a straight partnership anymore. Instead, a close corporation is formed with the partners as shareholders. A close corporation means that stock will not be issued to the public nor traded on the open market and, depending on the state of incorporation, the number of shareholders might be limited.

This book is not intended as a definitive legal work, nor am I a lawyer, however, over the years, I have formed several partnerships for myself as well as for clients and have always used the close corporation as the medium. I find it convenient and inexpensive. Not only does the corporate form provide some shelter from personal liability, it also makes agreements between the partners a lot cleaner. A cumbersome Partnership Agreement can be reduced to several easy-to-understand, one- or two-page contracts, each covering a specific point between the partners. As the business grows and more partners are added, it is a simple procedure to issue new shares of stock and write additional side agreements. Occasionally, depending on the current mood of Congress, there are even some potential tax savings by using the corporate form (more on taxes in the next chapter).

To Incorporate or Not. A corporation is a legal entity. It has its own life and can take actions separate from its shareholders. It can sue and be sued, pay taxes, declare bankruptcy, and live forever, with or without the owner(s). Many times it's easier to do something as a corporation than as a group of individuals. For example it's much easier to set up benefit programs—retirement and profit-sharing plans, group health and life insurance programs, liability and casualty insurance coverage, and so on.

Without trying to encompass all the advantages and disadvantages of the corporate form, the following are some of the more pertinent pros and cons for the potential buyer partnership.

On the plus side—
- If you ever want to get out, it's a lot easier selling your shares back to the corporation or to another partner than to dissolve an entire partnership.
- Psychologically, a seller would rather deal with a corporate entity than a group of individuals.
- Banks almost always prefer to deal with a corporation rather than individuals for both psychological and continuity of ownership reasons.
- Benefit programs for the partners can be more easily implemented through a corporation.
- It's easier to move money to and from the company in the form of loans.
- Accounting procedures are easier.
- There is limited liability in case of lawsuits.
- You can use an intermediary corporate holding company to hold stock in the acquired company which provides further shielding from personal liability.
- It is easier to plan your estate by providing for the transfer of your shares.

On the minus side—
- Costs to set up corporation.

- Additional state income taxes even though the corporation might report a loss.
- Annual agent fees and registration fees.
- There are more bookkeeping and corporate records required such as stock transfer records, board of directors minutes, and stock certificates.
- Limited liability may not apply if the court breaks the corporate shield.
- There is a potential for double taxation.
- Corporate tax rates are higher than individual rates if an S corporation is not used.

Nearly everyone has heard of how a corporation can be sued but shareholders cannot be. They are protected by the corporate shield. Although this remains true on the surface, with increasing frequency, courts have been piercing this shield and allowing personal lawsuits against shareholders. It nearly always happens in Chapter XI bankruptcy filings. It frequently happens in suits brought by the IRS. And it can happen if a disgruntled employee, or even a customer, claims misuse of corporate power. So even though many times the corporate shield will protect you in the event of lawsuits, in other cases it will not. Check with your lawyer for the final word on this very complex interpretation of personal liability.

It's easy to form a corporation. Nearly any law firm will be happy to do the incorporating and filing work for you; however, fees can run from $400 to $2,000 for this service. Registration fees to the state, and annual agent fees to be represented in that state, are additional.

Over the years, I have formed 12 corporations for my own use—and many more for clients—and used a lawyer only once. There are many companies whose only business is to form corporations for others and then act as registered agents to meet the legal requirements of the state of incorporation or other states you may do business in. They advertise in the Wall Street Journal nearly every week. Many are reputable; some are shysters. The ones that have been around for a long time are fairly easy to ferret out and these are the best. I have used a Wilmington based company called The Company Corporation for most of my work. It can be reached at: The Company Corporation, 725 Market Street, Wilmington, DE 19801, (302) 575-0440.

Complete incorporation forms and a brochure describing their services can be in the mail within a day. If asked, they will also do a computer search to guarantee the name you choose for your corporation and they'll incorporate in any state desired. Total cost for a Delaware corporation is about $150.00—$66.00 to the state and county for registration fees, $25.00 to The Company Corporation for the first year's registered agent fee, and about $60.00 for a gold embossed corporate minute book, imprinted stock certificates, stock transfer records, and a corporate seal. The annual agent fees run about $50 to $60 for subsequent years. They are less expensive than standard attorney's fees, and very reliable.

You can incorporate in any state you wish, and the decision can be independent of where the company does business, where the headquarters are located, or where the facilities may be. You don't even need a legal address in the state of incorporation—the registered agent provides that. Choosing the right state of incorporation should be determined by how much it will cost to do it, what the state tax laws and licensing fees are, and what state invokes the least amount of harassment. State laws governing officers and directors liability should also be investigated because they do vary.

Although state laws change from year to year, Delaware has always been a favorite. Many Fortune 500 companies are incorporated in Delaware, as are thousands of small companies, principally because of the pro business attitude of the state government. Costs of incorporating are low and state taxes are minimal. Recent legislation has also been enacted to afford further legal protection to officers and directors. Nevada is another favorite state with minimal costs and taxes. Recognizing that Delaware and Nevada are making good money from incorporating foreign businesses, other states have tried to get into the act by reducing fees and making it easier to become registered. To my knowledge, however, none offer the liability protection nor are as pro business as Delaware and Nevada.

Some states should be avoided. Minnesota with its reputed anti-business philosophy and legislation is one. Complex tax laws and voluminous reports make New York and California undesirable. Massachusetts and Connecticut have high tax rates. In Michigan and Wisconsin there is the risk of pro-Union legislation.

If a partnership is used to make the acquisition, either in its virgin form and as a close corporation, the one important contractual agreement you can't get away from, in addition to the standard Partnership Agreement, is the Buy-back Agreement. This is a written contract specifying how to handle a partner's share if he wants to get out of the partnership for any reason.

The idea is to agree going in that if a partner wants out, dies, or becomes disabled, the partnership (or the corporation if you are using that form) will purchase his entire interest at a predetermined price. Some agreements stipulate an independent appraisal at the time of withdrawal or complicated formulae, but I have always preferred the simple approach: either previous year-end book value plus an agreed upon premium, or a flat amount which can be adjusted every year. The latter really works best because no auditors or other outsiders get involved and there is less chance of argument. In the Appendix you'll find a rather complicated Agreement I have used a couple of times. Even though it's cumbersome, it works. You don't necessarily need a lawyer for a buy-back agreement. The sample form included or another you construct yourself will save you the cost of legal fees.

AN INVESTMENT BANKER AS A PARTNER

The distinction between venture capital firms and investment banking houses has blurred over the years. Originally, venture capital firms were only interested in financing high tech start-up companies and investment banking houses in handling major corporate acquisitions. But times have changed and now both types of financial institutions invest in companies for their own account in addition to acting as financial sources. And the distinction between start-up and existing companies has vanished. For purposes of structuring an acquisition organization, you can treat the two as the same.

In the past five years, the investment banking industry has grown to enormous proportions. Today, it is probably the single most important force in financing acquisitions of both large and small companies. Chapter 12 covers the use of investment bankers as a source of financing but here let's stick with the role they can play in the organization structure.

There are five common ways to structure an acquisition vehicle with an investment banker:

1. Between you as an individual and the investment banking firm.
2. Between a partnership of you and one or more partners and the investment banking firm.
3. Through a separate corporation.
4. By allocating the shares of the acquired company between you or your group and the investment banker.
5. Through a limited partnership with the investment banker as a limited partner.

There are probably other ways as well because the investment banking community is very creative, but these are the common formats. A partnership with an investment banking firm can be a real plus in putting together an acquisition as well as in managing the company after the close.

Because of his unique position in the business community as a source of funds, a deal maker, and an investor, an investment banker can be invaluable to the entrepreneur.

- He can help in the acquisition search.
- He can put together the financing package.
- He can provide sophisticated corporate finance skills in relations with banks and the Securities and Exchange Commission (SEC).
- He can contribute management expertise to operating decisions.
- He can usually act as the underwriter for an initial public stock offering (IPO).

Because an investment banker is in the merger and acquisition business himself, not only providing financing to third parties but also investing in companies for his own account, he most likely will have ideas and even contacts when you get around to doing the target search.

Not too long ago a small group of investors engaged me to perform a search for a manufacturing company in the water transport industry. I was familiar with the industry and had already accomplished several successful searches for similar types of companies so I certainly didn't expect any difficulty this time around. The timing was off, however, and prices had skyrocketed. It was truly a seller's market. Everything I looked at was either way overpriced, or dead wood.

Running out of ideas, I contacted a small investment banking firm. I knew they had contacts in several East Coast utilities and thought they might have some ideas.

Introductions were made and the conversation quickly got around to structuring a joint venture—not only could they help with the search, but they wanted a piece of the action for their own account. We finally agreed on a fifty-fifty partnership along the following lines:

- The investors formed a close corporation and this corporation would own 50 percent of the shares of the acquired company. The investment bank would get the other 50 percent.
- A board of directors would be elected for the acquired company with seats equally divided between the two parties.
- In exchange for these ownership interests the parties would split responsibilities as follows:

The investment banking firm agreed to:

- Head up the search effort for divestitures with their contacts in New York Stock Exchange and American Stock Exchange corporations.
- Assist me in the search effort with private companies.
- Put together a financing package for the deal.
- Review proposals from the investor group for potential targets.
- After closing, provide technical assistance in the areas of corporate finance and banking relations to the investor management group through Board participation.

The investor group agreed to:

- Continue to work with me in searching private company targets.
- Submit recommendations of proposed targets.
- Perform all due diligence investigations.
- Prepare the business plan for a mutually agreeable target.

- Coordinate legal, appraisal and accounting activities for the closing.
- Provide management for the acquired company after closing.
- A buy-back agreement stated that if either party wanted out within the first five years, the other party would buy his shares for book value plus a 10 percent premium.
- Both parties would work toward an initial public stock issue (IPO) targeted for year four or five of ownership of the acquired company.

The parties never closed a deal because the timing was so bad that even the investment banker couldn't come up with a good target that was reasonably priced. These partnership provisions have been used with other clients, however, and such an arrangement proves very effective.

An alternate way to structure ownership is for the two parties, the investment banking firm and the investor group corporation, to form another third party corporation with equal ownership, or some other negotiated split. This new corporation then becomes the buying entity in the same manner as a partnership of individuals forming a close corporation as a holding company. This adds another corporate layer for protection from lawsuits, but it also adds costs and accounting complexities.

Chapter 12 is devoted to the use of investment banking firms for sourcing financing and should be read in conjunction with the role such a partner can play in the search to decide if this path makes any sense for you.

A LIMITED PARTNERSHIP

The use of limited partnerships is not a new concept although during the 1980s this vehicle has become very popular as a tax shelter for investors. In fact, over the years limited partnerships have been a major catalyst for investments in commercial real estate and oil and gas field development. A limited partnership is a combination of the partnership and corporate forms of doing business and borrows some of the features of each. It always has at least one general partner, although there can be more, and an unlimited number of limited partners. The general partner(s), being the controlling force in the organization, is responsible for all operating activities and assumes full liability for the actions of the organization. Limited partners have no voice in management and are, in effect, merely investors—much the same as preferred shareholders in a corporation. Therefore, these partners cannot be held liable for the actions of the partnership. The term limited is used to designate limited legal liability—much the same as the corporate shield. Typically, limited partners receive a predetermined fixed distribution of profits and losses while the general partner draws a salary or other compensation for his efforts and is entitled to the leftover profits after distribution to the limited partners.

Limited partnerships became popular for tax shelters because the law allowed losses, as well as profits, to be passed through directly to the partners for inclusion in their personal tax returns—the same way an S corporation works, which we'll look at in the next chapter. Although current tax laws have effectively plugged this as a tax shelter, in their heyday limited partnerships afforded a way to raise equity and permit the investors to absorb start-up costs for personal tax benefits. In effect, Uncle Sam returned the investor's cash through tax savings.

There are too many variations on this theme to cover them all, but that's the general idea.

In the acquisition game, limited partnerships are another way to raise equity funding. Instead of selling stock in a corporation to raise cash, partnership units are used. Units may be sold to friends or business associates, or the investment banker may underwrite the sale of units to outsiders. Limited partnerships can be used in either partnerships between individuals or partnerships between an individual or an investor group and an investment banking firm. For larger acquisitions, say companies with a price over $15 million, when large amounts of equity funding are necessary, limited partnerships are extremely popular. Many times a small investment banking firm will be willing to participate in equity funding but unwilling to assume any legal liability for the operation. They will also want a preference position in the event of liquidation. A limited partnership share solves both problems.

FINDING A PARTNER

Unfortunately, there is no magic formula for finding an acquisition partner. As with Josh, most of our friends don't have funds lying around just waiting to acquire a company. In fact, most people never even think of buying a company as an investment or if they do, for one reason or another they can't get off dead center. So saying you need a partner to make a bigger acquisition is well and good, but where do you find him?

There are only five good sources that I have found at all practical:

1. Previous business contacts—an ex-boss or co-worker.
2. Old school friends and affiliations.
3. Investment clubs.
4. Lawyers and CPAs.
5. Advertisement in local newspaper or trade journal.

Previous business contacts are in general a pretty good source for a potential partner. Maybe one of your old bosses or somebody you worked with as an employee. If some of your corporate friends are reaching retirement age or threatened with redundancy they might very well be interested in investing in your venture—or even joining in the management of your new company. The basic problem remains the same, however. Even with the desire to be an entrepreneur, most people either do not have the personal financial resources or the risk-taking initiative to be an entrepreneur, or they don't think they do. You might be able to interest a number of people to be investors at say $10,000 each where you can't get anyone at $100,000.

Perhaps an old school chum would be interested. If you are active in your alumni organization, chances are that someone in the same group has both the financial resources and desire to become your partner—as long as you blaze the trail. If you've been out of school 15 to 20 years you'll probably be surprised how much interest can be generated in your age group of college alumni. Remember the American dream of owning a business. As long as you take the initiative and do the planning—which you are already in the process of doing—finding at least one or two alumni to invest shouldn't be that difficult.

Investment clubs were very popular 15 or 20 years ago as a vehicle for small investors to play an active role in choosing and watching their investments. Some of these groups are still active. If you can find one in your locale they might be interested in your venture, particularly using a Limited Partnership structure. These people are already attuned to playing the investing game, most have fairly sizable incomes and are looking for tax shelters, and many want the type of investment they can see, touch, and feel rather than merely watch its movement in the financial pages or on the Big Board.

I have had terrific luck interesting practicing lawyers and CPAs in investing in acquisitions. None want to actively participate in the management, but all want to sit on the board or be advisors. CPAs are especially receptive, probably because of their close proximity to small business tax work. Limited partnerships work great here but are not always necessary. With a role as board member or advisor, these professionals are able to keep their finger on the pulse of the business without complicated agreements. They usually insist on some fixed arrangement for annual distributions, however. If you can get either a lawyer or a CPA on the board, it will help immeasurably in financing the deal. It will also be beneficial to get free professional advice after the close.

As a last resort, try an ad in your local newspaper or a trade journal. This can be a very risky business, however, and if you resort to this means, be very cautious with any responses. And of course, if you find someone, be absolutely certain to check as many personal, business, and financial references as possible.

Finding an Investment Bank Partner

If it appears that an investment banker might be a viable partner, rather than merely a financing vehicle, stay away from the big boys. Chances are they won't be interested anyway, so don't waste time.

A number of small houses can be contacted directly with a proposition. You'll get better results, however, by making contact through a lawyer or CPA. References are important in this business, and your reception will be far warmer if the investment banker knows in advance who he is talking to.

The Appendix lists over 100 investment banking and venture capital firms I have either worked with directly or been referred to by other consultants or commercial bankers. Some are large houses, some are small. Some specialize in one industry or another. And their portfolios keep changing so what one may be interested in today, might be blasé tomorrow. If you must go in cold, try to get one of the many current books listing investment banks by size and type of industry affiliation. *Venture* magazine publishes books periodically and *The Arthur Young Guide to Venture Capital*, TAB Books, Inc., 1988, is a good starting point.

Finding the right acquisition partner is not easy. It can be a painful, time-consuming search. But going after a larger deal, you probably have no choice. Just remember, you initiated the acquisition process so you should maintain control over the selection of who goes with you. Don't let some banker influence you into taking on someone you're not entirely comfortable with. You'll pay the price later on. Now let's go on to examine some of the tax implications in buying a business.

4

Beating the IRS
Minimizing the Tax Bite

"Do it wrong and you'll owe Uncle Sam more than the banks!"

CONSTANTLY CHANGING TAX LAWS—BOTH FEDERAL AND STATE—PRECLUDE THE possibility of a layman ever becoming expert in minimizing taxes. Even full-time tax lawyers and CPAs have difficulty providing competent tax planning for more than one year at a time. As soon as someone discovers a possible way to reduce taxes even by a microscopic amount, Congress quickly reacts to revise the Code and close the so-called loophole. On the other hand, simply because the laws keep changing, doesn't mean you, as a buyer, can stop worrying about how to reduce tax burdens both for yourself and your newly acquired company.

Before getting into some of the methods currently used to minimize the tax bite for the entrepreneur, I must make it clear that I am not an expert in any kind of tax work. For this reason, as we look at several of the more common ways to deal with income taxes, there will be continued admonitions to check with your own tax advisor before taking any action. The odds are high that before you can implement the ideas in this chapter, the laws will have changed again and what is permissible now, will not be then and vice versa. Nevertheless, no book about buying a business would be complete without an examination of at least the more common tax treatments of transactions affecting the entrepreneur.

When buying a company there are three major tax implications to recognize:

1. Tax matters affecting the seller and thus looming as major negotiating hurdles.
2. Tax treatment of cash draws by the buyer after he becomes the business owner.
3. Tax planning for the day the new business owner decides to get out of the business.

NEGOTIATING HURDLES

There is a truism in buying a company: both buyer and seller must be satisfied that it is a good deal. In other words, if both parties aren't satisfied with the structure, price, and terms, it probably is not beneficial to either side. This doesn't mean the buyer should give in to each and every negotiating point raised by the seller. If he does, the odds are high he's paying too much for the company or payment terms are too stringent to match the cash flow. But a buyer shouldn't expect the seller to concede to every one of his points either. When that happens, one or more skeletons probably lurk in the wings ready to descend upon the buyer after closing.

The best acquisition contract is a win-win deal where each side walks away satisfied that even though he didn't get everything he wanted, the deal will be manageable and beneficial. This philosophy is especially true in the tax area.

Other than price and payment terms, two specific parts of the contract affecting the tax liability of both parties must be negotiated with vigor:

1. Determining whether it's a stock sale or asset deal.
2. If a sale of assets, deciding the allocation of purchase price between each asset—recorded and unrecorded.

There is no allocation question in a stock sale. The entire price is for shares of stock. The seller pays taxes on the gain between the tax basis of his shares and the sale price—which is a capital gain. No negotiations required.

Sellers feel strongly about making it a stock sale. Buyers can be just as adamant about buying assets for both liability and tax reasons. To resolve the issue, many are willing to pay extra to accomplish this, as in the case of two New York innkeepers. Rick and Mary Stienet located the perfect country inn near the Finger Lakes in upper New York. The business broker warned them that the seller wanted to sell stock but Rick and Mary were confident they could negotiate an asset deal. For them, purchasing assets was mandatory. Previously purchasing a small motel in the Midwest as a stock deal, within three years they had forked over $300,000 in unrecorded liability claims. Never again, they told themselves.

Negotiations went smoothly until they came to the structure of the sale. The seller was adamant for tax reasons. So were they for liability reasons, but also to take advantage of favorable tax treatment. It looked like the deal would fall through until Mary suggested the following compromise.

- The deal had to be an asset sale.
- To compensate the seller for extra tax liability, they would pay an additional 20 percent of negotiated price—about twice what they estimated the seller's excess taxes to be.
- The seller would take this 20 percent over a 10 year period—the first three years in the form of a consulting contract and the next seven on an earn-out agreement.
- The seller would be available for consultation whenever they needed him during the first three years, but only when asked.

Although skeptical, the seller agreed and the deal closed. Six years later, he is still getting paid and Rick and Mary have successfully expanded with two additional inns, as we'll see in Chapter 17.

One major new provision in the tax code to be especially wary of is the built-in gains provision. The Revenue Act of 1986 concocted a scheme whereby if the assets of an S corporation that was once a standard C corporation are sold within 10 years of making the election, the corporation is taxed on the built-in gains resident in all of its assets as of the date of the S election. Retaining ownership of the corporate stock, the seller also retains this tax liability and ends up with a double tax problem: gains taxed to the corporation and again to the seller when distributed.

Although in an S election all profits and losses are passed through to the shareholders, the built-in gains provisions make an exception. Here, the corporation itself will be liable for a tax on the difference between the fair market value and the tax basis of the assets at the date of the S election.

Even though a buyer is in the clear, he must be cognizant of the seller's position during negotiations. Just as increased costs in producing a product are passed on to the customer in higher prices, so must a buyer be prepared to compensate the seller, at least partially, for this additional tax burden.

In spite of the built-in gains provisions resulting in tax problems for the seller and therefore a potentially higher price to the buyer, there are two important reasons to buy assets rather than stock:

1. A stock purchase means the corporation stays intact and all liabilities—recorded, contingent, and unknown—stay with the corporation and become the buyer's responsibility. Of course, hold harmless clauses for unrecorded liabilities can and should be included in the Buy/Sell Agreement, but even at that, the cost and effort to collect against the Agreement might outweigh the benefits. You're still stuck with paying the bill. Obviously, a seller will want to sell stock for this very reason—and hence, further negotiations.

2. In an asset purchase, allocation of the purchase price to assets that can be depreciated or written off allows the buyer to recoup some of the higher price through tax savings in future years.

Unless the sale price is less than book value, a buyer always gains and a seller loses with an asset sale. The reverse holds true for a stock sale.

ALLOCATION OF PURCHASE PRICE

Assuming an asset sale can be negotiated, a second important negotiating point affecting tax liability is the allocation of purchase price against the asset categories being acquired. Even though tax laws change, the following general rules continue to survive intact, although whether this will be true in the future is questionable.

Receivables
- For buyer, cost recovered when receivables are collected.
- For seller, no income. He merely trades cash for receivables.

Inventory
- For buyer, cost recovered when inventory is sold.
- For seller, ordinary income realized if sold for more than the tax basis.

Land
- For buyer, cost recovered only when land is sold.
- For seller, capital gain.

Buildings
- For buyer, cost recovered through depreciation. Current depreciation life is 31.5 years.
- For seller, capital gain, but the gain equal to the difference between prior years' accelerated depreciation and the straight line method is recaptured as ordinary income.

Machinery and Equipment
- For buyer, cost recovered through depreciation. Current permissible lives are five to seven years.
- For seller, capital gain, except for the gain equal to the amount of prior years' depreciation which is recaptured and treated as ordinary income.

Non-Competing Covenant
- For buyer, cost recovered through amortization over length of contract.
- For seller, ordinary income.

Goodwill (including customer/client lists and files)
- For buyer, cost is not recoverable until business is sold.
- For seller, capital gain.

During negotiations the seller will try to allocate as much of the price as possible to goodwill. This is the only asset other than land where he gets full capital gains treatment. A buyer, on the other hand, should argue for allocations to inventory first, non-compete covenant second, machinery and equipment third, buildings fourth, and as a last resort land and then goodwill. Remember, neither side can have what it wants. Usually, the greater the amount allocated to goodwill, to help the seller's tax position, the lower the price. The more allocated to the non-compete covenant to help the buyer, the higher the price.

Unfortunately, under new tax legislation, the amount of negotiating room is severely limited—especially for the buyer when he pays a premium for the business. Once again Congress has penalized the entrepreneur by providing the IRS more information to second-guess the business buyer. Both seller and buyer must now file Form 8594 showing the allocation bases. Traditionally, part of the excess paid has been included in the basis for depreciable property. Now, the IRS has one more tool to interfere with negotiated terms and insist that amounts paid in excess of book value and the non-compete covenant be charged to non-depreciable goodwill.

Once again, check with your tax advisor about current regulations for treating each asset category. Don't try to be too creative on your own or you might end up with the type of mistake I made when I purchased my first financial services company.

Back in those days, I considered myself somewhat of an expert in tax matters. The idea of consulting a real tax authority never entered my mind. When the seller and I negotiated the allocation of price to asset categories, he was adamant that most of the price was goodwill—after all there were only a few pieces of office equipment, no inventory, a few receivables, and a leased office. Knowing that I could not deduct amortization of goodwill, I argued that what the seller called goodwill was actually payment for client files and staff personnel. The seller agreed, and that's how the contract was written.

The first year when filing my tax return, I showed a balance sheet consisting of $40,000 for client files, amortized over three years, and $50,000 for personnel, amortized over five years. A year later when the IRS agent showed up to audit the return, he blew his top. "What in the hell are these assets called 'Client Files' and 'Personnel'?"

I pulled out the Buy/Sell Agreement and pointed out how we had carefully allocated these amounts to those specific assets. I argued that although the accounting fraternity wouldn't recognize client files or personnel as recorded assets, in this business they certainly were. Without personnel there wouldn't be any business and therefore they were as much an asset as an office machine. Furthermore, I estimated that labor turnover being what it was, these people would leave within five years and that was justification for the five year amortization schedule. The client files were the same. Without the files there was no business and they had a useful life of three years.

Suffice to say, the IRS agent objected, wrote a deficiency report, and sent me a bill for taxes due. I argued with his boss for six months until I finally gave up, recognizing I couldn't fight city hall, and paid the tax.

As a footnote, the IRS agent left the Service midway through our negotiations and a year later I met him at a seminar. When queried why he had resigned, his response was that my case was so far out and such a struggle to resolve that he couldn't take the pressure anymore. Also, he happened to agree with my logic even though it was contrary to tax law.

CURRENT TAX REGULATIONS

This is probably a good place to describe the key provisions of the current tax regulations affecting most buyers. It's important to keep in mind, however, that these rules will change, and before negotiating a deal, check with your tax advisor. The three features to be covered here are tax rates, classification of income, and timing.

Changes in 1986 and 1987 have had the biggest impact in the area of tax rates. What was once a 46% maximum tax rate for corporations is now 34%, and what was once a top rate for individuals of 50% is now 33%.

The rates break down as follows:

For Corporations:

Income up to $50,000	15%
The next $25,000	25%
Over $75,000	34%

For Individuals (married filing joint return):

Income up to $29,750	15%
The next $42,150	28%
Over $71,900	33%

Traditionally, income classified as long-term capital gains received preferential tax treatment. Corporations paid a minimum tax of 28% on net long-term capital gains and individuals paid a maximum rate of 20%. The whole purpose of capital gains preferences was to encourage investment in long-term capital assets—real estate and production equipment for businesses, securities and real property for individuals. Investment in long-term capital assets furthers the economic growth of the country and for years this was considered beneficial to everyone. Now, however, Congress has seen fit to eliminate preferential treatment for long-term investments. The capital gains tax rates are no more. Gains on the sale of capital assets are taxed at the same rates as any other income.

There does remain one advantage in converting ordinary income to capital gains, however. To the extent that an individual has other capital losses, he may net these against capital gains and pay taxes only on the difference. Without the capital gains offset, only $3,000 of such losses are deductible in the current year—although the excess may be carried over for potential future deductions. So from the seller's perspective, it might still be preferable to allocate the purchase price to capital assets rather than ordinary income categories. Tax laws keep changing, however, so a buyer might gain in the future by this same allocation—except for goodwill.

Timing the recognition of income on the sale of capital assets has remained virtually untouched by the changes of 1986 and 1987. Installment sales are still recognized as a viable way for the seller to spread income to later years and possibly fall into a lower tax bracket. Obviously, you as a buyer would love to pay the entire price over future years to conserve cash. Because both sides win in deferred payment provisions, this should be a primary objective during negotiations. The seller could very well save taxes, and you can conserve cash. Assuming you can convince the seller that he will eventually get his money, this is a win-win situation. The exception—and isn't there always an exception?—is for that portion of the sale price allocated to non-capital assets. This is ordinary income and taxable in the year of the sale regardless of when the seller gets the cash.

CASH DRAWS AFTER CLOSING

The biggest tax problem for a buyer has nothing to do with structuring the acquisition deal. No matter how the price and terms are negotiated, once he takes over the company, his most difficult tax problem is how to get cash out without double taxation. As long as the draw is classified as salary or other compensation for services rendered, the amount is deductible to the corporation and taxable to the individual. But as soon as the IRS decides that amounts withdrawn are in excess of reasonable compensation, they are declared dividends. Such payments are not deductible to the corporation but are taxable to the individual—hence double taxation.

The problem escalates when there are multiple partners in the acquiring group—some active, some passive. Passive investors are not entitled to any compensation, just dividends, and thus all payments to them are always subject to double taxation.

Entrepreneurs have struggled with this dilemma for years. Although with the new, lower rates the tax is lessened, thirty plus percent times two is still too much to pay Uncle Sam.

There are three principal ways to resolve the issue—the first two straightforward, and the third one gray:

1. Elect to be taxed as an S corporation.
2. Structure the acquired company as a limited partnership.
3. Have the company treat as many personal expenses as possible as company expenses.

THE SMALL BUSINESS CORPORATION—"S" CORPORATION

Advantages of electing to be taxed as an S corporation have fluctuated over the years as Congress continues to manipulate the Code to please special interest groups. At times an S corporation has been a real help to small businessmen. With other revisions to the code, benefits have been negligible, or even a hindrance. Congress continues to favor the large lobbyists to the detriment of the entrepreneur and it's impossible to know what schemes will be concocted next. Under current revisions, however, there remains one provision under the S corporation rules still advantageous to the business owner. All income or losses to the corporation are taxed directly to shareholders rather than to the corporation with the exception of built-in gains.

An S corporation receives the same treatment from the IRS as a partnership. Corporate income or loss passes through to the shareholders in the same form as it was to the corporation. Each shareholder receives that proportion of income or loss that their stock holdings bear to the total shares outstanding. This pass-through occurs whether cash is distributed or not. If cash is not distributed until later tax years, it is done so tax-free at that time because the tax on earnings has already been paid. Because the corporation pays no tax at all, there can be no double taxation.

As in all tax laws, what Uncle giveth with one hand he taketh back with the other. The major disadvantage in using an S corporation, other than the built-in gains provisions, is that cash can only be distributed in the same proportion as the stock holdings, whether or not the shareholders are active or passive. So if you as an individual are the only active partner in a deal and own, for example, 60 percent of the shares, for every dollar distributed over and above salaries and bonuses, forty cents must go to other shareholders. There are also "at risk" provisions applying to the deductibility of losses.

S corporations are especially useful to small retail or personal service businesses when the corporate form of doing business makes sense for legal or other non-tax reasons. The S election provides a way to operate the business as a proprietorship or partnership for tax purposes and still benefit from the protection of a corporate shield.

To make an S corporation election, all shareholders must agree. The procedure is simple requiring only the filing of Form 2553, and except for very unusual circumstances, the IRS always grants permission. There are three problems to be aware of in making the election, however:

1. The Form must be filed within 75 days of the beginning of the tax year to which the election applies.

2. If the corporation reverts back to be taxed as a standard, or C corporation at a later time, it must wait a full five years to once again make the S election.

3. If you start out with a C corporation and then convert to an S corporation at a later date, and then decide to sell the company within 10 years of the election, built-in gains provisions apply.

If an S corporation seems possible, attention must be paid to the structuring of the buying entity before closing the acquisition deal. A corporation owning at least 80 percent of the shares of another corporation cannot make the S election. Therefore, to make it work, you must buy the shares of the target directly without using a parent holding company. On the other hand, if you buy assets rather than stock, then you can form a new corporation to be the owner of the assets and this corporation may file an S election.

If you purchase a small retail or service business or a professional practice and elect to operate as a proprietorship rather than a corporation, there is no problem of double taxation. All income from the business is taxed to you as an individual on Schedule C of Form 1040. All business cash is your cash and there are no problems with the classification of income or timing.

LIMITED PARTNERSHIPS

Assuming that you will conduct business as a corporation, either because you buy the stock of an existing corporation or your legal counsel advises incorporating a new company, and the purchase will be made with one or more partners, a limited partnership is another way to get money out of the company without double taxation.

As described earlier, limited partnerships have become a popular acquisition structure for a multiple buyer group where one or more individuals are general partners and an investment banker or other passive investors are limited partners. Limited partnerships were very popular during the seventies and eighties as tax shelters for wealthy investors—particularly for start-up businesses, real estate, or oil and gas investments—where the operating entity could expect substantial losses in its early years. These losses were then passed on to the limited partners for use as deductions on their personal returns. The advent of the "at risk" rules eliminated this benefit. No longer can passive investors deduct losses from a business in which they do not participate actively in management (except as an offset against passive income).

Limited partnerships are still popular as a means of avoiding double taxation on cash distributions, however. "At risk" provisions for losses—which dictate that a partner must have actual investment in the partnership equal to the losses he deducts on his personal return—are not applicable to profits distributed to the partners. Pass-through provisions operate virtually the same as in an S corporation. Profits of the business are taxed directly to the partners on their personal returns independent of any cash distributions. Cash may be distributed in later years tax free.

The proportionate share distributed to each partner creates a fundamental difference from an S corporation, however. In an S corporation a shareholder receives his share in proportion to his stock holdings. In a limited partnership, special provisions may be written into the Partnership Agreement specifying the distribution share for the limited partners as a group and the general partners as a group—and they need not be in proportion to share holdings.

Tax laws affecting limited partnerships are extremely complex and continually changing so if you use this method, be sure to consult a tax advisor well versed in structuring limited partnerships as well as in current and potential new tax implications of using this form.

PERSONAL EXPENSES

I call this a gray area because, although expenses incurred by a business owner on behalf of the business are perfectly legitimate deductions by the business, the reverse is not true: personal expenses of the owner paid by the business are not deductible by the business but are included as income to the owner. On the other hand, to be practical, in a very small business many expenses that are really personal are deducted as business expenses for tax purposes—even though, if detected by the IRS, they will be disallowed. Chapter 15 illustrates how many small retail business owners pay for certain types of personal living expenses out of the business even though contrary to tax laws.

In certain situations where the operating business is owned by a holding company, the owners might treat their compensation as consulting fees rather than salary. Under this arrangement, they could establish Keogh Plan retirement funds—another way to reduce personal tax liability—although then they are subject to an additional self-employment tax.

Although the deductibility of automobile expenses, and travel and entertainment expenses has been substantially curtailed under the current tax laws, these expenses may still be paid and deducted by the corporation under stringent rules. Other expenses normally considered personal might very well be paid and deducted by the company—but I'll let your imagination conjure up what they might be for your specific business. I certainly don't want to recommend anything which would be considered contrary to the tax laws. Whatever expenses can be legitimately handled in this manner, however, become another way to get cash out without double taxation.

Benefit plans can also be set up and funded by the company. Such benefits as health and accident insurance coverage or SEP and 401(k) retirement plans are still permitted by the IRS.

TAX PLANNING FOR A GETTING OUT POSITION

Why worry about tax planning for selling a business when you are just now getting into one? Because taxes can take such a substantial bite out of the proceeds of a sale, it only makes sense to begin tax planning to minimize this bite right away.

Getting Out: A Step-by-Step Guide to Selling a Business or Professional Practice addresses the requisite tax planning in structuring the best ways to dispose of a business. It would be redundant to explore the subject in depth here. If you are planning to sell or otherwise get out of your business within the next five years, I suggest you pick up that book for some helpful planning ideas for minimizing taxes at the point of sale. But here we are concerned with buying a company and there are only a few caveats to worry about now. The first has to do with built-in gains provisions of the S corporation election.

Many small business owners have converted to an S corporation in anticipation of selling their company and thus avoid double taxation. In an effort to plug this loophole, Congress has come up with built-in gains provisions. The built-in gains rules specify that gains realized on assets sold within 10 years of an S corporation conversion from a C corporation will be taxed to the corporation—not its shareholders—even though it is an S corporation. The calculation of the gain is based on the difference between the fair market value of the asset and its tax basis at the date of the S election. Because gains are taxed first to the corporation and then a second time when the proceeds are distributed to the shareholders, double taxation results.

If an S corporation seems like a plausible tax vehicle, the only way to avoid the built-in gains provisions is to make the election in the beginning and negotiate adjustments in purchase price with the seller. This provision applies only to the sale of assets, however, so if you sell stock when you get out you won't have the problem. With the fluidity in tax laws, by the time you get around to selling the company, these rules will probably have changed several times and hopefully, you won't have to worry about built-in gains.

The only other item to worry about at this time relative to a getting out position concerns estate planning. For years, estate planning advisors recommended a small business owner give shares of stock in his company to his spouse, children or other beneficiaries to reduce estate taxes after his death. The S corporation was a convenient vehicle to accomplish this, as were irrevocable trusts specifically designed for this purpose.

Once again, however, Congress has seen fit to complicate life for the entrepreneur. Under certain complex provisions of the current law—to be effective in spreading assets for estate purposes—the business owner must give away his entire ownership, not just a portion of the shares. And he must do this three years before his death. Once the shares are transferred the business owner can have no active relationship with the business, even as an employee. Circumstances invoking these provisions are far too complex to go into here, but if this seems like a viable option, be sure to check with a competent tax advisor first. There are ways around these special restrictions and either immediately before closing or right after you take over it would be a good idea to begin estate planning actions with your tax advisor. For most entrepreneurs, the acquisition of a business quickly escalates their estate assets to a level requiring careful planning that might not have been necessary before.

A Tax Checklist

As a help in overall tax planning after closing, the following checklist points out what questions to ask your tax advisor. The list keeps changing as the laws change so just because you review it now, don't forget to keep updating it each year.

TAX SAVINGS QUESTIONS

1. Should I use a holding company as the acquisition parent?
2. Should I use a limited partnership?
3. Should I incorporate the business?
4. If incorporated, should I elect to be taxed as an S corporation?
5. Should I consider a fiscal year end for my company?
6. Should I put my spouse on the payroll to take advantage of additional IRA deductions?
7. Is my salary and my spouse's salary reasonable for this size business? Can I increase it? Should I decrease it?
8. How about director's fees—should I pay myself and my wife to qualify for Keogh retirement plans?
9. How can I best draw out cash without double taxation?
10. Should I implement a medical reimbursement plan?
11. Should the company have a group-term life insurance plan?
12. Should I set up a 401(k) or a SEP retirement plan?
13. Is there any benefit in setting up new IRA plans?
14. Would setting up an ESOP be of benefit?
15. What record keeping should I have for travel and entertainment expenses to meet IRS requirements?
16. Can I make additional contributions to charities and save some taxes?
17. What is the most beneficial depreciation schedule to use?
18. How can I get a deduction for my car?
19. Should I sell or scrap unused equipment?
20. Can I gain anything by writing off old inventory?
21. Do I need to worry about foreign tax credits?

22. Can I use a Foreign Sales Corporation (FSC) for export sales?

23. If I can, how do I set it up?

24. Can I use a stock redemption agreement?

25. Should I have a contractual agreement in place to dispose of the company if I become disabled or die?

26. Should I sell or give some of my stock to my spouse? my children? a Trust?

27. Should I have key man life insurance?

28. Is there any way to shift either income or expenses from one year to the next?

29. Is there any way to shift income or expenses between myself and my company?

This list isn't inclusive—the number of possibilities for tax planning are limitless—but it will at least get your tax advisor thinking along the right channels.

So much for a brief look at the tax implications in buying a business. One last time: check with your tax advisor in the beginning, and keep checking every step along the way. Taxes are the biggest business expense you'll have. Don't take the chance of paying more than you absolutely have to. Just as the IRS is obligated to collect everything they can, you the taxpayer are obligated to pay only those taxes required to conform to the law.

5

The Search Begins
Locating a Candidate

"I haven't seen so many dogs since the kennel show."

SO FAR, NINE KEY QUESTIONS LEADING TO AN ACQUISITION HAVE BEEN examined:

1. Are you making the jump to entrepreneurship for the right reasons and do you recognize the concurrent risks?
2. Do you have the mental and emotional strength to be an entrepreneur?
3. Are your people skills honed to manage the difficult acquisition process?
4. Have you set personal goals consistent with owning a business?
5. Does buying a business meet these goals better than starting one from scratch?
6. Is the timing right?
7. Have you analyzed the right location for the business?
8. Will you make the acquisition alone or bring in a partner or two?
9. Do you understand the tax consequences of your objectives?

If all these questions have been answered in the affirmative, then it's time to begin the acquisition journey in the following nine-step sequence:

1. Prepare an Acquisition Plan.
2. Perform a target search.

3. Negotiate price and terms.
4. Investigate details of the target company.
5. Prepare a business plan.
6. Put together a financing package.
7. Draft and negotiate language for the Buy/Sell Agreement and other closing documents.
8. Close the deal.
9. Execute transition management procedures.

A CASE STUDY

Because of the complexities in making any acquisition—large or small, retail, service, manufacturing, or a professional practice—the easiest way to get a picture of how each of these steps comes together in the overall process is to look at an actual acquisition from start to finish. For most of the remainder of this book we will follow an entrepreneur through each of the steps he follows in the acquisition of a manufacturing company in the water products industry. This is an actual case history. Although some of the facts and names have been changed to protect the confidentiality of the companies, financial institutions, and people involved, the steps, sequence, and results are real.

The case centers around the acquisition of a mid-sized company, small enough for one person to handle, but large enough to provide income commensurate with the buyer's needs. While this target is significantly larger than many entrepreneurs will need, or even want, the acquisition process and the transition of ownership are very similar to smaller retail or service businesses. There are differences however, and as we move down the road, minor variations will be pointed out. In addition, Chapter 15 examines major differences in buying a smaller business. The purchase of a professional practice requires a completely different approach and for readers interested in this possibility, Chapter 16 describes the structure, valuation, and financing of such an acquisition.

John E. Joe is 48 years old, living with his wife and daughter outside Princeton, NJ. His background includes over 20 years in marketing and manufacturing of a variety of consumer and industrial products including wooden toys, industrial pumps, and water filters. For the past five years he has held the position of Vice President, Marketing for a multi-million dollar producer and distributor of metal components utilized in ground support equipment by the U.S. Military. His company recently lost a major contract and John now finds himself out of a job. He has always dreamed of owning his own business and now, with the support of family and friends, John decides to take the big step. Through prudent investment in the stock market and by a careful savings program he has put away $500,000 which he can invest in an acquisition. His father-in-law is willing to loan him another $500,000 on a long-term note. John calculates that with his wife teaching in the local school system, he will need to earn about $75,000 annually to continue his current standard of living. He can't think of anyone he'd like to form a partnership with and therefore decides to do it alone. Most of John's working life has involved spanning the globe, so a little more travel won't make any difference, therefore the only location criteria is that the target be within a reasonable drive of a major airport. If absentee management isn't feasible his family has agreed that relocating wouldn't be too bad and are willing to support him in any way they can.

THE ACQUISITION PLAN

John carefully weighed the economic, stock market, and industry statistics, and trends and decided that the timing was right to begin the search. Although ready to start earlier, he decided to wait out the bear market with the hope of catching early indicators of a turnaround. In October the first indications of such a turn began to surface. Interest rates stabilized for a while at least, and Federal Reserve monetary policy seemed to be headed in the right direction. John doesn't agree with the Government's fiscal policies of increased deficit financing, but that may go on for many years to come, and he certainly can't wait for a change there. Leading indicators reflect a recovery in the construction industry and even though the Unions are still screaming about high unemployment rates, it looks as if the recession has run its course and business should be looking up.

If his economic prognostication is correct, the turning business cycle will encourage profit improvements by the end of the first quarter next year, which means that he must be in a position to begin the negotiating process by mid-April, or May at the latest. Now he must put together an Acquisition Plan to see if this is possible.

An Acquisition Plan should be set up in a sequential outline of major steps with go, no-go decision points and estimated costs for each milestone. Search, investigation, and closing expenditures can then be budgeted and controlled to the progression of the plan. John constructed the following Acquisition Plan:

ACQUISITION PLAN OUTLINE

Action	Start Date	Finish Date	Estimate Cost
A. Survey Industry/Product/Market	10/31	1/1	$2,000
1. Economic growth curves—historical and future			
2. Market dominance—competition and pricing			

3. Foreign competition
4. Economics of user applications
5. List of companies
6. Sales literature and financial data of companies in industry
7. Trade Association Interviews

B. Target Search   1/1   4/1 $3,000
   1. Brokers, consultants, lawyers, accountants
   2. Investment bankers, venture capital firms, commercial banks
   3. *Wall Street Journal*, trade journals
   4. Unsolicited mailings
   5. Personal contacts

C. Preliminary Due Diligence
   1. Target #1   4/1   4/15 $800
     a. Meet with seller
     b. Facilities tour
     c. Obtain financials and sales literature.
   2. Target #2   4/15   5/1 $800
     a. Same sequence as #1
   3. Target #3   5/1   5/15 $800
     a. Same sequence as #2

D. Negotiate Price and Payment Terms for the Best of the Three Targets   5/15   6/15 $800
   1. Valuation of the business
   2. Earn outs, contingencies, hold backs
   3. Buyer paper

E. Perform Detailed Due Diligence   6/15   8/15 $5,000
   1. Financial—three years historical audit reports and monthly internal reports
   2. Prepare pro forma financial statements.
   3. Organization chart
   4. Meet management and second facilities tour
   5. Customer data—competitors, pricing, market size and share
   6. Outstanding lawsuits or claims—government, employees, customers, etc.
   7. Contracts in force—Union, vendor, customer, employee, leases

F. Source Financing	6/15	9/15	$5,000

F. Source Financing   6/15   9/15 $5,000
1. Prepare comprehensive business plan
2. Commercial banks
3. Finance companies—commercial and asset-based lenders
4. Investment banks and venture capital firms
5. Others

G. Final Due Diligence   9/1   9/25 $20,000
1. Update pro formas financial statements
2. Appraisal of equipment and real estate
3. Audit review by CPA firm

H. Write Buy/Sell Agreement and Other Closing Documents   9/15   10/15 $7,000
1. Engage legal counsel
2. Negotiate final language and terms of sale
3. Coordinate with financing parties

I. Attend Closing   10/31

Total time to make the acquisition will be 12 months from start to finish and budgeted costs amount to about $45,000. This looks like a worst case budget. John certainly should be able to close a deal in less than 12 months and keep costs under $45,000. It's far better to be conservative and plan for the worst, however. Remember Murphy's Law.

With an Acquisition Plan, John can see that he will have to plan on possibly a full year with no income and expenditures of between $30,000 and $45,000. He might also have to deal with the mechanics and cost of relocating his family, but won't worry about that at this stage. Any relocation will occur after the acquisition closes; and then a new plan can be prepared.

One word of caution about planning; the only thing certain about a plan is that it will be wrong. The future is unpredictable. If you could accurately predict what would happen next year or the year after, you certainly wouldn't worry about making an acquisition. So just because you've labored over an Acquisition Plan, don't expect it to be accurate. It should be used as a guideline and only a guideline and don't be upset if some dates are missed or if the budget is out of whack. The main purpose in planning is to force a mental discipline and to organize your thoughts and actions down a directed and meaningful path.

Planning and People

But planning does more than merely point the way toward achieving goals. If properly constructed and executed, it also influences the goals themselves. Planning and organizing a sequence of events has a major impact on other people. How these people react strongly influences what future events will occur. It's important to let people know what you expect of them, when you expect it, and what steps you will take to help them. It is man's nature not only to want to know what will happen in the future, but to be directed along some predetermined path of action to reduce the amount of effort, uncertainty, and indecision. Associates, peers, and employees will welcome a planned direction and respond to guidance along the planned route with favorable actions.

Most people—lawyers, accountants, bankers, and employees—feel you have a greater caring and concern for their problems if they see an effort made to try to plan future events affecting them. There is a camaraderie established when one person believes another cares enough to try to anticipate his needs and desires—and that is exactly what a plan does.

There isn't much literature yet about the effect of planning on human relations but as more people grow to realize the correlation between planning and solving people problems, experts in the field will evolve. There are already an increasing number of books and seminars concerning the relationship of caring and compassion to success in the business world and it's a natural step to go that extra inch and incorporate planning as a method of demonstrating these people concerns.

Without a plan, the probability of influencing future events becomes close to zero. If personal goals and objectives are well thought out and as many contingencies as possible are planned for, the results will be amazing. Future events can be influenced; sometimes modestly, often with profound results. However, even though planning is the cornerstone of any successful acquisition, a plan is only a plan, and must not be substituted for on-the-spot business decisions made as conditions continually change.

STARTING THE SEARCH

"It's like looking for a needle in a haystack," said Jerry as he and Marty were having coffee one morning in the local diner. (I happened to be sitting next to Marty and couldn't help overhearing the conversation.)

"You mean to tell me you've done all this planning to buy a company and now can't find one for sale? You must be looking in all the wrong places. The *Philadelphia Inquirer* is full of business opportunity ads every Sunday," answered Marty. "All you need do is pick up the phone and call one of those business brokers and you should have plenty to choose from."

Jerry replied, "Sure, if I wanted a gas station or a bar. But I'm looking for a bigger company; one big enough for me to make some money from it—and they don't advertise."

I couldn't resist interrupting, "Jerry, have you tried using an M & A consultant, or the *Wall Street Journal*, or have you asked your accountant for assistance?"

"No. Why should I go to someone else. I can do it myself, given enough time."

"Sure," I replied, "given enough time; how about five years?"

Now that goals have been established, an Acquisition Plan for sequencing the steps prepared, and the timing seems appropriate, it's time to begin the search. That means facing two key issues: 1. what type of target to go after, and, 2. how to find such a target available for sale. Let's see how John E. Joe does it.

Defining the Target

Because of his work experience, John decided to look for a manufacturing company distributing its products through manufacturers reps and distributors to a wide customer base. Potential for the development of an export sales program would be highly desirable. There should be key management in place and willing to remain with the company after closing. Ideally the target will have proprietary products and hold a unique position in the market place, either because of the nature of the products or because of the superiority or differentiation in its distribution channels. It should sell into a market large enough to permit an increasing market share but not so large as to encourage domination by very large multinationals. It would be perfect if the company was a market leader, but lacking that, a number two position would certainly be acceptable.

The industry should be in a long-term growth mode but the target should not rely on research and development to keep or increase market share. An R&D program requires too much working capital and with his limited resources, John must stay away from high tech companies.

With $1 million to invest as equity capital, using the four to one debt to equity rule, John can afford a cash purchase price in the neighborhood of $4 million. Assuming he can negotiate a price equal to book value and using the standard ratios of one and one-half to one, debt to equity, and a two times asset turn, the probable sales volume for an acceptable target will be in the $18 to $20 million range.

Location isn't a major concern. If the target is not local and absentee management isn't practical, John can relocate wherever necessary. He realizes he can't be too choosy about location going after an acquisition of this size. Opportunities are bound to be limited in any one geographic area and he must be flexible. The right company, at the right price, with the right cash flow are more important criteria. Most important of all, John wants to stick with industries he knows.

John finally zeroed in on the residential water purification industry as a good starting place. Many of the products are machined and assembled, fitting nicely into his manufacturing background. Distribution channels match his marketing criteria. And the size of companies seems about right to provide his income level.

The next step is to conduct a survey and do some market research to determine the industry's size, economic characteristics and competitive nature. A good place to begin the research is the local business library. The friendly librarian will be happy to recommend journals, catalogs, company listings, and industry statistics. Another good source of data is the local Department of Commerce office. This office usually has shelves of sparsely published data and statistics about every industry and industry segment imaginable. With the right direction, the librarian can produce more than enough data on almost any industry to get you started.

WHO CAN HELP?

Once you bone up on the economics and statistics of your chosen industry—in John E. Joe's case residential water purification—it's time to get started looking for the right company.

During his research, John discovered a number of products produced for the residential water purification markets: filters (both metal and fiber), tanks, testing instrumentation, and measuring instruments. It really doesn't make much difference at this point which of these products a company manufactures as long as it has a strong marketing organization.

Next he must determine what companies make these products, who controls the sub-markets, which are divisions of larger parent companies or under private ownership, and, of course, which ones are available for purchase. But where to start?

John recognized he didn't have an unlimited amount of time—time is money—so wisely decided to ask for help from an M & A consultant in this long, often frustrating search process.

M & A Consultants and Business Brokers

The fastest way to find the right house to buy is to explain your needs to a qualified real estate agent and let him do the legwork. Using an independent insurance agent usually results in the least cost and best coverage. If you want to refinance your house a wider choice of lenders can be reached by working through a mortgage broker. The same principle applies to buying a business. There are individuals and companies who make it their business to serve as agents for both buyers and sellers of businesses. Regardless of the size or type of business or its location, using a qualified agent is generally the fastest and most efficient way to proceed.

Agents are divided into two classes:

1. Business brokers who handle small retail and service businesses in a limited region, and,

2. Merger and acquisition consultants who deal with larger businesses covering a wide geographic area.

One word of caution, however. Real estate agents and insurance agents are usually required to qualify their expertise, either through passing an exam or by years of experience, or both, and the proof of this expertise is a license to do business. Through licensing the State attempts to control not only the qualifications but also standards of compliance governing conduct, and to a lesser extent business ethics. Unfortunately, most states do not require licensing of either business brokers or M&A consultants. Anyone can call himself a business broker or consultant and hold himself out as an expert. Consequently, incompetents and charlatans abound and these pretenders tarnish the reputation of reputable agents. Although trade organizations, such as the National Association of Merger and Acquisition Consultants (NAMAC), try to set ethical standards, the best way to choose either a broker or a consultant is through the interviewing process. Compare candidates by interviewing at least three before signing any contract. The following questionnaire can be helpful as a guide.

QUESTIONNAIRE FOR M&A CONSULTANTS AND BROKERS

1. Is he listed in the telephone directory (it's amazing how many are not!)?

2. Has the Better Business Bureau and the Chamber of Commerce ever heard of him?

3. What professional organizations does he belong to?

4. How many deals did he close in the past 12 months? (If less than three, go elsewhere.)

5. Get the names of these sellers and ask them for a reference.

6. Get the names of the buyers and ask them for references.

7. Get at least two references from banks financing deals he has closed.

8. Has he ever closed a deal involving a company of similar size and industry?

9. How does he plan to locate a target? Networking? Advertising? Personal contacts?

10. How long does he estimate it will take to find a viable target? To close the deal? If he says less than 180 days, forget it and look elsewhere.

11. Does he insist on an exclusive listing? He should.

12. What information does he want from you? He should want bank and trade references.

13. What is the fee arrangement? Compare this to the others you interview. Brokers should all charge about the same. M&A consultants may

vary but never pay more than the Lehman Scale (a formula explained within this chapter).

14. What type of contract will he want you to sign? It should be inclusive and guarantee how much time he will spend on your deal—5 days per month, one week, four months, or whatever. If he refuses to commit his time, go somewhere else.

If he is too articulate or well groomed—or conversely, slovenly and crude—or if you sense any lack of business etiquette or honesty, walk away. Pretenders are usually either too smooth or very rough. Trust your intuition, use the questionnaire, and you should be safe.

Business Brokers

Business brokers do exactly what the name implies. They list businesses for sale on one hand and advertise them for sale on the other. Fees are nearly always contingent on closing the deal and usually, but not always, paid by the seller, not the buyer. The amount ranges from 10 percent of purchase price to a modified Lehman Scale formula. A business broker does little to investigate the businesses he lists. He usually provides the prospective buyer with a one or two page sheet of financial and other data about the business given him by the seller. Business brokers generally handle only small local businesses in retailing, wholesaling, restaurants and bars, small hotels and inns, service firms, and some small manufacturing and assembly companies. They are listed in the yellow pages of any city telephone directory. More about business brokers in Chapter 15 when peculiarities of buying a small retail or service business are covered.

M & A Consultants

For larger companies—in excess of $2 million sales—merger and acquisition consultants can be a valuable source of targets. M&A consultants do more than merely list businesses for sale. Their primary goal is to offer consulting advice to either buyers or sellers about how to structure a sale and where to get the financing. They also assist in negotiations and valuation procedures, and of course, try to locate the right target company. They usually have a broad knowledge of the acquisition market. Some specialize in a particular industry such as larger hotels, plastics manufacturing, metal-working companies or health care. They keep track of parent companies considering a corporate restructuring that could result in divestitures of divisions and subsidiaries. Many consultants specialize in smaller companies in specific industries and maintain a network throughout the country of owners currently interested in selling. Many are also regionalized, however, and intimately familiar only with the markets in their areas. So if you're interested in buying a company in Southern California or Chicago, you're probably better off working with a consultant in either of those locations than choosing one from New York.

Some M&A consultants work on a contingency fee basis—which means no fee unless a deal closes with a candidate they introduce. Most M&A consultants' fees are on the Lehman Scale formula. The Lehman Scale was developed several years ago by Lehman Bros. brokerage house and works as follows:

5% for the first $1 million of sell price
4% for the second $1 million
3% for the third $ 1 million
2% for the fourth $1 million
1% for the fifth $1 million
1/2% for the excess over $5 million

Because a contingent fee gets paid at closing and out of financing funds, don't include it in the Acquisition Plan. It's exactly the same as a real estate commission paid on the sale of a house: the mortgage company figures this fee into the closing costs of the deal and merely adds it to the amount of funds borrowed. The same applies to buying a business, so don't worry about how to pay it.

On the other hand, many M&A consultants won't spend time searching for targets unless they know they will earn some fees for their efforts, and accordingly, insist on a monthly retainer. This retainer ranges from $2,000 to $15,000 per month and offsets against the Lehman Scale fee at closing. It should be included in the Acquisition Plan because it's out of pocket cash and can't be recovered unless and until the deal actually closes.

Having been an M&A consultant for a number of years, I strongly recommend the retainer fee arrangement even if the money must come from your own pocket. It is the fastest and surest way to close a deal. Not only will the consultant do all the legwork during the search phase, he can also be invaluable in assisting with negotiations and in arranging a financing package with known sources. He'll even assist in the transition stage after the close.

If you're going after a smaller target, however, don't waste money on an M&A consultant. A good business broker knows more about local markets and can provide a much greater variety of candidates. But for anything over $2 million in sales, an M&A consultant is the way to go.

Try to locate a member of NAMAC in that part of the country where most of your targets are centered. For example, Michigan and Ohio have the majority of drop forge companies, so going after one of these would dictate picking a consultant in Detroit or Cleveland. If you don't know yet where the industry may be concentrated choose one from a large metropolitan area such as New York, Philadelphia, Chicago, or Los Angeles. They usually maintain fairly good connections nationwide.

When engaging a consultant be sure to clarify that you will be doing some of the search work yourself, such as answering ads and direct mail campaigns. Explain that you want him to work through his network for available targets but not incur costs for travel or computerized database listings without prior approval. He should also be prepared to assist in negotiations at the appropriate time. If you're not confident of sourcing financing for the deal, let him do this as well. Most M&A consultants have favorite financial institutions with good track records in handling leveraged deals.

By paying him a retainer, the consultant will work with you from start to finish. It can't hurt to try to negotiate a contingency arrangement, but a qualified consultant, working from beginning to end on a deal, probably won't agree to it. However, nothing ventured, nothing gained. If he does agree, he'll probably want an exclusive listing which means he gets paid the contingency fee at closing whether he brings the target company, you get it yourself, or it comes from some other source. This isn't too unreasonable. He's entitled to be compensated for his time, and over a six to twelve month period he'll spend a lot of time with you that could be put to productive use elsewhere.

Investment Bankers and Venture Capital Firms

We've already seen how investment bankers and venture capital firms can assist as a partner. Even without a partnership arrangement, however, they can be of help. For deals over $5 million, unique businesses requiring complex financing structures, or small, glamorous start-up type companies, investment banking or venture capital firms can be amazingly creative. Every so often a deal one of these firms has been working on, either for their own account or as a financing source for someone else, falls through. Some of the smaller firms are happy to pass on this type of referral. It can't hurt to ask. Again, though, don't bother if you're looking for a smaller target.

It's a good idea to stay away from any mass contact with investment bankers or venture capital firms at this stage of the acquisition process, however. You may want to go back during the financing stage with a business plan and a proposal and these firms don't like to be bothered twice.

Some investment banking houses, and even some venture capital firms, accept an acquisition search engagement directly. If they do, however, it's with the understanding that when a target is found and agreed upon, they will arrange financing and get an equity interest in the deal. Additionally, investment bankers charge retainer fees significantly higher than M&A consultants—starting at $10,000 per month and going up from there. They will also want a closing fee based on the Lehman formula, part of which can be offset against the equity share. This gets very expensive, and unless the deal goes beyond your financial means and additional equity funding is required, stay away from investment bankers during the search. For a larger deal, the partnership route works even better.

Commercial Banks

Commercial banks tend to be too busy with their own interests to be of much help as a source of targets. Occasionally, however, it's possible your friendly banker might hear of an available business—maybe one of his own customers—and if so, should be willing to pass the information along. After all, he expects to keep the accounts with his bank and establish a line of credit if and when you do buy a company, so why shouldn't he help? If a banker does provide leads, the information is free and passed along on a friendship basis rather than as a result of an unsolicited inquiry. Once again, with a working relationship at a local bank, it can't hurt to ask.

Lawyers and Accountants

Performing tax services, estate planning, and suggesting investment opportunities as they do, it would seem that both lawyers and professional accountants should be good sources of target leads. However, while it's true that lawyers and accountants by the very nature of their professions, come into contact with both large and small businesses for sale, they seem unwilling to supply many solid leads. These professionals pride themselves on client confidentiality and seem to be somewhat ambivalent about passing along information about a client—particularly financial information. Also, they don't really want to get involved in this type of endeavor.

A good friend has been a practicing attorney for over 25 years. We had a discussion one day about this very topic. I asked him, "For as long as we've been friends Bob, why is it that you've never once given me a solid lead during a target search? I know you have known of businesses for sale many times but whenever I ask all I ever get is 'I'll keep my eyes open.'"

"Well," he answered, "you've given me many referrals for legal work and I've given you many referrals for consulting work, which is the way it should be. I'm a lawyer and you're a consultant. But just like you don't help me research a brief, I don't help you perform a search."

Practicing accountants are a bit better, but not much. But once again, if you don't ask you'll never know, so it can't hurt to try.

Wall Street Journal Ads

Many small companies already on the market advertise in the Business Opportunities section of the *Journal*. This can be a good starting point for small retail or services businesses particularly. They probably won't be located in your area, however, unless you happen to be in New York, Chicago, Los Angeles, or Dallas. Once in a while there will be a corporate divestiture, but most are single owner businesses. Consultants and business brokers also place ads in the *Journal*, so answering one might very well lead to a valuable contact with one of these agents. But be alert to the unscrupulous. He advertises here also. Don't sign any fee agreement or contract without first checking references and conducting an interview.

Answering ads requires letterhead. If you have a corporation or partnership make sure the letterhead bears its name, address, phone number and a spiffy logo. Pick a snappy name and be sure it's eye-catching but dignified.

Answer these ads faithfully. It takes a while for the responses to come back and even then there won't be many. Some will be dogs to be thrown out. But all it takes is one good one and you're in business. So be absolutely faithful to this campaign. Answer the ads as soon as you can each day. Remember, Wednesday and Thursday are the big days in the Business Opportunities section so don't forget to buy the *Journal* on those days at least.

Personal Contacts

Although current friends or associates might not know of any leads, how about some of the old gang from your last job? Or perhaps an ex-boss? Chances are they would be thrilled to hear from you and more than willing to help. Don't ask for money—just advice. I keep a telephone directory of business cards accumulated over the years and it's amazing how many times it has served me in good stead. People love to hear from old friends and occasionally can be very helpful.

On one such occasion, while trying to get information about companies in the cut glass industry, about which I knew nothing, an old contact came through in the clutch. Cut glass companies are those small, low profile firms specializing in making cut glass windows for churches, museums, and some homes. I ran up against a brick wall in my search and couldn't even begin to locate a source of data for specific companies.

Out of desperation, I thumbed through my old card directory. Sure enough, there was a card from an old acquaintance of 15 years earlier who at one time was in the church maintenance business. A short phone call solved the problem. "Sure, Larry," he replied. "I've got a trade association bulletin which lists all the members complete with addresses and telephone numbers—but it's almost three years old. Will that make any difference?"

I was jubilant. He had just saved me untold hours of research. Within three weeks the acquisition search began in earnest.

Unsolicited Mailings

Unsolicited mailings are either very beneficial in uncovering available businesses not yet on the market or a time consuming lost endeavor. Most of the time, however, at least some leads can be garnered. Even if none come to fruition, knowledge gained about a specific industry can be invaluable. The only costs involved are postage, letterhead, and databases.

A number of vendors supply databases complete with company names and addresses together with the names of the Chairman, President, and other officers. Some of the best are sold by computer on-line companies such as Dialog Business Connection, 800-334-2564, 3460 Hillview Avenue, Palo Alto, CA 94304, and Dun & Bradstreet in New Jersey. These databases can be downloaded directly to your computer and will save man-days of time. Additionally any reputable mailing list company (such as Ed Burnett Consultants, Engelwood, NJ) provides hard-copy lists customized to your specifications. These purchased databases vary in cost from a few hundred dollars to several thousand depending on the number of companies listed, number of sorts required and special services such as mailing labels or computer discs. Be sure to specify the selection criteria and the different data sorts you need, and get quantity price quotes to judge how far you can afford to go.

Even though it's more time consuming, the most direct way to learn of companies in a given industry is to build a personal database from library and industry sources. It's a good education. As a minimum, a great deal of data can be found for listed companies. If a second mailing is required—and it probably will be—data gathered from library sources cut down on the size of a purchased database. Standard & Poor's, Moody's, Value Line Investment Service, and local Business Directories are all helpful in compiling this list.

Sales literature and catalogs used to promote and sell a company's products are an often overlooked source of information. Once you get the name and phone numbers of interesting companies, give them a call. Tell them you are interested in learning more about their particular product lines and would they please send some sales literature, catalogs and price sheets. Usually the receptionist will do this but sometimes the sales department gets involved. By the way, this can be a terrific source of information on competitors and pricing when it's time to write the business plan.

Industry trade associations are another good source of listings. Sometimes, but not always, they will send out membership rosters on request. You might have to join the association to get the listing—but that's relatively inexpensive.

Once the mailing list is compiled, either from a data base or list company or from the library and personal sources, compose an eye-catching, sales oriented letter, designed to attract the attention of even the most jaundiced financial executive. By the way, it's best to address such mailings to the chief financial officer for a listed company and the chairman or president if privately held. It's important to use the person's name in the address, not just a title; this seems to compel an answer.

Make the letter sound as if you are the most important prospect he has ever met. And be sure the letter conveys the impression that you are financially viable and able to make an acquisition of the size defined in the letter. There's no need at this point to mention that you are a single entrepreneur trying to buy a company for yourself. This tends to turn people off (there are just too many "tire kickers'' bothering these executives). Don't lie, just don't mention any more than the reader has to know to elicit a response.

If composing a good sales letter stretches your capabilities, or if your address doesn't sound important enough, ask a friend in the consulting, accounting or legal profession to help with the composition and maybe even use his mailing address. I've found small ad agencies to be most helpful in this endeavor.

Don't be disillusioned if there isn't a bag full of replies. A return of 15 percent is outstanding. An average of eight to ten percent replies is customary. Of these, 80 percent will be ''thank you, but no thank you'' letters and 20 percent will be curious enough to want to hear more. Expect a number of phone calls too. Many people want to find out about financial viability and level of sincerity before taking the time to dictate a letter. If you don't have an answering machine on your telephone, get one, or use an answering service. Don't leave the phone uncovered during this critical search phase.

Other Sources

There are several organizations purporting to list hundreds—even thousands—of businesses for sale of every size and shape all over the country in monthly newsletters, magazines, listings, or directories. Typically, a company listed for sale in one of these sources means that it has been on the market for quite a while without any takers—and that either means it's a dog, there's something seriously wrong with its business, or the price and terms are way out of line. You're far better off using a consultant, a broker, *Journal* ads, or unsolicited mailings.

Although I've never had much luck with the following sources, they are listed here for completeness: • trade journals • insurance agents • real estate agents • *Wall Street Journal* ''Businesses Wanted'' ads • local newspaper want ads • *New York Times* want ads • commercial finance companies.

INCORPORATING THE BUYER

Before answering ads or sending unsolicited mailings, decide what the structure of the buying entity will be. Will you buy the stock of the target as an individual (assuming it is negotiated as a stock sale)? Will you personally buy the assets? Or should some other organization be structured to hold ownership? Chapter 4 pointed out one very good reason for making the purchase as an individual: an election can then be filed with the IRS to have the company treated as an S corporation for tax purposes (again assuming a stock purchase) and the profits or losses of the corporation are reported on your personal return. Remember, this is a good way to pass money directly from the business without double taxation.

Whether assets or stock, if an individual makes the purchase, he will be personally liable for all of the acquisition debt. Financial institutions seldom allow the leveraged target to carry that debt on its books.

An alternative is to form a close corporation and use this holding company to hold title, as discussed in Chapter 2. Even though the S corporation election is lost, a holding company provides one more corporate level between the buyer and the operating company. Although not a foolproof method, it does add a measure of protection for personal assets in the event of lawsuits against the operating company. Additionally, a holding company can be very useful down the road for subsequent acquisitions. And such a corporation can carry the acquisition debt on its books.

Even with a holding company, personal guarantees will probably still be required. Collecting against a personal guarantee, however, is significantly more difficult than foreclosing directly against a corporation.

A corporation will look better to prospective sellers, consultants and bankers. Even though merely a shell, people seem to feel more secure dealing with a corporation than an individual, particularly for larger target companies in excess of $10 million sales. Remember, part of the acquisition process is showmanship. At times the look right is more important than the be right, and psychologically it looks better for the buyer to be a corporation than an individual.

Whatever form of buying entity seems reasonable, it's now time to get moving. Build or buy the databases and mailing lists. Interview a few reputable M&A consultants or business brokers. Begin answering those *Wall Street Journal* ads. There are many seven-day work weeks ahead and time is money.

And by the way, don't forget to let your friends and acquaintances—old and new—as well as anyone else you can think of, know what you are doing. Talk to any bankers, lawyers, or practicing accountants you may know. The results can be surprising. Most everyone will really try to help.

6

The First Look

Choosing the Target and Preliminary Investigations

"It sounded like a great company until I met the management."

BILL ROSCOE WANTED TO BUY A COMPANY IN THE AUTOMOTIVE PARTS distribution business. He recently lost his job as Manager of Traffic and Distribution with a mid-sized AMEX company as a result of a merger with a large NYSE conglomerate. Bill was in his late fifties. He and his wife planned to move to the British Isles when it was finally time to retire. With Bill's early termination, they decided the time to make the move was now rather than later. The couple needed a stream of income to supplement his truncated pension, however, so Bill started looking for an acquisition in England. After reading a number of books about buying companies, he embarked on his search, armed with check-lists of do's and don'ts, library references, $10,000 of free cash to finance travel and out-of-pocket expenses while searching, and the normal optimism and enthusiasm characteristic of the entrepreneur making his first acquisition.

I met Bill a few years earlier at a social function. Although we never did any business together, one night I received a call from this casual acquaintance. "Mr. Tuller?" I heard the slightly broken voice on the other end of the line. "You probably don't remember me, but we met at a Wharton Alumni dinner a few years ago, and I remembered that you were in the M&A consulting business."

"That's right," I replied, trying to place the man, "and I still am. What can I do to help you?"

"Well, I've been trying for four months to find a company to buy in England, because that's where my wife and I want to retire, but I'm not having much luck. I remember some comments you made at the dinner that you have done several acquisition deals in Great Britain. Could we meet for lunch and discuss the matter?"

The next Friday we met and I was astonished at the change in the man from what I remembered. His face was drawn, his hand shook and he puffed on one cigarette after another.

"What's the matter Bill?" I inquired during lunch.

Then he launched into his story of frustration and anguish in trying to find the right company. Bill had spent four months commuting to England searching for his automotive parts distributor. He followed up on every lead from his English solicitor, his accountant, bankers, friends and acquaintances, chasing one after the other. Most of the targets were either not for sale, losing money, or priced out of reach.

"I've never seen so many losers," he stated between gulps of his martini. "I've been down one dead end after another. I've spent nearly my entire cash reserve and I'm no closer to finding a company now than when I started. What's worse, my wife is panicky. She wants me to drop the whole idea and try to find another job, but I think I'm too old for that. I don't know where to turn and I thought you might be able to give me some pointers."

"How about financing the deal?" I asked. "Have you thought about that?"

"That's another problem," he answered. "I assumed I would find a company first, and then worry about financing. But now, the sellers of the only viable candidate refuse to negotiate with me because I can't present them with a personal financial statement showing a net worth of $2 million, the asking price of the business. They claim I'm not a financially viable buyer!"

I suggested to Bill that he was experiencing the normal "acquisition blues" and that he had made the same mistake so many would-be buyers make in trying to do a difficult acquisition without professional assistance and adequate planning. I explained that if he wanted to buy a house in England he would probably contact an estate agent first. He would let the agent do the leg work and arrange a mortgage rather than try to do it all himself. The same principle holds true in acquisition work—particularly in an unfamiliar location.

After spending more time trying to calm him down, I finally offered to put him in touch with an associate of mine who was intimately familiar with the English acquisition market as well as British legal and financing practices. Undoubtedly he could help Bill locate the right candidate. He followed this advice and within four months closed a deal. Bill and his wife moved to England and are still happily and profitably running a small parts distributor in the Midlands.

This true story illustrates an axiom of acquisition work: Don't get discouraged when the going gets tough. By this time you are probably getting a bit weary of this whole exercise. In the beginning, it sure didn't appear that buying a company was going to be this much work or take this much time. But remember, no one said it would be easy. Buying a company can be one of the most difficult undertakings a person will ever face, and also the most frustrating. Even with professional assistance and a well thought out Acquisition Plan, you have probably already lost a good many leads and followed a number of dead-end roads. And how many dog candidates have been presented by brokers and consultants as the perfect match? How many people have said you don't have enough money or are not financially viable to even enter into a serious discussion with? How many times have you thought you had a great target only to learn that key personnel were related to the seller and planned to leave when he does? Also by this time, your spouse is probably becoming just a bit worried about family income and beginning to question the wisdom of sending out resumes again.

TEN RULES FOR A SUCCESSFUL SEARCH

So often, an entrepreneur starts looking for a company to buy without guidelines or parameters defining what he wants. This leads to an enormous amount of wasted time and money and invariably to failure. Some years ago, in an effort to establish standards against which to begin the search, I developed the following ten rules. Once you decide the timing is right, try to keep these rules in mind and the search period should be shortened considerably.

1. List the types of businesses matching your background. Put them in priority sequence with the one you are most comfortable with at the top. Discard all those beyond number five. Concentrate your search on the first one or two.

2. Don't look at companies located beyond a one hour commute from your home—unless you are willing to relocate the business or move yourself.

3. To judge the size of the company, follow the rule of thumb that $25,000 income to the owner (before debt service) can be generated from retail sales of $100,000, service business sales of $50,000, and manufacturing sales of $1,000,000.

4. Look for uniqueness. There should be something different or unusual about the company to give it market advantage—a proprietary product, unique service, superior quality, or prime location.

5. The annual return on your investment, after debt service and your own salary, should be at least 15, and preferably 20 percent, before taxes. (Most investment bankers demand 30 to 40 percent.)

6. The company should have increasing profits for the past three years.

7. The customer base should be broad with no one customer accounting for more than 10 percent of total sales.

8. Key employees must be competent and willing to stay after you take over.

9. There should be no outstanding lawsuits or claims against the company.

10. Most important of all, your intuitive judgment must tell you the current owner is honest.

MEET THE CANDIDATES

Now let's take a look at how John E. Joe is doing, and follow his search for that elusive target. So far he has reduced the number of viable candidates to three and it's time to narrow that list down to one. Here are his three candidates:

Candidate # 1

John's first candidate, a metal water filter manufacturer, sells its products primarily to the rural residential market for use in in-line filtration between the well and the residence. It also sells several small product lines for industrial uses. The company maintains a minor R&D program to develop filtration systems for use by small water utilities. It markets principally through distributors and enjoys profitable annual sales approaching $20 million. One shareholder owns all the stock which he wants to sell for $5.2 million cash. Included real estate houses the manufacturing facility and offices. Management ranks the company number two or three in the industry although they are not sure what public statistics prove this. They do not know the actual size of the industry but guess about $150 million sales domestically. The company is located in Chicago.

It's amazing how much information can be garnered about a company by telephone and letters without ever leaving the office. It appears that this target might be a logical candidate for John and the price isn't that far away from his $4 million budget. He can't determine the real value of the company, however, until he actually sees the facility and obtains some historical financial statements.

On the other hand, rarely will a private seller give out company financial statements without first meeting the buyer and determining his true level of interest. So maybe John must settle for summary financial statistics at this time and wait until completing his preliminary review for the complete financial statements. But how can the seller expect John to have genuine interest until he sees the financials? It's a Catch-22 situation.

LEVEL OF INTEREST LETTER

The best way to deal with a hesitant seller is to send him a non-binding Level of Interest letter—also called a Letter of Intent—indicating a desire to proceed with negotiations for the acquisition within a broad price range (which includes the seller's asking price) but contingent on the satisfactory completion of a due diligence investigation. I have used the following letter many times and it seems to get the job done.

Letter of Intent

This letter will confirm the intention of xxxxxxxxxxxxxxxx ("Buyer") to proceed to draft an Offer to Purchase all of the assets and/or common stock of xxxxxxxxxxxxxxxx ("Company") as soon as negotiations concerning the aggregate purchase price and terms of sale have been negotiated.

Buyer is prepared to proceed promptly to negotiate such price and terms, to draft and present such an Offer to Purchase, to perform the formal investigations and "due diligence," and to negotiate and draft as rapidly as possible a definitive purchase agreement acceptable to both parties. It is understood by both parties that Buyer will make a detailed review and analysis of the business, financial conditions and prospects of the Company and that Buyer must be satisfied in all respects with the results of its review and analysis prior to the execution of any definitive purchase agreement.

Upon acceptance of this letter, Seller agrees to furnish Buyer with sufficient information regarding the condition and affairs of the Company to enable Buyer to proceed with the abovementioned Offer to Purchase and to negotiate to conclusion such price and terms as will be mutually acceptable. Seller further agrees that until such time as negotiations are terminated by either party, Seller will not continue nor begin any negotiations or make any business disclosures with or to any potential buyer other than the Buyer, as defined herein.

Neither party shall have any legal obligation to the other with respect to the transaction contemplated herein unless and until the parties have executed and delivered a definitive purchase agreement, at which point all obligations and rights of the parties hereto shall be governed by such agreement.

SELLER   BUYER

_____   _____

Date_____   Date_____

Also execute a confidentiality agreement at this time. This is a binding contract specifying that you will not reveal any of the seller's confidential information to third parties. Most sellers accept this type of indication of interest as a genuine desire to proceed and cooperate with financial statements.

The following sample agreement might be helpful in drafting one for your deal.

Confidentiality Agreement

Dear Mr. XXX:

This letter is written with respect to the furnishing of certain information to xxxxxxxxxxxxxx ("Buyer") regarding buyer's possible acquisition of xxxxxxx-xxxxxxxx ("Company") from xxxxxxxxxxxxxxx ("Seller").

In consideration of Seller furnishing to Buyer certain information, all of which Seller regards as confidential ("the Confidential Information"), relating to the Company's business, assets, rights, liabilities and obligations, Buyer hereby agrees as follows:

1. The Confidential Information will be used solely for the purpose of evaluating a possible transaction between Buyer and Seller, and such information will be kept confidential by Buyer and its advisors; provided, however, that (i) any of such information may be disclosed to Buyer's employees and representatives who need to know such information for the purpose of evaluating any such possible transaction between Buyer and Seller (it being understood that such employees and representatives shall be informed by Buyer of the confidential nature of such information and shall be directed by Buyer to treat such information confidentially), and (ii) any disclosure of such information may be made to which Seller consents in writing.

2. The restrictions set forth in paragraph 1 shall not apply to any part of the Confidential Information which:
   a) was at the time of disclosure or thereafter becomes generally available to the public other than as a result of a disclosure by Buyer; or
   b) was at the time of the disclosure, as shown by Buyer's records, already in Buyer's possession on a lawful basis; or,
   c) is lawfully acquired after the time of the disclosure by Buyer through a third party under no obligation of confidence to Seller.

3. Buyer will not disclose to any person either the fact that discussions or negotiations are taking place concerning a possible transaction relating to the Confidential Information or any of the terms, conditions or other facts with respect to any such possible transaction, including the status thereof.

4. At any time, upon the request of Seller, Buyer shall return the Confidential Information to Seller and shall not retain any copies or other reproductions or extracts thereof. At such time all documents, memoranda,

notes and other writings whatsoever prepared by Buyer relating to the Confidential Information shall be destroyed.

Sincerely,

President

Occasionally, the seller may want some proof of a buyer's financial viability to complete the transaction. A reference letter from a bank should suffice; however, the seller may want more, such as personal financial statements. In my opinion, this is an unreasonable request at this stage and you should not oblige. So far only a preliminary interest in the target has been expressed and you certainly don't want personal financial statements circulating to parties unknown. Here, an M&A consultant can be of real value in dealing with an obstinate seller. As an independent third party, he should be able to convince the seller that you are, in fact, financially viable and can prove it at the appropriate time. He can also be of immense assistance in drafting the level of interest letter and confidentiality agreement. If the seller insists on personal financial statements, drop the target candidate from further consideration and go on to the next one.

Assuming the seller can be convinced of your sincerity and financial viability, schedule a meeting at the facility location. Most business owners are more than pleased to show off their operation. A facilities tour should be the starting point so that at the first meeting with the seller, you'll have some idea, at least, what his operation looks like.

Yes, I know, you've been in more offices, warehouses, stores, and manufacturing plants than you can count and after a while they all look pretty much alike. However, as you know, each assembly area, stocking room, display area, lay-up operation or production process is slightly different. It's important that a buyer be able to discuss what the seller believes are unique characteristics of his operation.

THE FACILITIES TOUR

Pay particular attention to the cleanliness of the facility. Even in the messiest manufacturing processes, a well maintained and organized shop, with trash in trash containers, and work areas swept up at the end of a work shift, are indications that personnel care and have pride in their operation. This attitude passes from supervisors to workers, and customers are much happier knowing that the workers really care about maintaining high levels of quality in the product. On the other hand, a dirty, messy working environment indicates a lack of interest by management and probably quality problems.

Also take a close look at the workers in the production area. Do they appear to be busy and at their work stations? Does the principal leading the tour chat with the workers as he passes? Does benevolent management seem to be present? Is there an air of productivity permeating the environment? Or are many people walking around somewhat aimlessly, standing in small groups, smoking cigarettes, and reading newspapers? Does the tour guide ignore the workers? You can tell a great deal about the efficiency and productivity of a business simply by being observant on this first tour. A negative attitude on the part of the workers indicates there is something seriously wrong with management/labor relations and signals a need to dig much deeper during the detailed due diligence investigation.

A client asked me to review the manufacturing facilities of a target candidate producing iron plumbing fittings—elbows, tees, and unions. He toured the plant several times and each time observed only a fraction of the workers on the shop floor that were listed on the manpower reports. Upon asking the plant manager where all the people were, he was told that there were a number of cubicles, alley ways and small rooms in the old facility, and he could be assured that all workers were present and accounted for.

I made an appointment with the president of the company to show me through the plant. He was eager to do so knowing that I represented a serious, potential buyer. I observed a messy, dirty machining area with metal chips everywhere. Cigarette butts covered many of the work areas. A general sloppiness prevailed throughout the plant. When confronted with this observation the president explained it away as being normal in this type of business. "No one can keep a clean shop when they cut metal."

As diplomatically as possible I mentioned, "I understand your problem. It's difficult to get people to pick up after themselves, particularly when their job demands constant attention. But what about your janitors?"

"We had to lay off all our janitors last month to cut costs when the order rate fell off."

"Oh, the order rate has fallen off?" This was new information my client had not uncovered. "It must be a pretty serious drop to cause massive layoffs."

"Well, you know the economy is bad all over and the fittings business has been hardest hit of all," was his reply.

Now I knew why my client could not reconcile the people count on the floor with the manpower reports—they were not there. The president related that 35 percent of the workforce were laid off just two weeks earlier. Obviously the reports we had seen were outdated. And contrary to what the president was telling me, although the economy had been flat for several quarters, I knew that the plumbing and heating contracting business was surviving quite well. Some of his competitors were actually increasing business by replenishing distributor stocks.

Clearly there were problems with this company that needed to be rectified. As a result of this visit and plant tour, I advised my client to drop the target unless negotiations could reduce the price substantially. Furthermore, I suggested that he should not make the acquisition at any price for a cash deal. A major portion of the price must be held back for at least a year until these internal problems could be corrected; or alternately, the seller should take a substantial part of the price in long-term buyer paper.

As a consequence, the deal fell through. A shame, but it's better to be cautious in the beginning than to recognize these problems after closing. So be observant during the facilities tour. Notice the housekeeping. Do some mental arithmetic to count heads. It's possible to discover more at this time than in weeks or months of detailed due diligence.

Before leaving the facility be sure to get financial statements—income statements and balance sheets, audited if possible—for the past three years. These will be necessary to calculate the value of the business prior to negotiating a purchase price, and later on when preparing the business plan.

Also, pick up whatever sales and product literature or price sheets might be on hand. This looks right to the seller and also provides a chance to update your files with current data. Conditions may have changed since receiving the first batch of literature.

Candidate #2

John's second target boasts sales of $16 million and manufactures water holding tanks. These tanks have an internal filtration system to segregate impurities before the water enters the plumbing system of a residence. Although similar tanks are imported from Germany and France, there are only three domestic manufacturers of such systems. The single owner wants to retire and is asking a sale price of $4.5 million cash. The company, located in Atlanta, has earned a strong reputation with competitors and plumbing contractors alike.

This looks like it might be the right candidate. It serves a small market niche with little likelihood of entrance by any large competitor. Selling a system rather than individual products strengthens its market position.

The first meeting with the seller went smoothly. John collected summary financial statistics for the past ten years and toured the facilities. The seller openly discussed the close correlation between his business and the residential construction market. Distribution stretches nationwide, although certain markets such as Florida, Texas, Michigan, California, and parts of New England predominate because the highest proportion of new well drillings occur in these states. When the residential construction curve rises, the company does very well, but when it falls they struggle to maintain profitability.

Even though the owner wouldn't allow John to meet the key management personnel, he told John up front that he knows his quality control manager and plant manager plan to resign when he sells the business. He also related that his controller should be replaced. So right away John knew he would have a people problem.

Recruiting key management personnel can be one of the most time consuming and difficult jobs a new owner faces. It's particularly difficult when he must do it immediately or shortly after closing. There will be a myriad of problems to be dealt with—not the least of which is learning the business—and a new owner certainly shouldn't be called upon to face these problems without a complete cadre of key supervisors.

ORGANIZATION STRUCTURE

Many entrepreneurs never seem to understand the importance of sound organization planning and structure until it's too late. Any business organization is only as good as its people. Certainly you have heard that old aphorism many times dating back to business school days. Unfortunately, a meaningful and workable organization structure can be extremely difficult to evolve and once reached, even more difficult to sustain. Books written on organization structure are so numerous it's hard to pick one over the others as the best reference; however, I developed my own theory of organization structure that worked for me running my own operating businesses.

I prefer to think of a management organization structure as being composed of three classes of people: the thinkers, the doers, and the analysts.

The thinkers are those who originate ideas to solve problems. Their minds work in mysterious ways creating "what if" situations on blackboards, around conference tables, or while sequestered in small rooms. Most of the thinkers' ideas won't work in practice, and their lack of patience with other people less endowed mentally makes them terrible managers. The thinkers are often unpopular with others on the management team because they are loners, not team players. But make no mistake, any management organization structure must have thinkers to be effective. They are the ones to turn to in times of trouble. Their advice must be heeded because the one idea out of twenty that works might be the solution to save the company. But, don't put them in leadership roles! They'll foul up every time. As presidents, thinkers often lead the business down troubled paths. On the other hand, they make excellent number two people, or board members.

The doers are the real managers of the company. They can get something done, on schedule and right the first time. Not overly creative (we have the thinkers for that), they are aggressive and understand how to manage people. The doers should be in charge of such functions as sales and marketing, manufacturing, personnel, and quality control. Doers also make good company presidents because they can make decisions quickly and accurately. The ideal combination is a doer as president, a thinker as executive vice president (or board member), and an analyst as chief financial officer.

The analysts manipulate ideas and data. They take the thinkers' "what if" ideas, quantify them, and then play "what if" games of their own using simulation models. Analysts match up the doers' aggressive plans with the thinkers' creative ideas and try to meld the two into a total company program. Analysts should not be put into management roles that require quick decisions—they are not well known for that characteristic. In fact, many analysts can never make a decision, but only report the facts and make recommendations. An analyst generally makes a good CFO or chief engineer because he can be trusted to weigh all the facts from all the sources before making recommendations.

If you are a thinker, then make sure you surround yourself with doers and at least one analyst. If you are a doer then find a thinker as a "number two," and if you are an analyst, find a doer as a partner and let him be president after the closing. It's important during the preliminary due diligence phase to sort out what the organization structure will look like after the closing and where the holes are. If there are too many holes, or the mix of thinkers, doers, and analysts is incompatible with your abilities, it's probably a good idea to drop the target as a viable candidate. An effective organization structure really is that important.

Candidate #3

John's third candidate assembles electronic instrumentation used to detect water impurities and unsafe levels of water contamination. It produces a pre-tax profit of over 8 percent on sales of $10 million. Water utilities use these products to monitor source water. Large apartment complexes and hotels use them to evaluate water used in pools and from private wells. An overseas market in Third World countries also exists. A major multinational NYSE conglomerate owns the target. The asking price of $8.5 million seems high, but the parent's restructuring plans create a need to sell so maybe there's room to negotiate price. The management team will remain after acquisition.

Now this looks like a terrific opportunity if only John can get the price down. Not only should the profitability provide adequate cash flow but the many patented products create unique market niches. And on top of this an export program is in place and working.

DEALING WITH THE LARGE CORPORATE PARENT

Assuming the corporate hierarchy believes John's financial viability, initial meetings for a facility tour and getting historical financial statements should not be problems. But somehow he must deal with this high price. This could be a deal breaker because in a large corporation negotiating decisions are hard to come by. But if he can't get the price down he can't possibly handle the deal financially.

A similar situation occurred during an acquisition search engagement near the peak of the last business cycle. A major AMEX corporation offered one of its high tech divisions for sale. A real glamour candidate, my client was so enchanted with the opportunity to buy this business that he overlooked the price tag of twenty-two times earnings. He went through the complete due diligence phase before trying to negotiate a more reasonable figure. When he finally came to realize that he couldn't possibly afford such a high multiple he tried to get the CFO of the parent to sit down and negotiate something lower. The two met several times in the seller's offices but no conclusions were reached. The CFO kept deferring decisions to the president. Although seldom available, when the president and John finally did meet, he deferred all decisions on pricing to the board of directors—which only met every other month.

Needless to say my client was beside himself. Here he had spent thousands of dollars and several months of time on this candidate and now couldn't even begin to negotiate the price—nobody could or would make a decision. Undaunted, he continued to play their game and waited two months for the board decision. After the board meeting, the CFO politely announced that the answer was no, they would not reduce the price, but, if the stock market began to slip they might reconsider. In a couple of months the market did turn down and my client called the president (by this time he had learned to by-pass the analyst-type CFO).

"Yes," said the president, "at the last meeting the board voted to reduce the offering price to twenty times earnings but will go no lower."

That was the end. My client finally realized he had wasted valuable time and funds on an acquisition that could never happen. He gave up this target and went on to less glamorous but more reasonably priced candidates.

Bear in mind that dealing with a divestiture from a public company requires different tactics than dealing with a private seller. Even though establishing a meaningful valuation, quickly and easily, with freely accessible annual reports and SEC filings, leads to a readily calculable purchase price, if the seller's asking price isn't in line, drop the candidate like a hot potato. Meaningful price negotiations between an entrepreneur buyer and a large corporate seller will probably be impossible. You have little or no leverage so don't beat your head against a wall trying to do something that's not possible.

PRELIMINARY DUE DILIGENCE

Once three or four targets have been identified, a preliminary investigation of each candidate must be done to decide whether or not to proceed. Experts in the acquisition game call this investigation "performing your due diligence." The following checklist of data to gather and questions to ask during this preliminary phase should help. (Chapter 8 presents a complete checklist for the full, detailed due diligence process together with key questions to ask each department supervisor.) This preliminary investigation checklist consists of two categories: (1) data you must have to make a decision, and, (2) information helpful at this stage but not really necessary for a go, no-go decision.

CHECKLIST FOR PRELIMINARY DUE DILIGENCE

Data to Gather and Questions to Ask

Decision Data

1. Listing of products or services offered for sale.
2. Location of facilities.
3. Sales for prior three years.
4. Profit before tax for three years.
5. Real estate included in deal—owned or leased.
6. If leased, monthly rent and terms of lease.
7. Number of employees.
8. Either total monthly payroll or the average hourly rate and number of people by function.
9. Position in market.
10. Assets included in deal—inventory, receivables, machinery and equipment, real estate, and so on.
11. Brief history of company.
12. Who owns the company.
13. Is it a corporation, proprietorship, or partnership.
14. Type of sale—stock or assets.
15. Meeting with seller.
16. Facilities tour.
17. What makes company unique.
18. Asking price.

Additional data

1. Three years financial statements—audited if possible.
2. Tax returns for three years.
3. Organization charts.
4. Personal resumes of key employees.
5. Any outstanding lawsuits or claims.
6. Last year audited by IRS.

7. Meetings with supervisory personnel.

8. Company financial forecasts for five years out.

9. Strategic plan.

10. Description of distribution channels.

11. Listing of competitors.

12. Size of markets.

13. Description of export program.

Enough data must be gathered during preliminary due diligence to decide which one of the group of targets looks the best. It's important to get as much as possible at this stage because the next step will be to negotiate price and terms. That happens before a buyer has a chance to thoroughly investigate the markets, financial data and personnel. Obviously, the seller has the upper hand at these negotiations because he knows the company—you don't. Yet, in most cases he will not be willing to turn a buyer loose with his records and personnel until a deal appears fairly certain. So you end up negotiating price and terms from weakness, not strength. The more data gathered during preliminary due diligence the more accurate the valuation calculation, and hence the more effectively you can plan negotiating strategy.

Some sellers press for an Offer to Purchase at this stage before negotiations even begin, making the assumption that the offering price and terms are fixed. Don't believe it. If a seller takes this path you know right up front that he wouldn't be so anxious unless something is wrong with the deal. It's like the used car salesman who wants you to sign a purchase contract before test-driving the car.

The most difficult part of this preliminary stage is getting enough financial data to prepare preliminary financial forecasts. You can't possibly know what a reasonable price would be without determining what cash flow the business can generate. Almost without exception, unless it's a corporate divestiture where much of the financial data is public knowledge, the seller will hesitate disclosing full financial statements without an Offer to Purchase. Now, once again, a third party such as an M&A consultant or business broker can be invaluable. He acts as the intermediary to convince the seller you cannot proceed without enough financial data to determine cash flow.

Unfortunately, in many small retail or service businesses, because of poor record keeping, financial statements might never be prepared and tax returns provide the only source of financial data. For an unincorporated business, this means Schedule C from the owner's personal return, and most likely he will refuse to turn this over at this stage. Now the intermediary must come up with enough financial statistics from the owner—on scratch paper if necessary—to permit the calculations. Don't worry about accuracy of the data at this time. If gross misstatements are uncovered during the detailed due diligence phase, you can always either back out of the deal or renegotiate price or terms to compensate.

Rory Janes targeted a small laundromat as a potential acquisition. The seller provided sales figures, headcounts, and the number of washers and dryers included in the deal. He would go no further, however, without a binding offer to purchase. From his own knowledge and research of the market, Rory prepared preliminary cash flow forecasts but guessed wildly at rent and utility amounts. He asked the broker to get this data for the current year, but the seller adamantly refused.

Using his best estimates, Rory decided to proceed, negotiated a deal which could be financed, and issued an Offer to Purchase letter. During his detailed due diligence, he discovered that actual fixed expenses were about twice the amounts he had estimated. Presenting this finding to the seller, he demanded a reduction in price. The seller held that an offer was an offer and wouldn't let Rory back out of the deal.

Fortunately, Rory's Offer to Purchase letter was contingent upon getting financing for the deal, and when the bank saw the real fixed expenses, they refused to participate. The deal fell through and Rory was out several months of search and investigation time, as well as $4,000 of expenses. For his next target, Rory made sure he had enough accurate financial data to reach a reasonable forecast before negotiating a price.

On to Negotiations

In our case study, John E. Joe obtained the necessary data to make his judgments and complete the preliminary due diligence for each of the three targets. Of the three, Candidate #1 looked like the best deal, and John proceeded toward negotiating a deal for the purchase of Make Money Filter Corp.

Before negotiations can begin, however, John must calculate a meaningful valuation of Make Money and determine how far he can go in price and terms. The next chapter gets John through these next critical steps.

7

The Debate Begins
Negotiating a Purchase Price

"Pride is to negotiating what salt is to an open wound."

ARMED WITH DATA GATHERED DURING PRELIMINARY DUE DILIGENCE, IT'S TIME to prepare to sit down with the seller and negotiate price and terms—or rather, tentative price and terms. Whatever the results of this negotiation, be very careful to make the agreement contingent on satisfactory completion of a thorough and complete investigation of the company's records, facilities, people, and markets. Ordinarily the seller doesn't object to this proviso. He knows what skeletons will come out during detailed due diligence and, if he has been honest, realizes there won't be any major surprises. If, on the other hand, he insists on a firm Offer to Purchase at the conclusion of this first round of negotiations, there is something important he hasn't revealed and you better back off fast.

Four things are needed to begin negotiations:

1. A perception of the seller's personality, needs, and objectives.
2. An estimate of the value of assets and liabilities.
3. A calculation of the value of goodwill.
4. A perspective of the financeability of the deal.

THE SELLER AND THE HUMAN ELEMENT

To negotiate any contract effectively you must know the opposition. It's virtually impossible to conclude a mutually satisfactory contract without a grasp of the underlying objectives of the other party, especially in buying a company. When a seller puts his company on the market, he faces severe psychological trauma. He has decided to sell his baby—a business nurtured and developed over a number of years which has become a major part of his life. Whether profitable or in financial trouble, in his eyes, the company manifests characteristics reminiscent of family. He has weathered storms, taught employees, promoted goodwill, and risked everything to make the company survive and grow. Now, he feels like a mother cutting the umbilical cord attached to her baby. And this feeling inevitably has a profound effect on a seller's demeanor and actions at the negotiating table.

Assisting a client negotiate the purchase of a plastic extrusion company in Connecticut, it became painfully clear early that we had missed something during our preliminary due diligence. Buyer and seller began negotiating and quickly closed the gap on price. My client was willing to pay all cash at closing, and more than anxious to close the deal within the time frame established by the seller. But we couldn't seem to get off dead center on a minor point involving a consulting contract with the seller. My client wanted a one year contract; the seller wanted two years.

A full day discussing this apparently moot point yielded no movement on either side. That evening while reviewing strategy for the next day's meeting, we mulled over why we couldn't get the seller to budge. "Do you suppose, Larry, that he really doesn't want to sell?" my client interjected.

"It's possible, I guess, but then why waste everybody's time negotiating? And I don't see how he cannot sell. His bank has refused to expand the line of credit and without additional working capital he'll never get that big export order shipped next year."

"Well, there's no sense in wasting more time if he isn't serious. I'll bring the point up first thing in the morning."

The next day, my client asked the seller, "It seems to us that we're bogged down on a very minor point and before we go any further, I'd appreciate it if you would tell me honestly, do you really want to sell?"

The seller responded, "I did in the beginning, but the further we get into the deal the less enthusiastic I become. Remember, I started this company from nothing 12 years ago. It's been my life ever since. My wife is gone, the kids are all grown up, and I don't know what I'll do if I sell out. So I guess the honest answer is, no I don't want to sell. Sorry to have troubled you. Would you like a ride to the airport?"

The human element will affect everything you do in an acquisition from dealing with professional advisors and bankers to effectively negotiating with the seller. Especially so with a privately held company. Most deals are closed because of a mutually satisfactory merging of personalities of buyer and seller. Negotiations proceed more smoothly and substantially quicker by cultivating the seller and trying to understand his motivations. There are six key issues about the seller that should be judged prior to negotiations:

1. Does he really want to sell? In the case of the Connecticut plastic extrusion company the answer to this first question was crucial.

2. What are his motivations in selling? The seller's objectives and motivations are often hidden, but need to be uncovered. What subjects seem to excite him and which ones does he brush off as inconsequential?

3. Does he personally need a large cash settlement? If he really does need a cash deal and you're not prepared to handle it that way there's not much sense in proceeding.

4. What are his plans after the sale? Many sellers get cold feet about selling when they realize that after the close they will have nothing to do but play golf or tend their garden. The inactivity of retirement, even with a large cash settlement from the business, can scare off even the most enthusiastic seller. If this seems a problem, try structuring a deal to keep him on as a consultant, board member or even an employee.

5. What are his feelings about his employees? Most private sellers are very concerned about the continuity of their company after closing. At some point during the process they invariably ask "Do you plan to keep the existing people on the payroll or will you bring in your own people?" This concern for the welfare of his employees is more typical in rural America than in the larger metropolitan areas but even in New York and Los Angeles, I have heard this question asked of the buyer.

6. Is he basically honest in his dealings so far? The need for honesty in such a major transaction is obvious. If you have any doubt about the seller's honesty and openness, back off right now and go look for a different target. Even if agreement is reached on price and terms, the odds are high you'll never reach satisfactory language for the representation and warranty section of the Buy/Sell Agreement.

Honesty is a two-way street. It's important to be honest with the seller right from the beginning. There may be special conditions that you either will not or cannot cope with—perhaps a recalcitrant customer, or a landlord's threat to not renew the lease, or EPA questions about the continuation of existing production lines or facilities. These are all important considerations to resolve, not only for making the deal, but to manage the company after takeover.

If the plan is to lay off some of the seller's personnel and bring in your own people, tell him up front and get the issue out of the way. Either he will proceed knowing you have been honest with him or he will back out of further negotiations to protect his employees. Whatever the reaction, get it over in the beginning so you won't waste your time and his.

Chances are the seller is going through an even greater emotional upheaval selling his business than you are in buying it. Have compassion and understanding. Let him know you want to help his people and his company, not destroy them. Don't be afraid to share your dreams and aspirations. He has probably gone through the same dreams in his lifetime and would welcome the openness. And above all, try to be patient with him and work with him, not as an antagonist, but as another human being worthy of your concern and caring.

WHAT ARE YOU BUYING?

Whether it's an asset or stock deal, before a reasonable purchase price can be determined the specific assets and liabilities of the business must be identified. This sounds like pure rhetoric, yet buyers consistently enter negotiations without even the barest understanding of what they are buying. In a business acquisition you buy three things: business assets to generate products or services, liabilities incurred by the previous owner (if a stock sale), and customer goodwill. The tendency is to think only of how much cash the company can generate—and this is, of course, very important. But the assets and liabilities of the business will dictate how much of this cash you can take out and how much must be plowed back in. The following three examples illustrate what I mean.

The TBS Group targeted a $20 million manufacturer as their first acquisition. Preliminary cash flow projections indicated a cash throw-off of over $2.5 million annually—more than enough for debt service and a handsome return to the investors. As negotiations were nearing completion, one of the Group members asked the key question—What state-of-the-art equipment has been added in the past three years? The answer was none. It became immediately clear that for the first three years the TBS Group would need to plow back at least $1 million each year for new equipment—and the deal collapsed.

R.U. Levitts was anxious to buy an office supplies business and he closed the deal in a hurry, without bothering to take a physical inventory. After he took over and counted the merchandise, he found that at least one-fourth was stale and soiled from long shelf time. It cost him much of his first year's cash flow to re-stock this damaged and obsolete inventory.

Larry was ready to sign the contract for the purchase of a small accounting practice in the Midwest. He had questioned the seller early in negotiations about the quality of the outstanding receivables and was told that all were OK except for the largest account, an automobile jack manufacturer, who was slow but always eventually paid up. Six months after he took over, this account—amounting to half the total receivables—liquidated its business and Larry had to write off the account. Because of this, he had to borrow to meet his payroll and never did pull out of the disaster. Eventually he had to sell the business at a substantial loss.

Know what you're buying and buy only what you know is there.

CALCULATE GOODWILL

Once the assets and liabilities have been defined, you'll want to know the likelihood of continuing to make the profits and cash flow the seller enjoyed. The unrecorded but nonetheless very real asset permitting this is called goodwill. It might also be called customer lists, client files, or any number of other labels. Whatever you call it, there must be some way to quantify how much this goodwill is worth to a buyer and therefore how much he is willing to pay for it.

When we speak of valuing a business we have to ask the question, "What will the valuation be used for?" If it is to determine the amount of fire insurance to carry, then clearly, the cost of replacing the assets in kind is relevant. If you plan to sell the assets at an auction, then auction value should be used. If the assets are to be used as collateral for a loan, then loan value is important. If you are buying a business, you'll want to know not only what the assets are worth, but also the value of goodwill—and the doors open wide.

There are volumes of books written about different methods to use in valuing a business. Hardly a year goes by without someone coming up with a new scheme to fit the exigencies of the moment. Fortunately, all methods begin with some basic premises which have been accepted for years as viable ways to value a business and these methods are what we will focus on.

Special valuation techniques applicable to small retail businesses and professional practices are treated in Chapters 15 and 16. For mid-sized companies there are only four sensible ways to calculate the value of a going business:

1. A multiple of the average cash flow generated in the past.
2. A multiple of the average cash flow it can generate in the future.
3. Net asset value.
4. Current published price/earning ratios for similar businesses.

Let's look at each of these methods using the financial data John E. Joe has gathered from Candidate # 1 in our case study. Complete financial statements for this target can be found in the Appendix. But first, some definitions to make it easier to follow:

1. *Net Asset Value.* A business, just like an individual, has certain assets of value: cash, investments, inventory, accounts receivable, real estate, and machinery and equipment. It also has assets which are of no value to the

buyer such as unamortized organization expense, prepaid expenses or deferred income or basically any asset on the balance sheet not used to generate profits for the business. Just like an individual, there are also liabilities—trade accounts payable, accrued expenses, short-term bank debt, long-term mortgages, and notes payable. The difference between total assets of value to the buyer and total liabilities to be assumed is the net asset value of the company. This is similar to book value, but excludes non-productive assets and liabilities recorded for accounting purposes only, such as Unfunded Pension Liability. Therefore it is similar, but not the same as book value.

2. *Cash Flow*. Profits create cash which can either be withdrawn from the business in the form of dividends, bonuses, owner's draw, and so on; or plowed back as working capital or invested in long-term assets (real estate, machinery and equipment, long-term investments); or used to pay debts. In the context of pricing a business, cash flow is calculated as follows:

Pre-Tax Profit		XXX
Add:	Depreciation and amortization	+ XXX
	Dividends, bonuses, owner's draw	+ XXX
	Interest expense on short and long-term debt	+ XXX
	Adjusted cash profit	XXX
Deduct:	Income taxes on adjusted cash profit	– XXX
	Adjusted after tax cash profit	XXX
Add:	Decrease in working capital	+ XXX
	Sale of long term assets	+ XXX
Deduct:	Purchases of long term assets	– XXX
	Increase in working capital	– XXX
	Net cash flow	XXX

Interest expense is not considered as a deduction from profits nor are principal payments on short or long term debt considered as cash expenditures because the buyer will probably not assume these liabilities; he will incur new debt through his acquisition financing and the creation of a new operating line of credit.

3. *Projected Net Profit*. Annual profit after tax projected over the next five years based on historical profitability of the company and the historical economic curves and market trends. Projected net profit is that profit which the current ownership and management would produce if left intact and does not reflect efforts of the buyer to increase market share, cut costs, develop new products, and so on.

4. *Historic Profitability.* Annual after-tax profits as reported by the company in the prior full year of operations.

Candidate # 1—The Best Deal

John E. Joe is four months into his acquisition search and has finally settled on the company he wants to buy. The metal water filter manufacturer seems the best bet of the three. According to his Acquisition Plan he's about two months ahead of schedule and has committed only $5,700 of the original $7,400 budgeted to date—not bad. Now John really needs to get moving, though. The business cycle continues to improve and it's fairly obvious that the economy is on the way up. The stock market shows bullish tendencies and preliminary indications from the analysts say that first quarter earnings for many companies will show a marked improvement over last year. If he doesn't move expeditiously, John will lose his timing advantage.

John's choice is named Make Money Filter Corp. and manufactures filters for residential markets. The company was founded in 19XX as a result of a merger of the Wire Frame Products and the Water Gasket divisions of Big Boy Parent, Inc., a publicly traded (AMEX) company located in Kansas City. Big Boy organized Make Money as a highly autonomous subsidiary and chartered the company with the mission to become the market leader in mid-sized residential metal water filters. The newly formed company never got off the ground and three years later, under a reorganization program, Big Boy sold Make Money Filter Corp. to its present owner.

The company is one of only three major competitors designing and manufacturing metal water filters for use in in-line filtration systems between the well and the residence. Products are sold through plumbing wholesalers and distributors. Make Money owns all the real estate occupied by the manufacturing plant (130,000 sq.ft.), warehouse (15,000 sq.ft.) and administrative offices (15,000 sq.ft.).

So much for the background, now let's look at the four valuation techniques.

FOUR VALUATION METHODS

The most widely used of the four techniques is the historic cash flow method. The major advantage in looking at historic cash flow is that, at a minimum, a buyer should be able to generate as much cash as the previous owner. If he doesn't believe he can, he shouldn't buy the business. If the timing is right, however, both the national economy and industry curves should be heading upward. Therefore, even in a stable business, and even if he can't implement policies to increase growth, he should do better than the previous three years. This method yields a minimum value for the company. Note that the historic cash flow method, along with the next method, forecasted cash flow, includes the value of the net assets along with goodwill. There is no separate add-on for asset value.

Historic Cash Flow Method

Account Category	(Dollars) Actual		
	Year 1	Year 2	Year 3
Pre-tax profit	1,685	1,751	1,855
Add:			
Depreciation	700	700	700
Bonuses & owner's draw	300	350	350
Interest expense	525	502	480
Adjusted pre-tax profit	3,210	3,303	3,635
Less: Taxes @ 34%	(1,091)	(1,123)	(1,235)
Adjusted after tax cash profit	2,119	2,180	2,400
Add:			
Decrease in working capital	1,061		
Less:			
Increase in working capital		(1,364)	(1,537)
Purchase of fixed assets		(600)	(740)
Net Cash Flow	3,180	216	123
Average cash flow three years		1,173	
Multiple		× 5	
Historic Cash Flow Valuation		5,865	

Three points should be noted. The current tax rate of 34 percent is used rather than actual rates in effect during each of the years to reflect the future results if all other conditions remain constant. Changes in working capital and fixed assets are included as normal operating expenditures of the business. Owner's draw, which was subtracted from the published statement of income is added back and dividends to the owner are excluded. If you owned the company you would most likely structure a different compensation package.

The multiple of five is purely arbitrary. Some may prefer three, or seven, or some other factor. Current practices, however, use this multiple to reflect recovery of initial investment in five years.

Cash Flow Method—Forecast

Normally the future prospects for the company are more relevant than its history. History is all right for a guide, but a buyer should be able to do better in the future. Forecasted results should be your own estimates, however. Don't use a seller's forecast. It will always be more optimistic than yours. Again, in this calculation, the value of assets is included with goodwill.

| | (Dollars) | | |
| | Forecasted | | |
Account Category	Year 1	Year 2	Year 3
Pre-tax profit	1,706	1,794	1,845
Add:			
Depreciation	700	700	700
Bonuses & owner's draw	300	350	500
Interest expense	458	436	414
Adjusted pre-tax profit	3,164	3,280	3,459
Less: Taxes @ 34%	(1,075)	(1,115)	(1,176)
Adjusted after tax cash profit	2,089	2,165	2,283
Add:			
Decrease in working capital	1,389		
Less:			
Increase in working capital		(150)	(600)
Purchase of fixed assets			(500)
Net Cash Flow	3,478	2,015	1,183
Average cash flow three years		2,225	
Multiple		× 5	
Future Cash Flow Valuation		11,125	

When a purist values future cash he will apply a discount rate to arrive at its present value. Such an approach certainly has merit: cash earned three years from now is not worth as much today as cash earned today. Personally, I prefer not to use the present value concept. It is too easily misunderstood and can be confusing to the layman. I find absolute values far more meaningful for the average businessperson. And again, the multiple in the illustration is purely arbitrary. Looking to the future, a five year recovery on initial investment is reasonable, however, and is used by most professional investors today.

Net Asset Value Method

Remember, net asset value is similar to book value—though not the same—and therefore the data used in this calculation comes directly from the target's most recent balance sheet. It includes only those assets productive for the buyer after takeover and the liabilities he will assume.

Asset/Liability Category	(Dollars) Amount
Cash	45
Accounts receivable	4,205
Inventory	4,850
Net fixed assets	3,156
Total assets	12,256
Less: Accounts payable	(1,006)
Accrued expenses	(1,025)
Net Asset Value	10,225

Normally, the seller's short and long term debt won't be assumed by the buyer and therefore no deduction is made for bank notes, mortgages or long term notes payable. Prepaid expenses and other assets are not included because presumably these intangible assets are of little or no use to the buyer. Similarly, if the company has other intangible assets such as purchased goodwill or unamortized organization expense, these would be excluded. The net asset value method uses figures which have nothing to do with replacement cost, fair market value, or liquidation value. They come straight from the balance sheet—presumably prepared using generally accepted accounting principles.

This method does not recognize any value for goodwill. The assumption is that any goodwill built up over the years will be meaningless to the buyer. In some businesses this may be true—such as certain one person personal services businesses—but surely, in a mid-sized business with products or services to be sold to the same customers, there must be some goodwill. Otherwise there would be no customers.

Profitability Method

I personally feel this method yields nothing but confusion to the negotiating process. Unless a stock is publicly traded there can be no published price/earnings ratio. To justify the use of a P/E ratio from a similar, but publicly traded company, is meaningless. Nevertheless, many sellers—and particularly publicly traded parent companies divesting a subsidiary or division—argue this as the only viable method. The best that can be said for it is its simplistic approach. Anyone can calculate it with a minimum of data.

	(Dollars)
After tax profit last year	1,224
Assuming a P/E ratio of	× 6
Value	7,344

CALCULATING LOAN VALUE

The best way to calculate how much can be borrowed for a leveraged buyout is to employ the same method used by financial institutions—the liquidation method. This method gives no credence to the company as a going business. It views the company as if there was no goodwill and in fact, not a going business at all, but merely a collection of assets with a market value. The theory is that if a buyer defaults, the bank's only recourse will be against the assets of the business. (They choose to disregard personal guarantees when making this argument.) Because the bank will want to make it's recovery as soon as possible, liquidation of the assets at a public auction is the most expedient process. The liquidation value of Make Money assets using the current year balance sheet looks like this:

Asset Category	(Dollars) Book Value	Liquidation Factor	(Dollars) Liquidation Value
Cash	45	100%	45
Accounts receivable	4,205	75%	3,153
Inventory	4,850	25%	1,212
Prepaids	10	-0-	-0-
Land and buildings	1,200	60%	720
Machinery & Equipment	2,456	80%	1,965
Other assets	45	-0-	-0-
Gross Liquidation Value			7,095
Less: Liabilities Assumed:			
Accounts payable			(1,006)
Accrued expenses			(1,025)
Net Liquidation Value			5,064

Liquidation Factors are those reductions from book value used by a bank to give it a cushion in the event of default and liquidation proceedings. Normally a forced liquidation appraisal number for the fixed assets would be used, but in lieu of that, book value (after accumulated depreciation) is a quick way to at least get a feel.

SETTING THE PURCHASE PRICE

Now for the tricky task of determining what weight to apply to each of these methods for Make Money Filter since they have each yielded such significantly different results.

Valuation Method	(Dollars) Valuation Amount
Cash Flow Method—Historic	5,865
Cash Flow Method—Forecast	11,125
Net Asset Value	10,225
Profitability Method	7,344
Liquidation Value	5,064

There is no right or wrong way to value a business. Each company has different characteristics. A high-tech, rapid-growth business justifies more emphasis on the future and thus the forecasted cash flow method makes more sense than a look at the past. A company serving a stable or mature industry should generally be valued closer to historic cash flow times a negotiated multiple. A manufacturing company utilizing substantial machinery and equipment or large blocks of real estate must give credence to the fair market value of its business assets. Ownership of a publicly traded company can be transferred, over time at least, at stock market price/earnings ratios. If a business is in financial difficulty or has suffered losses for several years, there is merit in looking at it without any goodwill and liquidation values might be appropriate. And on and on it goes.

In the case of Make Money Filter, the stock is not traded, the industry is very stable—growing at three percent per year, and it has significant machinery and equipment. It has been profitable for several years and therefore is not in a turnaround condition. So based on these facts, both the profitability method and the liquidation method are irrelevant. There is also a very real question about accomplishing future forecasts. If the current owner doesn't sell, it looks doubtful that he can improve results very much over past performance, so most likely forecasted cash flow overstates the true worth. This leaves net asset value as a reasonable measure of the company's asset worth and historic cash flow as a basis for judging the benefits of goodwill.

Obviously, the seller will argue that the net asset value method is right because that's what he has invested in the business. Additionally, by paying off the company's outstanding notes and mortgages totaling $4,250,000 before the close, he will net only $5,975,000 after liquidating these debts ($10,225,000 price less $4,250,000 debt) which is far less than he needs.

John's retort will be that the seller has essentially taken the proceeds of the loans out of the business in dividends, bonuses and other draws over the years and therefore why should John compensate him for amounts he has already withdrawn? Even giving the seller the benefit of the doubt, using his projections of net profits for the next three years, the average cash flow of $1,173,000 would require a factor of almost eight in order to justify a price of $10,225,000 and current factors of four to six are prevailing. If the business was in a rapid growth market or if significant new products were designed and ready to be released, maybe a higher factor would be justified. But the facts are that the residential water market has been growing at an average of three percent per year for the past 30 years. Even if the water purification niche grows faster, it certainly can not be called rapid. And there are no technologically advanced new products ready for release by the company.

Clearly negotiations could go on for a long time, so let's stop here and settle the issue. The seller is asking $5.2 million for a stock sale which means John would assume existing debt of $4.2 million, so the real asking price is $9.4 million. An asset-based lender will not lend in excess of 70 percent of liquidation value of $5 million. Because John has a very real limit on how much he can pay for the business—remember he has only $1 million of his own and his father-in-law's money to invest as equity—and much more than a three or four to one debt/equity ratio would be undesirable, he can probably go as high as $5 million in a cash out purchase price and still manage the debt service. But $4 million is more desirable. A $4 million price would equate to 3.4 times cash flow (still within reason) but is less than what the seller could theoretically get if he were to liquidate the business (before debt pay off). From the perspective of the P/E ratio, based on current after tax earnings of $1 million, a four to one ratio is probably slightly under what the stock market averages would show for this type of business near the bottom of a bear market.

Therefore, considering all the major factors of P/E ratios, cash flow—historical and projected—net asset value, and liquidation value, John should shoot for a $4 million cash price plus a deferred payout to give the seller at least liquidation value and something for goodwill. If this doesn't work then the only alternative, assuming he still wants the business, is to negotiate some type of deferred payout for the excess price over $5 million. Which brings us to the most common way to buy a privately owned business—by using future payments made from company earnings.

DEFERRED PAYMENTS

A buyer should always try to negotiate a portion of the price to be paid out over an extended period of time rather than all cash at closing. Better yet, negotiate a payout based on the company's performance over an ensuing period of years rather than fixed monthly, quarterly, or annual payments. There are three commonly used deferred payment plans: earn outs, other contingency type payments, and buyer paper.

Share the Profits

An earn out is a method of paying part of the purchase price out of company profits over a period of years. For example, if John negotiated a price of $6 million for Make Money but only $4 million was payable as cash at closing, he might be able to negotiate the balance to be payable over say a 10 year period as a share of company profits. Based on his forecast of an annual after-tax profit approximating $1 million a year, let's say he agrees to pay the seller 20 percent of profits each year for 10 years. If the annual profit actually hits $1 million each year, the seller eventually gets his entire $6 million price. If the profits turn out to be more than $10 million for the period, the seller ends up with more than $6 million, which would be more equitable. After all the seller is entitled to something extra for the use of his money.

A more common arrangement calculates the $1 million earn out payment at a simple interest rate, say 10 percent. The seller will then be entitled to earn not $2 million, but $2 million principal plus $200,000 per year as interest for a total of $4 million over the period. On this formula, and forecasting a $1 million annual profit, he would get 40 percent of the profits, not 20 percent.

Of course, the seller still runs the risk that the company will not generate the forecasted profit for such a long period. To guard against this risk, he might want a minimum payment each year of say $200,000—if profits fell below the $1 million mark. Or John could agree that in such a case the payment period would automatically extend beyond 10 years until the full $2 million principal and 10 percent interest is paid.

Whatever specific terms might be negotiated, an earn out provision for a portion of the purchase price is the best insurance you can get that the business data presented to you by the seller really is as it seems and there are no major skeletons in the closet. Remember, in his eyes, he is selling you future earnings potential and if he takes part of the price based on your realization of this potential, you can be assured that his confidence in the business is as great as yours. Additionally, banks love to see this type of deal. The more payments taken as profit sharing over a period of years, the more reliance they place on the projections of future cash flow, and the easier it is to get the financing.

If It Doesn't Happen You Don't Pay

Another form of deferred payment is contingency payments. Generally, contingency payment arrangements are negotiated when there are major unknowns at the time of close. For instance, if the company plans to rely on the receipt of a major government contract for a substantial part of its business in the future, a portion of the price might be paid only if, and when, the contract is booked. The amount of payment could be predicated on a matching of the contract value with the amount forecasted by the seller. Similarly, payment might be deferred until the settlement of labor negotiations or lawsuits in process at time of the close and could be contingent upon satisfactory resolutions thereof. Although sellers are generally reluctant to agree to such contingent payments, if the contingency is of major significance to the health of the business, you must insist on its inclusion as part of the deal. If the seller remains adamant, walk away from the deal. A significant uncertainty about the future prosperity of the company because of commitments made by the seller is a deal breaker. There should be no uncertainty about that.

A recent acquisition engagement involving a small government subcontractor was a classic example of the need for contingency payments as part of the Buy/Sell Agreement. The target had quadrupled in size over the past two years as the result of winning a Navy contract for the production of components for a shipboard missile protection system. This contract called for shipments to be delivered over a 24–month period with progress payments for material purchases. My client was very excited about closing the deal because if the two follow-on orders were awarded over the succeeding three years the cash flow from progress payments would be so significant that a second acquisition could be totally financed from this internal cash. The seller assured us that the receipt of these follow-on orders was merely a rubber stamp process by the Naval Procurement Office and that no other manufacturer could match his delivery schedule, quality standards, and pricing.

At the negotiating table we pointed out the uncertain characteristics of Navy procurement and that the product was specifically designed by the Navy so that several known subcontractors could produce it. A government agency would not likely single-source any weapons contract. Because of the critical nature of this follow-on business, we wanted 75 percent of the purchase price deferred to its receipt. The seller argued that the follow-on contract was a shoo-in and therefore no hold back was necessary. As a counter offer, he agreed to take a note from the buyer for 25 percent of the price payable over three years.

My client was so excited about the business he was ready to agree to these terms. He wanted the company at almost any cost. We recessed and I tried to reiterate the need for caution, finally convincing him to hold his ground for a contingency. He did finally walk away from the table as we reached a stalemate on this issue.

Six months later, the follow-on contract was awarded to a competitor who won the bid with a 10 percent price cut. The target company was almost out of business and today is little more than a small machine shop doing one-fourth the volume of that year.

Your Promise To Pay

For a variety of reasons on both sides of the table, it may be reasonable to negotiate a portion of the purchase price in the form of a promissory note. Payment of the note should not be contingent on any business occurrence or profit level. It can be structured to be payable monthly, quarterly, annually or with a balloon payment at the end. It could be for any length of time—three years, five years or longer. Of course there must be an interest rate applied to avoid IRS constructive receipt provisions. From the seller's position, this method defers taxable gains and from the buyer's perspective it conserves cash. From the viewpoint of financial institutions, such buyer paper gives assurance that the seller is comfortable with the financial projections and the buyer's credibility as a manager.

Although buyer paper is a convenient way for both parties to benefit, be aware that the seller may demand personal collateral other than the assets of the acquired business. Also, since a financial institution will want this same personal collateral as security, the note to the seller must take a second position to the banks. More on financing in Chapters 11 and 12.

When sitting at a negotiating table always remember that the general rule of thumb is, "seller's price but buyer's terms." Stick to your guns and if you can't lower the price, make sure the terms are something you can live with.

Taxes

The effect on both the buyer and seller of income tax regulations plays a major role in price negotiations as well as in setting the structure of a deal and the terms of payment. Both Congress and the IRS change applicable tax laws on a regular basis and probably will continue to do so. As pointed out in Chapter 4 it is very important to seek qualified tax advice during both the preliminary negotiations and final writing of the Buy/Sell Agreement.

Should you buy stock or assets? What will be the tax effect on both parties? Will depreciation recapture rules apply? How can you minimize taxes on future income by the structuring of the acquisition deal? Will the seller have capital gains or ordinary income? The questions go on and on. It might be that you can negotiate better terms for yourself causing a higher tax to the seller and for this he will want a higher price. Unfortunately, because the tax laws are changing so rapidly, it is impractical to set forth any firm rules to follow in this area except to caution you to be aware of the major impact of taxes on negotiations and to advise you to seek qualified tax advice throughout the process.

THE RULE OF THE FOUR P'S

One final suggestion for negotiating strategy and tactics. From years of learning negotiating tactics the hard way I have developed a set a rules called the Four P's. These rules are fundamental to successful negotiations, and no chapter on negotiating strategy would be complete without a description of this philosophy. The four P's are people, planning, perception, and patience:

1. Know the people against whom you will negotiate.
2. Plan your strategy in advance of negotiations.
3. Exercise your perceptive judgments and don't be afraid of your intuition.
4. Practice patience.

People

Know your opponents. If the seller does his own negotiating, it will be much easier to resolve issues. The human element comes into play with the seller far in advance of sitting down at the negotiating table. If understanding and compassion have been practiced thus far, you will arrive at a mutually satisfying conclusion to negotiations much faster and smoother. Many times, however, the seller elects to be in the background during negotiations. He may feel inadequate in dealing with financial measurements. Or perhaps he realizes that negotiating price and terms is really a selling job and feels inadequate in the persuasive arts. For many reasons, sellers utilize legal counsel, an outside accountant, or a consultant as the negotiator.

It's important to know just who will be sitting across the table in order to plan the appropriate strategy. If he's an accountant, you'll want to defend valuation calculations using sound accounting principles. You'll need as many accounting facts about the target as possible. And you'll want financial data from competitors, trade associations, government bureaus, and any other source to substantiate your number. Bring your own CPA to back up the calculations if it makes you more comfortable. As a minimum, bring a tax advisor. Don't be outflanked on tax issues: this is always a favorite ploy at the negotiating table.

If, on the other hand, the seller appoints his lawyer to do the negotiating, bring your own legal counsel. Lawyers love to out-fox wary layman. Argument and persuasion are the daily nourishment of the legal profession and you could very easily be outmaneuvered without even knowing it unless, of course, you have legal background yourself. But even then, your perspective comes from a business viewpoint, not legal, so let the lawyers debate the niceties of the law. Bring your lawyer. It will be well worth his fees to be certain to cover all the bases.

One word of caution, however. Don't let opposing lawyers negotiate with each other about business subjects. If they do, it's almost certain the process will go on for days with no decision ever reached. Lawyers are trained to advise, not to make business decisions, and they love to debate.

A consultant associate invited me to sit in on a negotiation as his guest. Two lawyers were negotiating price and neither of them had much of a financial background. Each tried to analyze the valuation calculation but neither could get very far with it. Finally, after a full morning of getting nowhere, they mutually decided that price could not be based on financial statements anyway. Therefore, they agreed to throw out the financial calculations and enter negotiations on the more esoteric subjects of customer goodwill, retirement plan funding (or under-funding), and how the Buy/Sell Agreement should be structured. No conclusions were ever reached during the two days I sat at the table.

Plan Your Strategy

As with everything else in the acquisition process, good planning pays off at negotiations. Before ever getting to the table, have your strategy worked out. Know what the numbers are and what the estimated debt service and cash flow will be. Regardless of the results of any valuation technique, you have a fixed amount of equity to contribute and there will be only so much cash available for debt service. A quick calculation determines how far you can go.

Try to estimate how the seller will proceed with negotiations. You should know something about him by now and be able to form some judgment about his degree of aggressiveness. Try to judge how low he will go for a cash price. This gives you a starting figure below the seller's drop dead number for bargaining room. I've found that the best method for planning negotiating strategy is to outline, on paper, your strong points and weak points and another outline estimating the same for the seller. Compare the two outlines and any items rated strong for you and weak for him or vice versa can be settled very quickly. When both sides are adamant about a point the matter must be negotiated with vigor. There's no sense spending time on moot points first. Get to the heart of the matter quickly. If you can't resolve the key issues you don't have a deal.

Also, make a judgment about what the seller is really after. Does he want or need a lump sum cash payment? Or would deferred payments be more advantageous to him? Does he have tax or other liens pending against the assets of the business? If so, then provisions of the bulk sales laws might apply and perhaps knowing this will give you some leverage on either price or terms. Are there family members employed by the company? If yes, then concessions might be gained by agreeing to employment contracts for these people. Such questions might be resolved prior to negotiations by asking the seller up front, in an informal atmosphere. The fewer issues to negotiate, the better, and the higher the probability of reaching an early agreement. Each case may be different, but the principle of planning is the same. Always, do your research and construct a planned strategy before entering negotiations.

Perception

Not much can be said about this third "P", perception, except trust your intuition. Generally, first impressions are the most revealing. A seller's conduct at the first meeting can tell you a great deal about how to negotiate with him. Your judgment of people and events is probably fairly keen or you wouldn't have progressed this far. If that's true, then now is the time to hone that perception to a fine edge. You'll need all the intuitive help you can get during negotiations. Don't be afraid to trust your instincts: most of the time they're right.

Patience—The Golden Virtue

Patience is a characteristic few entrepreneurs have. Yet, at the negotiating table patience can win more points than any other tactic. We've all heard the athletic coach tell his players that the best offense is a strong defense—and that's patience. Even the most hardened professional negotiators have difficulty coping with an opponent who waits them out.

Several years ago I was called upon to renegotiate a very oppressive construction contract with a major international Dutch contractor. It was clear that my client had an extremely weak position and legally could be held responsible for millions of dollars of materials he couldn't possibly deliver. The Dutch were tough negotiators. I knew I could never go toe to toe with them or we would certainly get scalped. Their negotiating team spoke fluent English, but I decided the best tactic was to pretend misunderstanding of their arguments. Negotiations shifted from Rotterdam to London to New York and stretched over four months. Most of the time I just sat and listened, playing the dummy. The Dutch were getting tired of doing all the talking. Finally, their lead negotiator bit the bullet.

"So far, Mr. Tuller, we haven't heard one concrete recommendation from you on how to solve this dilemma. If you can't deliver, how do you propose to settle this dispute?"

"Well, we would just as soon wait and see what develops over the next six months," was the best I could come up with.

"Not good enough!" shouted my adversary. "We must get on with the job. If your client can't produce, we'll find another supplier."

Negotiations ended, my client was out of the contract, and the Dutchmen went about their business—all because I had the patience to wait them out.

The Sin of Pride

Most negotiators have an abundance of pride. Unfortunately, pride can be the greatest detriment to a successful negotiation. Experience has taught me that pride has a way of turning friends into enemies, amicable discussions into fierce arguments, and rational negotiations into non-productive and inconclusive shouting matches. Pride is competitive; it gets in the way of sound logic and reason so that the only important goal is to win. It precludes the possibility of exercising care and compassion in dealing with other people. Pride prohibits understanding, it rules out compromise. Virtues key to the success of an entrepreneur—or anyone for that matter—are cast aside in favor of self indulgence and the need to win.

So many times people become frustrated and angry because they are afraid to admit they were wrong, or because they can't bring themselves to ask for help. Pride instills an overwhelming need to win. Pride blinds an otherwise kind, caring person to the hurt and pain he causes others. Pride gets in the way of reason and conscience. It is destructive and selfish. Pride inhibits those actions that can help people and fosters those that hurt. For these reasons, pride is truly the greatest sin of all.

Pride at the negotiating table will always be destructive. When two parties sit down to work out differences and one, or both, is more interested in winning than in reaching an equitable solution, no reasonable resolution can be reached. How many times have you known in your heart what was right but could not accept it because it wasn't your idea?

So even though there are really five ''P's,'' only four are worthwhile. The fifth, pride, can only destroy.

Assuming everyone controls their pride and mutually agreeable price and terms can be negotiated, the next step in the acquisition process is to issue an Offer to Purchase memorandum and then complete the investigation of financial and operating details of the target company. The experts call this the due diligence phase.

8

The Detective at Work
The Due Diligence Process

"When the doctor probes, the skeletons walk."

To recap where we are so far, let's look at the original acquisition steps from Chapter 2:

1. Define realistic goals.
2. Prepare a reasonable Acquisition Plan.
3. Review current tax laws for structuring the deal.
4. Develop a detailed plan for sourcing potential targets.
5. Perform a preliminary due diligence investigation.
6. Negotiate price and terms based on realistic valuation of the target.
7. Perform a thorough due diligence investigation.
8. Prepare a complete business plan.
9. Develop sources for at least three alternative financing structures.
10. Arrange for final updated due diligence investigation.
11. Write Buy/Sell Agreement and negotiate final language and terms of sale.
12. Attend the closing.
13. Plan the transition management period.

So far we've looked at the first six steps. Our buyer, John E. Joe, defined his goals, prepared the Acquisition Plan, reviewed the current tax laws, and hired an M&A consultant to help in the search. He also answered *Journal* ads and used an unsolicited mailing. After preliminary due diligence investigations, John identified Make Money Filter Corp. as the best choice of three potential targets. He's almost half way through the acquisition process.

Now he's ready to send an Offer to Purchase letter to the seller and then proceed with an exhaustive investigation into the affairs of Make Money.

OFFER TO PURCHASE LETTER

An Offer to Purchase letter must be submitted at this point. The seller won't reveal any more information about his company until he has a firm offer in hand and knows the deal will go through. Even though he has an executed confidentiality agreement, a seller is very protective of what he regards as proprietary information. Inevitably, he feels the buyer already has been provided enough data to make a firm commitment.

On the other hand, you can't make a firm offer without completing the detailed due diligence investigation and arranging the financing, which brings up a key point. Do not reveal to the seller that financing has not already been arranged nor discuss with him the source of the funding. It's none of his business whether you intend to use your own savings, borrow part or all of the purchase price, or bring in other equity investors. The seller will probe for the answer throughout negotiations trying to judge your financial viability and your capability for making the deal. But do not under any circumstances discuss plans for financing or indicate how much, if any, will be borrowed money. Many sellers are afraid of a leveraged deal because they really don't understand the concept. They might be willing to agree to earn outs or buyer notes as partial payment of the purchase price but get frightened off when they learn the buyer plans to use borrowed funds. They fear he might default at a later date and leave them with worthless paper and a financially disabled company.

The following sample Offer to Purchase letter can be used to get around this problem.

OFFER TO PURCHASE

This letter will confirm the intention of xxxxxxxxx (''Buyer'') to acquire all of the outstanding common shares of xxxxxxx xxxxxxxxxxxx (''Company'') from xxxxxxxxxxxxxx (''Seller'') for an aggregate purchase price of $_____, payable at Closing.

Buyer is prepared to proceed promptly to perform the formal investigations and ''due diligence'' and to negotiate and draft as rapidly as possible definitive agreements of acquisition acceptable to both seller and buyer. It is understood by both parties that buyer will make a detailed review and analysis of the business, financial conditions and prospects of the Company and that buyer must be satisfied in all respects with the results of its review and analysis prior to the execution of any definitive purchase agreement.

Seller agrees that in performing its due diligence, buyer and its representatives will be allowed full and complete access to the books, records, and facilities of the Company and that its officers, employees, independent accountant, and legal counsel will be made available, at mutually agreeable times, to review with buyer or its representatives such aspects of the business, financial condition or prospects as buyer deems necessary and that seller will keep buyer fully apprised of and informed with respect to the Company's business activities, financial condition, and prospects.

The definitive purchase agreement will contain terms, conditions, representations and warranties appropriate to the proposed transaction and it is presently contemplated that, in general, consummation of the proposed transaction will be subject to satisfaction of a number of other conditions, including principally the following:

1. A determination that there has been no material adverse disclosure or development concerning the financial condition, earnings or prospects of the Company which, in the judgment of buyer, makes the culmination of this transaction undesirable;

2. The Seller will exert his best efforts to preserve the relationship of the Company with its employees, customers, suppliers and all other parties necessary in running the business until Closing Date;

3. A mutually satisfactory resolution of all legal, tax, accounting, regulatory or other similar matters;

4. The receipt of all consents or approvals, and the execution and delivery of such other contracts, agreements and documents, as may be deemed necessary or desirable;

5. All broker or intermediary fees for this transaction will be the exclusive responsibility of the seller;

6. Upon acceptance of this letter, the seller agrees to negotiate to conclusion and execute a definitive purchase agreement exclusively with buyer by _____ 31, 19XX, and seller will not continue nor begin any negotiations or make any business disclosures with or to any potential buyer other than the buyer, as defined herein, until after the above date or until and if negotiations of purchase between buyer and seller are terminated.

The parties to this transaction will each pay their own expenses in connection therewith, including, but not limited to, those costs and expenses incurred should the transaction not be concluded, for any reason.

Neither buyer nor seller shall have any legal obligation to the other with respect to the transaction contemplated herein unless and until the parties have executed and delivered a definitive purchase agreement, at which point all obligations and rights of the parties hereto shall be governed by such agreement.

SELLER _____   BUYER _____

DATE_____   DATE_____

It is perfectly reasonable to make an offer contingent on satisfactory completion of due diligence and verification of asset values and financial records. A seller should accept this condition knowing where all the skeletons are and that no serious problem will be uncovered. If he pushes too hard for a firm offer at this point—before a thorough due diligence investigation—chances are something is wrong with the business he doesn't want you to learn about. This is a deal breaker. If you can't break the log jam, walk away from the deal.

Again, do not under any conditions reveal how or with whom the deal will be financed. Sellers like to believe a buyer has enough personal wealth to stand behind the company in the event of difficulty later on. They also know that high debt levels can be very risky. Even without deferred payments, most sellers are concerned about the welfare of their employees and do not want to risk financial disaster because of exorbitant debt payments. Many a deal has broken down simply because the seller is afraid to close on a leveraged buyout.

Getting Started

The detailed due diligence investigation is such an important part of acquisition methodology and it is such a time consuming endeavor that you might consider enlisting the services of a CPA, or an M&A consultant to help. Most of your time will be spent at the target's location gathering data and then assimilating it into a comprehensive business plan—as we'll see in Chapters 9 and 10. Assistance from a CPA or a qualified consultant in the analysis of financial data and preparation of pro forma forecasted financial statements shortens the completion time substantially. Time is of the essence. One more negotiation phase remains—language for the Buy/Sell Agreement—and the longer it takes to get to this step, the tougher the seller will be in his language demands.

The first step in the detailed due diligence phase is to send the following checklist to the seller and ask him to have his people gather documentation for as many of the items as possible.

CHECKLIST FOR DUE DILIGENCE

A. Marketing
  a. Customer order backlog reports: by customer and product line as of each quarter for the past three years and current year to date.

b. Listing of orders received: by customer and product line for each month for the past three years and current year to date.

c. Listing of shipments: by customer and product line for each month for the past three years and current year to date.

d. Listing of outstanding customer contracts and outstanding customer bids: domestic, export, and international.

e. Listing and description of all manufacturer's rep organizations, agreements, and commission schedules.

f. Listing of buying sources: export and international.

B. Financial

a. Detailed statements of income and balance sheets by quarter (including annual reports) for the past three years and for each quarter of current year to date.

b. All supporting schedules to above statements of income and balance sheets for the periods listed, i.e. manufacturing overhead detail accounts, selling, general and administrative accounts, and detailed cost of sales. These schedules should be by major product line, if available, but as a minimum, separate schedules for export and international.

c. Aged accounts receivable by customer as of each quarter for the past three years and for each quarter of current year to date.

d. Physical inventory summary (if any) or detailed breakdown of inventory (raw materials, work in process—material, labor, overhead, and finished goods—material, labor, overhead.) as of each year-end for past three years.

e. Aged accounts payable by vendor as of each quarter for the past three years and for each quarter of current year to date.

f. Listing of accrued expenses as of each year-end for the past three years.

g. Federal and state tax returns for the past three years.

C. Personnel

a. All employment contracts or agreements, oral or written, including any severance or termination compensation arrangements with salaried, hourly, or collective bargaining unit employees.

b. All bonus, deferred compensation, stock option, profit sharing, or retirement programs or plans covering salaried, hourly, or collective bargaining unit employees.

c. If there is a pension plan, all documentation, including actuarial reports, tax returns, Trustee reports, population census reports, funding requirements, unfunded liabilities, and so on, for the past three years.

d. Schedule of hourly wage rates and number of personnel in each rate, by work center, department and geographic location.

e. Organization chart of salaried personnel, by location, showing function responsibility, tenure, age, salary, name, and title.

    f. All documentation relating to employee insurance coverages—health, life, AD & D, dental, etc.

D. Contracts, Agreements, Appraisals, Insurance and Litigation
    a. All contracts or agreements with vendors and customers.
    b. All contracts or agreements with employees.
    c. All contracts or agreements with collective bargaining units.
    d. All contracts or agreements with other third parties.
    e. All recent (within three years) appraisals of real estate or machinery and equipment.
    f. Listing of machinery and equipment.
    g. All insurance claims outstanding.
    h. All patents, copyrights or license agreements.
    i. All non-compete covenant agreements.
    j. All lease or purchase agreements for machinery and equipment, autos or real estate.
    k. Legal descriptions of all real estate including deeds, title reports, title insurance documentation, together with documentation of any lien thereon.
    l. Listing and description of all outstanding litigation or anticipated litigation.
    m. Is Union contract transferable? If yes, then description of mechanics of making transfer—such as required approvals.

Before the Buy/Sell Agreement can be written all this data must be assimilated anyway, so he might just as well begin now. In many cases a seller balks at what he considers to be proprietary information, because he really isn't sure the deal will go through. He'll probably say some of it is superfluous. It's important however, to persuade him that the more data he furnishes the first time around, the more succinct the final contract will be and the shorter the time period before closing.

Complete financial statements for the last three years (preferably audited) and monthly internal reports of orders received, shipments, order backlog, and headcounts are of primary importance at this stage. Armed with this data your CPA or consultant can begin the financial analysis. Try to get the seller to mail these reports first, before making any trips to his location. That way the analysis won't be held up while you're digging for non-financial data.

Use a Computer

It should be mentioned at this point that a personal computer can be very helpful in saving man-days of recording and analyzing piles of data accumulated through the due diligence process. Use a strong word-processing package (Wordstar 2000 or Wordperfect) and a good spreadsheet program. I personally prefer

Lotus 123, but several other programs serve the purpose as well. If you don't use a PC now but can spend the time to learn at least spreadsheet software, make the investment. It will be well worth the effort, not only during the acquisition process but in managing the company as well. More and more entrepreneurs are becoming self-sufficient in this information-explosion economy. We have all learned that it's better to be safe than sorry.

MANAGEMENT AND ORGANIZATION

Most of the data can only be gathered at the location itself. The starting point is to schedule a trip to meet the management, see the facilities again and gather as much data from the checklist as possible. Be sure to schedule meetings with the seller and key employees first. Valuable insight into the peculiarities of the company and its products and markets can be gained just by spending time probing the minds of key managers. With the seller's permission, private meetings with each functional manager often yield the best results. At times, however, the seller might be reticent to allow this type of privileged communication, or else he will want to be present during the interviews. So be it. A buyer is at a seller's mercy in terms of procedures and methodology.

Try to get an organization chart immediately, or if there is none in existence ask for one to be prepared. Be sure to understand the responsibilities of all management, supervisors, and other key employees. Also, try to gain insight into the inter-personal relationships between the managers. Who are the thinkers, who are the doers, and who are the analysts? Who is the seller planning to promote, and why? Who is he planning to let go, and why? You may not agree with his assessments, and certainly after closing you will make your own choices, but probing the seller's philosophies about his people provides additional insight not found in documents.

With the seller's attention, this is a good time to ask about labor relations, employment contracts, personnel policies, and fringe benefit programs. Get the seller thinking that you really do regard his people as his most important asset and he'll almost certainly cooperate down the line in digging out manufacturing, marketing and financial data.

Try to get an understanding of management style. Is caring and considerate management practiced, or is the style more belligerent and antagonistic?

Also try to meet with the seller's legal counsel and CPA firm. They'll be hesitant to give out much hard information, but discerning their attitudes toward the personalities of the seller and his key employees might lead to problem areas needing research. And you never know, some interesting facts may slip out.

MARKETING

Assuming the seller has been an active manager and is conversant in general business conditions, the second most critical area is marketing. Order trends, industry conditions and market competition should be under the domain of the marketing manager. Ask questions such as:

- What are the capabilities of his organization?
- Is the internal sales organization functioning effectively?
- Are any competitors ready to introduce important new products to the market this year or next?
- What is his forecast of orders for next year?
- What can be done to improve the marketing effort?

He won't have all the answers but chances are he will welcome the opportunity to brag about how well his organization is doing. Or maybe it will be the opposite—what a poor competitive position they have, or how ineffective his organization is because of budget cuts, and so on. Marketing people love to talk and he probably has a better insight into the marketplace than the seller.

I remember one of my first acquisition engagements when I was asked to do the initial interviewing of the management team, after the new owner took over. During his due diligence phase, the buyer had not been allowed to interview these managers without the seller being present. He reported to me that the managers were very uptight and not at all helpful in clarifying a number of issues raised with the seller about the market share of the target company. However, he researched the company's position on his own and concluded that the slide in share over the past three years had been caused by ineffective marketing leadership. The buyer planned to replace the vice president of marketing as soon after closing as possible.

I interviewed this marketing man and listened to his tale of woe. When the business cycle turned down three years earlier, his boss, the seller of the company, forced him to lay off all in-house salesmen and cut his rep organization in half. All advertising was terminated and sales bonus programs eliminated. These actions not only demoralized the remaining marketing staff but alienated several large customers who subsequently established ties with his two largest competitors. At a time when business was slow, prices were dropping and the order trend plummeted, instead of bolstering marketing activities and increasing advertising, the seller did just the opposite. The decrease in market share was not a result of ineffective management by the marketing manager but rather short-sightedness on the part of the owner. Fortunately, the man was not terminated. Instead he was given license to strengthen his organization and increase the advertising campaign.

If my client had been able to speak with this man privately during the due diligence phase he would most likely have uncovered this condition, and it could have been a deal breaker.

PRODUCTION, ENGINEERING, QUALITY CONTROL

If possible, it's a good idea to interview the production manager separately and then talk to the engineering and quality control managers together (if there are such people in the organization). Whether the target is a print shop, publishing house, computer software developer, or a manufacturing company, the production manager is responsible for getting the product through the shop and shipped on schedule at the lowest possible cost. Therefore he is the one most concerned about shop efficiency and productivity. A true doer in the organization, he is often at odds with both the engineering manager (who always seems to design products difficult to make and routings making it impossible to stay on schedule) and the quality control manager (who is more concerned with making sure the product meets specifications than in meeting schedule and cost budgets).

When meeting with the production manager be sure to query him in five major production areas and listen carefully, for his answers may be different from the other managers:

1. What are the historical trends and current statistics of "promises kept" to the customer or to the production control schedule? This is an excellent measure of the effectiveness of the shop in meeting production schedules.

2. Is there a "Just In Time" (JIT) purchasing program in place for the buying of materials, or is the raw material warehouse overstocked?

3. What are the historical trends and current statistics of variances to cost standards? Is the shop running at least 85 percent efficient against the labor standards?

4. How is productivity or shop utilization measured, and what has been the historical trend here? The answer to this question provides a clue to the adequacy of current manpower staffing. A downward trend indicates too many people on the payroll in the face of declining orders. Or if the current productivity is less than 75 percent there might be problems in first-line shop supervision.

5. How good or bad are labor relations? What are the average number of grievances per week or per month? Have there been recent strikes or slowdowns?

The production manager most likely has the best insight into the inter-personal relationships between department heads. His responsibilities put him squarely in the middle of the organization chart. He must constantly perform a delicate balancing act between order input, material flow, scheduling of machines and labor, labor performance, customer demands, quality standards, equipment repair and replacement, and labor relations. In many facilities this job is the most crucial and demanding of all. It's vitally important that the manager is effective and can, in fact, get the job done. If, during the interview and subsequent meetings you determine that he is not an effective manager you might reconsider proceeding with the acquisition.

When meeting with the engineering and quality control managers, try to get answers to the following:

1. What is the process of entering engineering design change orders into the shop?

2. Who is responsible for determining and approving new shop routings?

3. What are the procedures for assuring compliance with engineering specifications and meeting quality standards?

If there seems to be a bottleneck between the engineering department and production it might indicate either a shortage of qualified engineers or questionable technical qualifications. Or it might merely indicate personal conflicts between the engineering and production managers—not an uncommon situation.

Also explore what new product development programs are in process or on the drawing board. Is there a planned new product development program in effect, or is the R&D effort merely one of catching up with competition? Are the quality standards written into the specifications more stringent or less stringent than the competition? There is certainly no need to produce a Cadillac and sell it at Ford prices if the competition is producing Fords. That is a sure way of reducing profit margins. Lastly, inquire about the presence of a Quality Review Board composed of all the department heads and the owner-manager. Such a Board should meet at least once each month to review current status and plans in the engineering and quality control activities. In addition to the quality control questions relating to the engineering function, ask the following questions of the quality control manager:

1. Is there a written Quality Control Procedures manual in effect?

2. What are the current material and product scrap rates and are they improving or deteriorating?

3. Where is the inspection performed—on-line or at the finished product stage? Are inspectors responsible for maintaining quality standards or are the operators held responsible?

4. Is the company using state-of-the-art quality assurance and testing methods? Is the Quality Circle procedure employed? Are testing gauges and other equipment up to date and adequate?

5. What has been and is currently the product returns rate? Is there increasing customer dissatisfaction with product deliveries or product quality? What is the field failure rate?

While meeting with these line managers responsible for the design, production and selling of the products, remember that the key questions are, how do these key employees interact with each other, and, what level of understanding and caring do they have for their subordinates? Of course, they must also have a detailed knowledge of the business and the industry. The factual details of the target candidate can be garnered through other phases of the due diligence investigation but these interviews and meetings are the only source for judging the human values in the company—the most critical consideration in the success or failure of any business organization. If you aren't satisfied that the company has strong, caring supervisors with the right human values, stop immediately and go back to the drawing board. The odds are heavily stacked against you as a newcomer anyway. To add personnel problems created by an uncaring management to an ever-increasing store of challenges after closing is an almost certain recipe for failure.

FINANCE AND ADMINISTRATION

The interview with the finance executive should be left until the end. A buyer probably already has financial statements, some internal reports, and a pretty fair idea of the profitability of the company by this time. Also, it's better to meet with the Doers and Thinkers first to get a broad spectrum of the business prior to hearing the generally conservative impressions of the analyst. Remember, being an analyst, the finance manager views the strong and weak sides of the business from a different perspective. He'll be more concerned with profits, costs, and cash than with production schedules, product design, and sales campaigns.

Administration (including the personnel function) is generally under the province of the finance manager. If the target has a personnel manager reporting directly to the President, however, then of course interview him separately.

The finance manager is the one person in the organization most likely to understand the impact of decisions by the rest of the supervisory personnel on the profitability and cash flow of the business. He knows about internal controls, cash requirements, collection activities, and unprofitable product lines. He can also explain the various functional cost relationships and define potential cost reductions areas. You'll be working with him in preparing the pro forma financial statements for the business plan so this is a good time to establish rapport.

There are a host of matters to discuss with the finance manager, so schedule at least one full day to get through everything. Don't hesitate to ask probing questions; you may not get complete answers but at least any serious problem areas should be spotted. It's usually convenient to group subjects within this activity into the following categories to make sure everything gets covered:

A. Financial
  1. What are the internal controls over cash?

2. Which customers are difficult to collect from—and why?

3. Are there any accounts in dispute?

4. What are the average days outstanding in payables—and is the payment policy 30 days, 45 days, longer? Why?

5. How much was the inventory write-down last year?

6. Is there obsolete or unsaleable inventory?

7. Is pension funding current?

8. How good are bank relations?

B. Systems

1. What type of systems are in effect? Mainframe, PC's; purchased software or customized; integrated or stand alone systems.

2. Any programming talent in-house? What are the capabilities of the data processing staff?

3. In general, describe the functioning of the labor and production reporting, order entry, inventory control, production control, and accounting systems.

4. What are the built-in internal controls in the systems?

C. Administrative

1. What are the employee insurance programs?

2. What are the mechanics of pension funding? Who is the Trustee?

3. What is the bonus or profit sharing program?

4. Who does employee hiring, firing, evaluation?

5. Is there a company policy manual?

The finance manager will be the hardest to get to open up. His natural tendency as custodian of the company's purse is to be extremely protective of what he considers to be proprietary matters. Although accustomed to being open with auditors and bank representatives about the pure financial results, he protects what he considers proprietary information from other prying eyes. Also, being an analyst type, he is not overly communicative to begin with. An intense probing, if not done discreetly and under the auspices of the seller, brings nothing but empty air.

While conducting these interviews, make an effort to establish a communications link with each of the key employees so that when it's time to write the business plan you can go directly to the source to get detailed questions answered. If the seller balks at direct communications with his supervisors, preparing the business plan can be much more difficult and time consuming. So take the time in the beginning to establish a friendly rapport with the seller and his team.

INTERNAL REPORTS

During the management meetings try to determine from each of the department managers what internal reports are prepared by their department or under their jurisdiction. Although internal reporting is quite different for each company, some reports are necessary for any business to function. Other reports, valuable only to a specific activity, are often designed by the department manager for his personal use in running his show.

In the marketing area, weekly reports covering orders received, order cancellations and shipments (or sales) by customer should be available, as well as the weekly or monthly backlog of customer orders. Try to get these reports for at least the past three years. Sales by territory, customer, and product line are usually prepared by or for the marketing department to assist the sales force in analyzing strong or weak markets and should be readily available. Industry statistics published by trade associations or other industry groups may or may not be of value but are generally available from the marketing manager. Reports tracking price changes, discounts granted and customer returns can also be valuable information. If they are not prepared on a regular basis, try to have the marketing department compile such reports for the past three years, even if they are incomplete.

One report prepared periodically throughout the year by every marketing manager for his own use is a forecast of orders and shipments expected over the ensuing six to twelve month period. Many managers don't formalize these reports for distribution but at least they mentally project the future and sometimes translate these thoughts to written memos or note pads. It's human nature to want to know what the future will bring; but it's also human nature not to want to be held responsible for predictions not coming true. Therefore, although sales forecasts surely exist somewhere in the marketing department they may not be made public. If you can possibly obtain such internal forecasts to verify your own sales projections against management thinking, this goes a long way toward building credibility with financial institutions.

In the production and quality control departments a sample of the reports which should be available are:

- labor hours incurred
- production units completed at each work station
- scrap and product failure statistics
- production schedules by day or by week
- delivery promises kept
- monthly manpower headcount reports by function

These dynamic reports continually change and are used primarily as management tools. Although such internal reports are not necessarily vital to due diligence procedures, it helps to at least see samples to judge the accuracy of the data obtained during the interviews with department managers. Remember, production managers are doers. Their focus is on the here and now. They are more interested in meeting today's or this week's production and delivery schedules than in seeing what transpired historically or predicting what will happen in the future. So don't look for forecasts from them.

Try to get copies of as many of the historical production and quality control reports as possible. All of them might not be needed, but once again, one or more might lead to problems or potential problems to be aware of before closing.

Don't forget that the real purpose of going through due diligence procedures is twofold:

1. To gather detailed information sufficient to prepare a comprehensive and understandable business plan with pro forma financial statements.

2. To uncover information, attitudes and maybe some skeletons in the closet, not readily available in hard factual form, to help judge whether or not to proceed with the deal.

The finance department is the most lucrative hunting ground for internal reports. After all, one of the primary functions of accounting is to produce reports. In fact there are usually so many reports that a buyer needs to pick and choose only those of benefit to his investigation. Be sure to pick up the annual financial statements for the past three years as well as the corporate tax returns. Some other internal reports of interest are those dealing with gross margin profitability by product line and by customer, labor and material variance analyses, and comparisons of actual expenses to budget by cost center.

Most mid-size companies have some type of formal annual financial planning process—usually prepared in the fourth quarter for the following year. Income statements, balance sheets, cash flow statements, and all of the supporting schedules of the last planning period can be very helpful in understanding the functional cost relationships, pricing and volume expectations, and capital expenditure requirements. You might not agree with management's sales forecast but at least it's a base to start from.

CLAIMS, CONTRACTS, AND LEASES

Unfortunately, most businesspeople do not think in logical formats such as lawyers; nor are they as cautious as lawyers about what contracts they sign or what they agree to with customers, vendors, employees, and others related to the business. If they did act more like lawyers there would be far fewer civil actions brought in the courts. That's not the case, however, and therefore a very important part of the due diligence campaign must be to ferret out any outstanding claims, lawsuits, and liens against the company or its assets. A good place to begin this search is with the target company's legal counsel. Be sure to inquire of all contracts—vendor, employee, customer, pension plan, labor union, and so on—as well as any outstanding claims or potential claims (such as third party suits) waiting in the wings but not filed. And what was the last year audited by the IRS and State taxing authorities?

Finally, get copies of all current contracts including leases or installment purchase contracts, so that your own legal counsel can review them later on. He might be able to identify more potential dangers than the target's counsel. This is particularly relevant for any government contract work.

Summary

- Once negotiations of price and terms are completed, issue an Offer to Purchase letter contingent upon satisfactory completion of the due diligence phase.

- Do not, under any circumstance, reveal how the deal will be financed.

- Send the seller a detailed due diligence checklist and ask that he begin to gather all data on the checklist relevant to his operation.

- Ask him to immediately forward audited financial statements for the prior three years. A CPA or consultant can then begin the analysis while the due diligence process goes on.

- Tour the facility a second time and look for improvements from the first trip.

- Meet with the seller and obtain additional information of overall company and market conditions.

- Meet with each of the key management employees—alone if possible— and ask all the questions from the departmental checklists.

- Gather all relevant internal reports produced by the company covering the past year—three years for marketing data.

- Try to meet with the company's legal counsel and outside accountant.

- Gather all data pertaining to lawsuits, claims, and leases. Pay particular attention to recent IRS audits and adjustments.

You might need to go back more than once. Most investigations take two or three trips before all the data is accumulated in a usable format. But keep pushing. This is the chance to get to know the company almost as well as the owner. It's the best opportunity to make a go, no-go decision. Be cordial, but aggressive. A legitimate buyer has a right to know everything about the company before he buys it.

Though complex and time consuming, the steps in the detailed due diligence investigation must be accomplished by a buyer of any size or type of business to be certain he understands all he can about the company before incurring the legal and financial risks of becoming an owner. It might appear that many of the areas covered in this chapter apply only to large companies or manufacturing type businesses. While it's true that each size and type of business places a different emphasis on each of the functional areas, most companies, large or small, must have the basic functions of marketing, production, and finance. Some won't have engineering or quality control departments but all worry about maintaining state-of-the-art techniques and selling only quality products and services. The smaller the company and the less complex the business, the fewer due diligence questions need to be researched. But all of the areas must be examined to be certain whether they apply or not to a specific company.

Back to Make Money

John E. Joe followed all the steps listed above. His investigation turned up some questionable items, but none serious enough to call a halt to the proceedings. His CPA began the analysis of the financial statements and by the time John completed his site work, the numbers were ready for him to begin preparation of the business plan.

9

Your First Book
Preparing the Business Plan

"Don't ask for money unless you have all the facts."

BY NOW MOST PEOPLE ASK IF BUYING A BUSINESS IS REALLY WORTH ALL THE effort, aggravation, and money. Don't despair. Finding the right company and negotiating a good price is usually the hardest part of any acquisition. Oh, there are still financing and legal problems to cope with, but the gut-wrenching work is done.

It's hard to know at this point whether all pertinent information has been gathered during the due diligence process. Probably not, but that won't be cleared up until the business plan gets put together. Any serious skeletons dug up during detailed due diligence should have been recognized and resolved by now, however, and a buyer should have a pretty good feel for the capabilities of supervisory personnel. It's time to get busy on the financing.

To many an acquisition-minded entrepreneur, arranging a financing package can be a confusing and wearying pursuit. If not done properly, it can also be a very time-consuming and frustrating process. Those so-called friendly bankers counted on to do the acquisition financing turn out to be anything but friendly when you try to borrow money. All the advertisements about "competitive interest rates," "loan closings in three days," and "excess funds to invest" turn out to be just so many advertising come-ons. In the real world of finance, no one loans money without a 110 percent guarantee that it will be repaid on schedule.

But an even bigger problem must be overcome. Many bank loan officers who either approve or disapprove loan applications, have very little experience in the management of an operating company and find it difficult to accurately assess the risk of any specific deal. Unless a banker has successfully dealt with a similar company before, he can't begin to intelligently evaluate a proposal. Rick Felleni learned this lesson the hard way.

THE BANKERS' DILEMMA

A large commercial bank in the Midwest was ranked in the top 20 banks in the country. My client, Rick Felleni, did his personal banking there for years and wanted to give them the first crack at his acquisition financing. He approached them with a request to borrow $8 million, fully secured, to buy a manufacturing company located in this bank's territory. I accompanied Rick on his first meeting with the senior vice president, a man with impeccable credentials in banking circles. A well-documented and comprehensive business plan demonstrated that the target company was number three in the water sports equipment market—boats, accessories, diving gear, and fishing equipment. The company was well known with a profitable history. The leisure time market, on a significant growth curve, appeared more recession proof than most other consumer products industries.

Cordial enough at our first meeting, the banker requested that Rick return the next week with personal references. Additional information requests continued unabated for the next seven weeks. Rick began to worry about the bank's continued procrastination. They couldn't seem to reach a conclusion and excuses about "needing to go to committee" became redundant. Finally the two of us met with the same senior vice president with whom we had started. I asked point blank whether or not the bank was interested in the deal and if they were, when could we expect a decision. Full of apologies for taking so long, the banker finally admitted that no one in the secured lending department really understood the boating business and suggested we go elsewhere. How much easier it would have been for everyone if he had merely acknowledged in the beginning that the bank would not loan on an unfamiliar business instead of beating around the bush for almost two months.

The one consistency throughout all the deals I have put together both for clients and on my own account is that most commercial bankers, both at senior levels and lower management positions, are extremely reticent to admit they have no background in general management. But without such experience, how can they possibly understand the intricate economic, operational, and inter-personal relationships present in an operating company? Most bankers begin their careers with a bank and remain in the industry for life. Although the profitable management of a bank requires many of the same operating principles necessary in a manufacturing, retail or service company, with little or no breadth of experience to draw upon, it's nearly impossible for them to cope with the myriad of daily operating problems always present. No wonder so many banks are in financial trouble today. Bank management cannot even run their own companies: how can we possibly expect them to understand the intricate workings of a manufacturing or retail business?

Human nature being what it is, it's perfectly normal to avoid any subject with which one is not familiar and if a banker has not had personal experience with your specific markets, or the target is not in a currently popular industry—such as the petroleum industry in the '70's or space technology in the '80's—don't waste time trying to get acquisition financing. The odds of a turn-down are too great. Far better to begin the search again, this time seeking industry knowledge.

There are a number of financing sources other than commercial banks, and every year the financial services industry spawns new companies and new, more creative financing becomes available. As long as money is available to invest—and short of a worldwide catastrophe there probably always will be—there are sources of capital for acquisitions. The trick is to find such a source quickly and expeditiously, when needed, and on affordable terms.

But first you need a business plan.

BUSINESS PLAN OUTLINE

No reputable financial institution will entertain a loan proposal without the submission of a comprehensive business plan. In addition to looking for skeletons in the closet, the due diligence effort was directed toward gathering data about the target company—the products, markets, competition, people, and financial results—to prepare such a complete, detailed business plan. Even though market research has probably led to a fairly thorough understanding of the company and its market forces already, it's not until a buyer actually sits down and assimilates all the facts, opinions, inferences, competitor research, industry statistics, and economic influences into a written document that he can understand the business completely. So the preparation of the business plan is not just for the financial institutions; it's also the best way to achieve a grasp of the target business in a comparatively short period of time. This knowledge becomes essential in preparing reasonable financial forecasts to project cash flow and debt service capability.

Many entrepreneurs spend substantial time and money out of their own pockets during the survey, search, negotiation, and due diligence phases of an acquisition. Yet the deal never closes because they are unable to get the necessary acquisition financing. This is almost invariably a result of poor preparation or presentation of the business plan. Financial institutions have no other way to judge the merit of either a debt or equity investment in a business except through an analysis provided by the business plan.

With a poorly prepared or sloppily presented plan—and presentation is almost as important as preparation—the reader will have difficulty believing the entrepreneur has the ability to effectively manage the business. Almost all secured creditors or equity investors place at least as much importance on their perceived ability of the buyer to manage the business as on the quality of the underlying assets. After all, the payback of the loan and the return on invested capital must come from the business. If the buyer lacks technical expertise or management ability he can destroy even the most profitable enterprise.

Most bankers will not loan or invest money for an acquisition unless they are comfortable that the buyer can and will make whatever changes are necessary to cause the business to grow both in sales and profits. Growth is the key word. Few financial institutions are interested in an acquisition loan if the pro formas project a steady or declining business. Banking mentality requires minimizing short term risk. Even though many businesses would be far better off over the long term by pruning product lines, eliminating certain market segments or paring back manpower levels in the short term, a decreasing business base gives the impression of increasing risk to the secured creditor.

The moral to all this is that the business plan must be prepared and presented to show a growth business over the next five years. If you have any question about how to do this or are reticent about putting pen to paper, hire a qualified M&A consultant or even a professional writer to do the writing. Even though it must be factual and conservative, the plan is still a selling tool. It must convey a growth message or financing will become a real chore, if not impossible.

By this time you are probably saying, ''Why make such a big production out of what is essentially just a written description of the business and some financial projections?'' The detail of the following outline should clarify that a business plan is more than this. Regardless of the size or type of acquisition, a professionally prepared business plan should include all the following:

BUSINESS PLAN OUTLINE

I. The Parent Company (or individual buyer)
   A. Background
   B. Objectives and Goals
   C. Capitalization Structure (or personal financial statements)
   D. Organization Structure—Present and Future Plans
   E. Personal Resumes and Background of Principal(s)
   F. Current Balance Sheet

II. Economic/Market Conditions/Timing Analysis
   A. Industry Background
   B. Historic and Current Economic Curves Influencing this Industry
   C. Historic and Current Market Conditions
   D. Timing of Acquisition Relative to Market Conditions

III. Proposed Financing Structure for Acquisition
   A. Purchase Price and Terms
   B. Sources of Capital—Equity, Long Term, Short Term, Mezzanine Debt
   C. Application of Funds
   D. Illustrative Return on Investment and Payback Based on Cash Flow

IV. Target Candidate
   A. Background and History
   B. Current Capital Structure/Ownership
   C. Market and Product Analysis
      1. Market Economics
      2. Competition and Market Share Analysis
      3. Product Applications and Product Life Cycles
      4. Pricing Policies
      5. Distribution Channels
      6. Marketing/Sales Organization—Current and Future Plans

   D. Production Analysis
      1. Plant Layout and Material Flow
      2. Production and Cost Systems
      3. Production Organization Chart
      4. Capital Expenditures—Historic, Projected
      5. Utilization and Capacity Analysis

   E. Personnel
      1. Total Company Organization Chart
      2. Personal Resumes of Key Management
      3. Historic, Current, Projected Manpower Headcounts
      4. Labor Relations/Union Contract
      5. Pension Plan and Other Benefit Programs

   F. Facilities
      1. Real Estate Description
      2. Listing of Equipment
      3. Outstanding Liens
      4. Real Estate and/or Equipment Lease Arrangements
      5. Current Appraisals—Real Estate and Equipment

G. Financial
 1. Three Years' Historical Income Statements, Balance Sheets and Statements of Cash Flow
 2. Corporate Income Tax Returns for Three Years
 3. Listing of Assumptions Made for Pro Formas
 4. Five Year Pro Forma Forecasted Income Statements, Balance Sheets and Statements of Cash Flow—with and without Proposed Acquisition Financing
 5. Calculation of Debt and Equity Return and Payback

THE BUYER

This lead-in section of the business plan gives the reader an early indication of the background and management qualifications of the buyer. Include a very brief, one-paragraph synopsis of your qualifications to run the business (a personal resume is included later). You can also expound on your overall goals and objectives developed way back in the beginning stages of the acquisition search. Don't hesitate to write a detailed discussion of the factors leading to the selection of industry, company size, pricing parameters, location requirements, and so on. The more complete the descriptions of yourself and your goals and objectives, the more likely the reader will continue to wade through the rest of the plan. On the other hand, if he gets turned off here, he is not apt to spend the time looking at the rest—and obviously will not be interested in granting the loan.

Financial institutions love to hear about optimistic plans for expansion, but don't expect them to believe the financial results. They expect the buyer to be optimistic so that when they apply their own risk factors and project their own significantly more modest growth curves, the financial projections still show sufficient cash generation to meet debt service requirements.

Capital Structure

If a newly formed corporation will be the acquiring entity the reader wants to know how it is capitalized. If he sees that equity contributions are reasonably substantial relative to outside financing, he'll know that the buyer appreciates the dangers in high leverage deals as much as he does. He also will realize that by making a substantial equity contribution the buyer is serious about staying with the company over the long haul and won't bail out when the going gets tough. Remember, a banker relies heavily on the new owner's ability to make the financial projections come true. If you are not locked into the deal he will feel very insecure with the forecasts.

A personal financial statement should be prepared but not included in the first submission of the plan. If a banker isn't genuinely interested in the deal, there's no sense in having your personal financial records distributed. When a banker does express a sincere interest, or if he asks for it, then deliver it to him personally.

Management

Presenting a picture of management competency right up front is extremely important. A personal resume or profile should highlight those experiences that qualify you to be an entrepreneur. Even though you might never have had the opportunity to run a company before, as a corporate employee you probably have managed a department or a project with creative results. The creative ability to solve operating problems along with evidence of supervisory abilities impress both bankers and investors. If there are other friends or business associates who might join the new business venture at a later date, as employees or minority shareholders, also try to include their brief resumes or personal profiles in this section of the plan.

A formal organization chart showing the proposed personnel in the parent corporation and their relationship to the operating people at the target is always welcome. Even if you are the only active participant now, an organization chart helps the reader understand how management might be structured in the future. At least it shows that thought has been given to management structure and this is a plus. If possible, show a controller or v.p. finance at the parent level. A banker's confidence level escalates when he sees this. He then has one more buffer between his money and the buyer. In his eyes this provides a measure of control over the use of funds in the operation of the business. This is particularly relevant when going after an operating line of credit with the same bank providing the acquisition funding.

ECONOMICS, MARKET CONDITIONS, AND TIMING

Here's the place to describe the economics of the industry and the inter-relationships of economic and business indicators to the target company. Recognizing that no two economists ever agree on the magnitude of economic swings or the timing of upturn and downturn fluctuations, feel free to expound your own theories. But be sure to document what conditions, facts, and assumptions lead to the conclusions advanced. Hardly anyone will agree with these conclusions, but at least it shows that a good deal of thought has gone into analyzing the business.

Few bankers really understand economic forecasting techniques. Most are familiar, however, with basic leading indicators such as residential housing starts, Dow Jones averages, treasury bond and corporate bond yields, consumer spending statistics, inventory accumulation versus sales, and so on. They also seem to understand the most widely used trailing indicators such as capital appropriations, non-residential construction expenditures, trade deficit funding, and petroleum drilling statistics. Therefore, stick with basic economics without becoming too sophisticated.

Try to quote current industry trends from trade journals, Department of Commerce statistics, and competitors' newsletters in the preparation of broad industry forecasts of activity for the out years. These projections may not be accurate, but they are more creditable than personal forecasts.

It also helps to discuss the current P/E ratios for public companies in the same industry—if you can ferret out meaningful comparisons. If published P/E's are in the 18 to 20 range and the purchase price calculates at 10 to 12, a banker views this great negotiating job as adding credibility to the buyer's management skills.

PROPOSED FINANCING STRUCTURE

Any reader wants to know early in the process how the buyer would like to finance the deal. Throwing the ball back to the banker is the worst approach to use. Being indifferent to the capital structure connotes financial immaturity in the buyer. The following statement only brings frowns: "Debt financing of $2 million is required; however, the structuring of interest rates, terms, and collateral is open." Not only does this indicate lack of sophistication in financial matters thus causing concern by the lender, but by not stating a proposal, the bank loses its chance to negotiate. For some reason, when reviewing a loan application, a lending institution always wants to negotiate such things as terms, collateral, and guarantees, rather than merely stating up front what they will or won't do. Without a proposal, there is nothing for them to negotiate from. This irritates the lending officer and may kill the deal right then and there.

Another rule of thumb: Always ask for more funding than really needed and for better terms than necessary. If a $1 million operating line is required, ask for $1.5 million. If long-term debt of $3 million will suffice, ask for $3.5 million. Anything above $3 million can be a cushion against additional equity requirements. When the banker says he needs a personal guarantee for the full amount of the loan, be surprised—even affronted—and maybe a limited guarantee can be negotiated.

Personal Guarantees

A word of caution about guarantees. It's becoming quite common for banks—particularly commercial banks and finance companies—to demand personal guarantees for the full amount of a loan. Many will also insist, in the case of an individual entrepreneur, that his wife or other relative sign as a co-guarantor.

Resist such commitments with a vengeance. Eventually a banker may win the full guarantee but under no circumstances give in to a co-guarantor. If he insists, pack up and try someone else.

This might sound unreasonable and inconsequential. After all, as everyone knows, a guarantee can only be collected if there are assets to seize. If life savings are already committed to the deal and a buyer is willing to pledge all the assets of the business, there won't be any free assets to collect against. Why would a lender feel so strong about full personal guarantees? Perhaps the experience John Rosmetti had in the early '80's will illustrate the point.

John Rosmetti purchased his company with over 90 percent leveraged debt. The asset-based lender insisted he sign a personal guarantee for the full amount of the loan and that his wife co-sign. (By co-signing, all assets held in joint ownership such as their house, car, and checking account, became pledged assets.) A couple of years later unusual external market forces forced severe losses. Cash was scarce and John missed one quarterly payment on his long-term loan. He tried to explain that this was a short-term dip in market demand and within two years, at most, the market should turn around—but the lender wouldn't listen. Because of the co-signed guarantees, all individual and jointly held assets were in jeopardy, and this provided the lender with the club he needed. John was replaced as CEO of his own company with a general manager the lender coerced him into hiring.

This is clearly interference by the lender in management prerogatives. It is also contrary to avowed banking philosophy and conflict of interest laws. With the threat of complete financial ruin, however, the lender prevailed and even now, several years later, John does not yet have control of his own company. John is currently suing, but against an army of hot-shot New York lawyers representing the lender, he doesn't have much hope of success.

Be very, very careful of any personal guarantee. Check with legal counsel before signing, and if your rights under the guarantee are not clear, ask him to explain until they are. If the terms are too onerous, go elsewhere for financing— and don't, under any conditions, let your spouse co-sign.

A BUSINESS PLAN FOR *MAKE MONEY FILTER CORP.*

Let's get back to Make Money Filter. The final negotiated deal called for a total purchase price of $6 million. Terms were $4 million cash at closing, $1 million in a promissory note, secured by the stock of the parent company (but second in priority to any secured lender position), and $1 million in a 10-year earn out. Liquidation value of the assets of the business was about $5 million, but $2.7 million was the maximum loan value these hard assets would carry. John needs an operating line of approximately $1.5 million so he certainly doesn't want to secure any long-term loan with working capital assets.

With these facts, he proposed the following financing structure.

	Millions
Purchase Price for 100% of the common shares	$6.0
Paid as follows:	
Cash at Closing—	
Equity from buyer	$ .7
Long-term debt, secured by all of the real estate and equipment; principal amortized over 7 years, payable quarterly, with interest at prime plus $1^1/_2$, payable monthly	2.7
Mezzanine note payable, secured by a second position on all real estate, equipment, and current assets, and a first position on the common stock of the parent company, payable annually in five equal installments, with interest at prime plus three points, payable monthly	.6
Total Cash at Closing	$4.0
Promissory note payable at the end of three years, with interest at prime plus one point, payable annually, secured by a second position on the common stock of parent company	1.0
Earn out of 10 percent of after-tax profits each year for 10 years	1.0
Total Purchase Price	$6.0

Additionally, a $2 million operating line of credit will be needed, with interest at prime rate, secured by a first position on all receivables and inventory with a borrowing base of 85 percent of qualified receivables and 40 percent of qualified inventory.

If John proposed equity participation from an investment banker he would also show in this section a calculation of how much the investor could expect to get as a return in each of the five years. He is trying to get along without a partner, however, so such a calculation will not be necessary at this stage.

With this proposal John still has $300,000 of uncommitted equity funds and $500,000 of operating line funds to concede during negotiations with a bank, if necessary.

Target Candidate

This is the meat of John's business plan—a discussion of the target candidate, Make Money Filter Corp. This discussion follows John's background and his proposed financing package. Potential lenders or investors are more prone to read the voluminous details about the target if they already see a potentially good investment. What return can they expect on their money? How qualified is the buyer to manage the business? Are the negotiated price and terms favorable to the buyer or will the deal be too highly leveraged? Many financial institutions regard the details of the business as less important than positive answers to these questions. On the other hand, even if these key questions are all answered positively, they still expect to see proof in the detailed discussion of the target candidate.

Background and History

This section should include the following:

- Historic changes in market share, profitability, ownership, and major product introductions.
- Target's product uniqueness.
- Key management progression.
- Profile of current owner/manager.

It's always best to begin with historic changes in the company and then jump into why it is so unique. For example, if it built airplanes during WWII, even though it no longer does, this is the place to mention it and pique the readers' interest. The background section should also include a discussion of key management progression. Credentials of the current owner/manager are only relevant to give the reader a comparison to the buyer's background.

Capital Structure/Ownership

A brief description of the net worth section of the target's balance sheet, together with the percentage ownership of outstanding common shares is sufficient here. If there is outstanding preferred stock, dividend terms would be included. Also, dividend payments or other distributions to the seller would be shown because cash draws—other than salary or compensation—usually show up as reductions of new worth or owner's equity in the balance sheet.

Market and Product Analysis

The market and product analysis section should include discussions on:

- Market economics.

- Competition.
- Market size and market share.
- Product applications.
- Pricing policy.
- Distribution channels.
- Marketing and sales organizations.

Here is where the reader must be convinced of the validity of assumptions about market growth and market share so that he can see the buyer didn't conceive them out of thin air. These assumptions must have a sound basis in fact and industry projection statistics as well as be related to expectations and growth programs of competitors.

In the Make Money plan, market economics of the residential water purification markets are well documented and fairly easily researched. Correlations between sales of purification systems and filters and residential construction starts are clear. Demographic data relating to population growth, underground water basins, and state and local government regulations controlling well drilling and contamination restrictions are all pertinent economic data. Quotes from the Department of Commerce relating to projected changes in this data is always impressive and John will include them wherever possible. Trade association projections and historical data are also valuable tools to illustrate economic forces affecting the market segment. Quotes from articles by noted authorities in the area of water contamination or ecological controls look good and will be used freely.

If possible, John should obtain or create graphs and charts to illustrate pertinent economic trends. A picture is worth a thousand words, and this is particularly true when writing for an audience neither sophisticated in the residential water purification industry nor particularly interested in reading columns of numbers.

In the discussion of competition and market share, John must present as much data as he has on each of the major competitors including annual sales, market share, unique market niches, location, and major strengths and weaknesses. For example, John should tell the reader why another company is the market leader and what keeps this competitor at the front of the pack. Why can't Make Money Filters be the leader? What must be done to improve its position in the market? How much will these changes cost and when can they be implemented? What will be the effect of these improvements on the financial statements? John wants to be sure to let it be known that he doesn't intend to sit back and let market share relationships remain constant.

One word of caution about market size and market share—substantiate both with hard data. Don't make guesses that can be proven wrong. If the seller or his management team make judgment calls, that's all right because you can assume they know their own markets. But don't under any circumstances make personal estimates of market size or market share.

The presentation of this data should be in a format that can be read at a glance and should not be so complicated as to be misunderstood. The competitors and market share for Make Money Filter are reported in the following.

MAKE MONEY FILTER CORP.
Schedule of Competitors and Market Share
As of March 31, 19XX

Product Line	Market Size	Competition	Mkt. Share
6" Single	$50,000	Make Money	25%
		Global, Inc.	45%
		Sanit, Corp.	20%
		Others	10%
3" Single	$200,000	Make Money	50%
		Sanit	40%
		Others	10%
6" Double	$5 million	Make Money	40%
		Global	60%
10" Double	$10 million	Make Money	30%
		Global	60%
		Mono-Type	10%
Double Systems	$100 million	Make Money	10%
		Forcehead	25%
		Makeready	30%
		Others	35%
Single Systems	$200 million	Make Money	2%
		Global	10%
		Makeready	10%
		Foreign Imports	20%
		Others	58%

A clear, well-documented picture of where the company stands relative to the field leads even an uninitiated reader to the right conclusions. Don't get too sophisticated. It would be pure chance to find a banker who thoroughly understood the market niches of your specific target company, even with some knowledge of the general industry.

In the product applications section, discuss the technical aspects of the various product lines. Don't go overboard with technical specifications or engineering structure but concentrate on the description of user applications. The reader is mostly interested in knowing where and how the products are used rather than how they are designed. A comparison of the target's products with those of its competition can give the reader an idea of the uniqueness of its products and why, with the proper marketing effort, its share of the market niche can be increased. This of course, assumes the company has some unique products. Most companies do. Although it's possible, in certain cases where the product lines are very standard and similar products are made by several companies, that the uniqueness is not in product differentiation but in distribution or service. Such was the case with a well-known manufacturer of plumbing and heating products.

This Ohio company has the major share of its substantial market because of the manner in which it warehouses its products throughout the world. Sales personnel supply customers' needs almost immediately upon receiving an order, regardless of location. This company recognized early that the products it sold could be purchased from a large number of manufacturers with no product differentiation. A decision was made to overcome this lack of product loyalty by giving the customer superior delivery service. Two central warehouses were strategically located to provide less than two days delivery to a chain of regional distribution warehouses throughout the country. The salesmen sold out of these regional distribution centers. If a customer needed quantities of one to one thousand, delivery was made the same day. For larger truck load quantities, two-day service was available. Such delivery service brought this company from an insignificant market position to a status of market dominance within two years.

In the pricing policies section, include descriptions of the pertinent cost systems and how they interact with pricing the product. Some buyers prefer to defer cost systems to the production or financial sections of the plan, and that works too.

Does the company price its products on cost plus a mark-up? If so, a discussion of the adequacy of the manufacturing cost system becomes mandatory and must be included here. Do they use price sheets and then discount by different percentages to different customers? If so, then point out the discount ranges and how customers are differentiated. Are the products made to customer order and therefore price is established at the time of quoting a job? In this case, a discussion of the cost estimating system is in order. As in other sections of the business plan, it's important to keep continuity in your discussion to avoid losing the reader. To be safe, assume that he has no experience in this type of company or industry.

Distribution channels and marketing organization discussions go hand in hand. It's difficult to talk about an organization responsible for getting the orders without also discussing how this same organization has responsibility for managing the delivery of those orders. Normally in small companies the marketing, sales, and distribution functions are all under the jurisdiction of one manager to simplify relationships with the customer. It's much easier for the customer to deal with one individual or one organization for all his needs than to be forced to communicate with one group for order placing, another for expediting, and a third for delivery.

In addition to explaining current organization, distribution channels, pricing policies, and competition, remember to fully discuss future plans for the marketing function. The reader must be sold on the idea that you can increase market share more than the seller did. Discuss positively what will change in the marketing area, how long it will take and what these changes will cost versus what benefits will be derived. As seen earlier, the only way to interest a financial institution is to convince them that this company can go farther and grow faster under your leadership than ever in the past. The marketing section must prove this point.

Summary

That finishes the first half of the business plan. By this time your reader is either hooked and will continue reading or the plan is already in the trash barrel. So far, the banker or investor knows:

- Who the buyer is and what qualifies him to make this deal.
- What the current and projected industry statistics look like and how the buyer assesses national economic conditions.
- What type of financing arrangement is proposed and how much he will need to kick in to make the deal fly.
- Something about the target's history and product lines.
- Why this target is unique and looks so good.
- The target's position in its market place, how its distribution system works, and what the marketing organization looks like.

If your reader has given the deal a passing grade so far, he will now want to keep reading and find out about how the product is made, what the personnel organization looks like, what's included in hard assets and how the financial statements shape up. Those are the subjects of the next chapter.

10

The Business Plan
Preparing the Second Half

"No one told me it would be a book."

"I DIDN'T REALIZE YOU HAD TO HAVE WRITING TALENT TO BUY A BUSINESS. I thought technical and management abilities were what counted!"

Mary Jo was frustrated. Reading books about how to buy a company, researching for weeks in libraries, attending seminars on entrepreneurship, and interviewing several successful owners of small businesses, she eventually bit the bullet. Mary Jo left her job as controller of a small hotel chain with plans to buy a natural foods emporium in Philadelphia. She found what she was looking for and negotiated a good price. When we met she was struggling with the business plan. "One thing I could never do well is write. It was almost my downfall in college, and now I'm faced with the herculean task of writing this business book," she complained over coffee one morning.

"There's no reason you have to do it yourself, Mary Jo. Hire someone to do the writing for you. It won't cost that much," I suggested. "In fact, I'd be happy to do it for you."

"It's all yours, Larry. Come over to the house tonight and I'll turn over my trunk of material to you."

Without writing talent or inclination, there is no reason to struggle with the detailed writing of the business plan. Plenty of talented people with excellent writing skills—and typing skills—are begging for work. If a well-written business plan can close the financing loop for an otherwise good deal, for goodness sake don't blow it. Most people don't possess good writing skills, so if the shoe fits, get on the phone and find someone else to do the actual writing. The fees are generally reasonable; a good writer can get it done rapidly; and with the proper packaging, you can quickly get on to the next step in the acquisition process— presenting the plan to financial institutions.

Some of the better sources of writers who could perform this service are:

- English teachers in a local high school.
- English professors at local colleges or universities.
- Work-wanted ads in professional writer's trade journals, such as *Writer's Digest* magazine.
- Work-wanted ads in the local newspaper.
- Place a help wanted ad in this same paper.
- Graduate students.
- M&A consultants—be careful here, however, some write worse than you do.
- A small advertising agency that writes its own copy.
- Small printing companies often know of free-lance writers.
- A practicing CPA for the financial section of the plan.

For a few hundred dollars the entire business plan can be professionally written and ready to turn over to an ad agency, publisher, or book binder for packaging—but more on the presentation format toward the end of this chapter. However you resolve the writing aspect, take the business plan seriously. The better it looks and the more complete it is, the easier it is to get the financing.

Some small business buyers try to get by without a business plan. This is a major mistake and costs the entrepreneur later on. Even if the seller carries all the financing and banks never enter the picture, a business plan should be prepared. It needn't be voluminous, nor is a fancy presentation necessary, but it should be complete, including descriptions of the business and financial forecasts. Those buyers who make the effort find that after they take over the business, reference to original assumptions and descriptions can be most helpful as guidelines in running the company, particularly for the first month or two. So regardless of the size of the business, translate your due diligence research into a formal business plan.

THE PLAN FOR MAKE MONEY FILTER CORP. CONTINUES

Now that the background and marketing sections of the business plan are completed, let's move on to the nitty gritty of writing the production, personnel, and facilities sections, and the all-important segment dealing with financial statistics and projections. Continue to bear in mind that although the business plan clarifies an understanding of the target, its main purpose is to influence a banker.

Production Analysis

Unless the banker has an engineering bent, keep the section on production as short as possible. This section is really more for your own information than to sell the package. Except for the data covering the organization, most of the items are of generic interest only. The following questions should be answered:

- What is the plant capacity versus current production levels?
- Is there enough floor space to meet projected volume increases?
- What were the capital expenditures over the past three years for real estate, equipment, or vehicles?
- What capital expenditures are planned in the future for these same items?
- How are production personnel organized?
- Is the facility laid out efficiently for smooth material flow?
- What type of cost system is employed? Is it computer based or manual? New or established? (Unless, of course, these items were covered in the marketing section.)
- What cost-improvement programs are planned in the next year or two?

Usually the largest group in the company, the production organization requires a more thorough analysis than other departments. Formal organization charts showing names, tenure, salary, and functional responsibility should be included. Also, headcounts of people in each of the production departments, both current and projected, should be shown.

Because every production activity is structured differently, it's unlikely the reader of your plan will understand projected cost reduction programs, labor efficiency improvements, forecasted productivity increases, or new-product development programs without a fairly clear description of what the organization looks like and how it interacts with other departments. Therefore, the major part of this section should deal with people—headcounts, educational cost improvement programs, technical qualifications, reorganization plans, and so on.

This is also the logical place to discuss current and projected new-product development plans; unless, of course, there is a separate R&D or development engineering department, in which case a separate section should be devoted entirely to it. A banker will always be interested in R&D plans. Ideas for developing new products or new services loom as major pluses in making a judgment of the likelihood of success in the new venture. Bankers seldom understand the inherent risks entailed in new-product development programs, however, and are enamored with the concepts rather than the practicalities.

Personnel

Everyone is interested in the people aspects of a business. Bankers, especially, must be convinced that nothing in the personnel area will prohibit or diminish the probabilities of success. This section should include:

- A complete organization chart for the company.
- Personal resumes for each of the key employees.
- Three year historic and current headcounts by department.
- A description of labor relations and Union membership.
- A description of major employee benefit programs with emphasis on any pension or profit sharing plans.

The marketing and the production organization structures have already been discussed. The purpose of the personnel section is to bring the total company organization together into a homogeneous operating structure.

Most readers prefer to see a formal organization chart complete with boxes, titles, and management names rather than a less formal listing, tabulation, or descriptive narrative. Personal resumes for key employees are important but should not take the place of a formal organization chart. Fortunately, there are some very inexpensive software programs on the market today to draw these charts automatically with a personal computer. You might as well get one because re-drawing an organization chart several times can be an extremely laborious and time-consuming manual task.

Even though everyone has seen or used an organization chart, few know how to draw one that presents a complete picture of the company for an outsider such as a banker. The trick is to show the interaction of one department with another without thumbing through a whole book.

For most small to mid-sized companies, there should be enough room on one sheet of paper to have one box for each of the salaried personnel. The hourly personnel can be included under each supervisor shown as the number of heads for each function. Each individual's box should include his name, title, function, tenure with the company, salary, and whether he is exempt or non-exempt.

Following is an example of what the box for a finance manager looks like:

Finance
Controller
R.P. Smith 11 yrs. — $55,000 (E)

A box for the shop foreman is drawn like this:

Tool & Die
Foreman
P.Q. Lawson 9 yrs.—$32,000 (E)

Immediately under the Foreman's box, show the number of production people reporting to him, detailed by job classification:

	Headcounts (N/E)
Machinists	10
Grinders	8
Tool Makers	11
Helpers	6
Total for Dept.	35

When drawing an organization chart, several pages may be necessary. Include the top management of the organization and the department managers on the first page. Then use a separate page for each of the departments. Don't use more pages than necessary, but be sure to be complete for the entire organization. All people should be accounted for—and paper is cheap.

Either as part of the appendix to the plan or immediately following the organization charts, include the personal resumes or profiles of each of the key managers. These vitae should include education, work experience—both with the target company and elsewhere—and ages. Preliminary judgments of capabilities or promotional possibilities can also be included.

The next subject in the Personnel section is a brief documentation of three-year historical and current headcounts for both salaried and hourly employees. These should be shown by department or major job activity. Projected personnel additions and deletions in the ensuing year or two can also be helpful if you have already developed those plans. Of course, if the financial forecasts include changes in manpower these changes must be included.

No need to go into a detailed accounting of grievances and policies relating to labor relations. But general comments should be made about the status of relationships between workers and management, together with any changes over the past few years. Have relations been amicable or have there been work-stoppages or strikes? What is the average tenure in the hourly ranks? What is the demographic curve of the work force? If most of the workers have long tenure and are in their sixties or seventies, labor turnover problems could occur before long and the costs of a training program should be planned for in the pro forma forecasts.

The age of the workforce also has a major effect on the funding of any pension plan and group insurance premiums, and a discussion of these fringe benefit programs should be included. If the pension plan is substantially under-funded based on actuarial calculations, reveal that now rather than springing it later.

Is there a union contract? If so, then present a brief description of its salient features. Don't reveal too much about contract terms at this stage, however. The mere fact that there is a Union will frighten off some bankers. No sense in rocking the boat until you're on firmer ground.

Facilities

Most financial institutions, but especially asset-based lenders, have great interest in the facilities section. Here they learn what type of hard-asset collateral is available for a long-term loan. Bankers love to have hard-asset collateral. There's something about being able to touch and see collateral that gives financial people a warm feeling. Yet, if they must foreclose on a loan they really don't want to end up with real estate or equipment on their books. That's why they keep the auctioneers in business.

Include the following material in the facilities section:

- Description of all real estate included in the deal.
- The most recent appraisal data for real estate.
- If real estate is leased, a complete description of the lease terms.
- A listing of all equipment and machinery.
- The most recent appraisals at fair market value and liquidation value.
- A complete description of lease terms for any major equipment leases excluding small office equipment.

In the real estate segment, a description of the property, blueprints of the buildings, and a plot map would be helpful. If such documents are bulky—and they usually are—merely stating that they are available for inspection at the offices of the target will be sufficient. Include comments about the visual appearance of the buildings—are they new, old, one or multiple-story, clean, well kept, and so on, to help the reader visualize the property. Pictures are very helpful.

Statements about the most recent appraised value of the real estate and the methodology used by the appraiser can be included. You'll need to get your own appraisal before final financing can be arranged anyway so there's no need to elaborate at this time.

If an assumption of the mortgage is part of the deal, a thorough description of monthly payments, interest rate, prepayment penalties, name and address of the mortgage holder, and number of years remaining must be included.

If the property is leased, include the same information—monthly rent, lessees obligations for maintenance and so on, term of the lease, and the name and address of the lessor.

If machinery, equipment, or vehicles are included as part of the business, a detailed listing of all items is mandatory. The reader will not be able to identify the use of each piece but just seeing a list gives him comfort. The longer the list, the more impressive, as Alvin learned.

Alvin was trying to acquire a small machine shop operating with predominantly milling machines—large CNC (computer numeric controlled) equipment—but few in number. We put together an equipment list for the business plan which totaled one and one-half pages. He submitted the plan to four different financial institutions and each of them expressed concern that there weren't enough hard assets to make the deal. Never mind that the appraised value of the equipment was over $3,000,000 and he was trying to borrow only $2,000,000. The list wasn't long enough. Alvin tried again with his second choice of candidate—a much smaller deal. This time the equipment list totaled eight pages of conventional machines with an appraised value of $2,500,000 against a loan request of $2,000,000. The bank jumped at the opportunity to make the loan.

Remember, just as with real estate, you'll need to order your own appraisal before final loan approval. Don't be too concerned about the values on the equipment list at this point. If the seller has had an appraisal within the past five years, both the fair market value and liquidation value (Chapter 13 defines these terms) would be helpful and should be included. Also comment on the age and general appearance of the equipment as well as the seller's preventive maintenance program.

If any equipment is leased, be sure to include a synopsis of the terms and conditions of the leases (except for small office equipment) together with a statement of any restrictions the leases place on a transfer of ownership of the company or its assets.

Financial

Last but certainly not least are the financial statements, forecasts, and statistics. The financial section brings everything together in quantifiable terms. No trouble with a banker understanding this section. Included are:

- A detailed listing of economic and business assumptions used in the financial forecasts (called pro formas).
- Pro forma forecasts of balance sheets, statements of income and statements of cash flow for five years.
- Three years of historical financial statements—balance sheets, income statements, and cash flow schedules.
- Audit reports for three years.

- Corporate federal income tax returns for three years, or Schedule Cs if the business is unincorporated.
- Calculations of debt payback and equity return on investment.

Even though a banker may not understand the business, he should be able to intelligently interpret financial statements. With that in mind be very careful that:

- all numbers tie into one another—that is, they are reconcilable from one period to another and between schedules.
- generally accepted accounting principles (GAAP) as dictated by the American Institute of Certified Public Accountants are used in the construction of the pro forma financial forecasts.
- the assumptions you have made are both reasonable and clearly stated.

If you do not have a broad-based financial background, let your CPA help with this section.

Economic and Business Assumptions for Forecasts

The following listing of questions should all be answered at the beginning of the financial section. All assumptions should begin with current data and cover the next five years.

Economic
- Projected curves of related economic indicators, both leading and trailing, such as residential construction indices.
  - What are the Department of Commerce, trade association, and other economic authorities predicting for the key indicators?
- Interest rate trends.
  - Will interest rates go up, down, or remain constant?
  - What is the timing of major changes?
- Inflation factors.
  - What are you projecting as inflation factors each year?

Sales
- Market growth.
  - What is your projection of the annual growth rate of the target's market?
- Market share changes.
  - What will be the annual change in market share?
  - What will cause these changes?
- Foreign competition.
  - Will foreign competition increase or decrease?

- • Will there be Government interference in the free market to cause these changes?
- Changes in distribution patterns.
  - • What changes are planned in the distribution system?
- Export program.
  - • When will an export program be established?
  - • How much annual sales will be contributed by exports?

Operations
- Cost reduction programs.
  - • What are the planned cost reduction programs?
  - • When will they be effected?
  - • What will be the amount of operating cost reduction?
- Pricing policies.
  - • Are any changes planned in pricing policy?
- Capital expenditure program.
  - • What are the annual capital expenditures each year?
  - • How much will be for maintenance programs and how much to support new products and processes?
- Average wage rates and salary increases.
  - • What is the current hourly wage rate?
  - • What are the projections for the next union contract settlement?
  - • What changes in the salary administration program are planned?
- Personnel changes.
  - • What positions will be replaced and when?
  - • What positions will be added and when?
  - • What are the headcount projections by year?
- Income tax rates.
  - • What are the forecasted tax rates?
- Receivables' days sales.
- Inventory turns.
- Trade payables' days.
- Management bonus program.
  - • Will there be any changes in the bonus program?
  - • How much cash is allocated each year to bonuses?

Financing
- Acquisition debt amount and payment terms.
- Operating line amount and terms.
- Owners draw and dividends by year.
- Management stock option program, if any.

PRO FORMA FINANCIAL STATEMENTS

The pro formas may be structured in any format that makes sense from the readers' viewpoint, but certain rules must be followed:

- The format must either be the same as used in the seller's historic statements or the seller's statements must be restructured to conform to the pro forma format.
- All forecasts must be prepared in conformity with GAAP standards.
- Three years of actual financial statements should be included on the same pages as the pro formas, in columnar format.
- The historic financial statements must be adjusted for any salary, dividends, other distributions, or major fringe benefits paid to the seller.
- No compensation or draw amounts for the new owner should be included.
- The net worth section of the balance sheets must be consistent with the profits from the statements of income from one year to the next.
- Historic financial statements must be reconcilable to the Federal tax returns.

Try to keep the structure of your pro formas as simple as possible while at the same time revealing everything you want the reader to see. The worst format conforms carefully to GAAP standards but prevents the reader from getting a thorough understanding of the financial condition of the business. On the other hand, you dare not venture too far from GAAP or a sophisticated reader will think you are trying to hide something, fool him, or that you don't know what you are doing.

One error commonly made even by experts—is to structure the pro formas creatively, but leave unchanged the historic data presented by the target company. This will always confuse the reader. The first thing he will do is try to trace the progression of the financials from historic to forecast. If he can't make the transition easily, you've lost his attention. To get around this dilemma, reformat the historic financial statements included in your pro formas to the same format as your forecast, always carefully following GAAP procedures. An audit trail remains mandatory, however, so the reader can get from the actual to the reformatted statements.

Another common error is to omit the opening balance sheet at the beginning of the post-acquisition period. Although many financial readers pay close attention to the cash flow statements, they all scrutinize the balance sheet. Not only must an opening balance sheet be part of the format, it must be restated using current accounting definitions applicable to the type of purchase being made. If it's a stock purchase and the price includes a premium over book value (or a discount from book), check with your CPA to be sure of the current procedures for what the accounting profession calls "purchase accounting." For several years now, purchase accounting has meant that, in the opening balance sheet the fixed assets are stated net of the depreciation reserve plus or minus any premium or discount from book value not allocated to inventory or other assets. Future depreciation is then calculated on this new balance of fixed assets which bears no resemblance to account balances on the target company books.

Another example of a confusing procedure mandated by the accounting profession is that when buying a company any unrecorded liability for unfunded pension costs must be recorded as a liability on the opening balance sheet after acquisition—even though there is no requirement for the target company to record such an amount on its books prior to the sale.

The list goes on, and almost every year the accounting profession seems to modify, add to, or delete from its presentation requirements for acquisitions. Check with your CPA to be sure of current accounting policy and then keep checking again and again—before beginning the pro formas and after completion. In fact, unless you are a CPA yourself, let him prepare the pro formas using your assumptions. It's costly, but well worth it in the end.

Experience is probably the best teacher and that certainly holds true when it comes to preparing pro forma financial statements. My first business plan—many years ago—was, I believed, a masterful job. With my background as a practicing CPA, I considered myself an expert in the application of GAAP. Gathering all requisite data, working man-days with calculator and workpapers (this was long before the advent of the personal computer), and finally producing the finished product, I was certain the banker would jump at the opportunity to finance such a sound investment. In about 10 days his call burst my bubble.

"How can I believe your forecast when I can't even reconcile historic net worth year to year? And what about cost of sales? How can I reconcile these cost variances with your headcount projections? And where is the projected cash flow schedule? The source and application of funds as submitted doesn't reconcile to balance sheet cash balances."

I had been guilty of four cardinal mistakes in pro forma presentation:

1. The pro forma statements were not formatted for ease of understanding by the reader. I was careful to use the target's standard cost format but forgot that the reader was not an expert accountant.

2. The beginning balance sheet did not flow from historic data.

3. So intense about conforming to GAAP, I missed a key element—defining the cash available to pay back the loans.

4. I was more worried about accounting niceties than about a forecast that made sense.

Needless to say, those mistakes were never made again.

The most important schedule is the statement of cash flow. This statement must illustrate exactly how the company will generate the requisite cash to pay back the loan or the required investment return. The cash flow forecast should be clean and straightforward without accounting jargon. The AICPA (American Institute of Certified Public Accountants) has yet to make a pronouncement about acceptable cash flow statements for private companies. Therefore, be flexible and make the presentation clear. But it must tie into both the statement of income and the balance sheet.

A banker defines free cash as follows:

Net profit after tax

Plus

Tax-effected non-cash items such as
depreciation and amortization

Plus

Interest and principal of existing debt service

Plus

Owner's draw, and dividends

Plus or minus

Changes in working capital

Include your own projected compensation, but keep it on separate lines to be easily identifiable. Always assume that the reader will recognize optimism and arbitrarily reduce available cash by some factor before calculating free cash for his purposes. Although expected returns change with current market conditions, a good conservative rule of thumb is that debt financing should carry an interest rate of prime plus three points and debt liquidation over a five year period. Equity financing should return cash of 30 percent to 40 percent on average over a five year cycle with investment liquidation either through payback or through a public offering at the end of the period.

Pro Formas prepared by John E. Joe for the Make Money deal are included in the Appendix. Try to follow this format when you do your own forecasts. It is acceptable to bankers and has worked many times in arranging financing for both large and small acquisitions.

Return on Investment

Let's take a brief look at how to format the calculation of investor rate of return. Don't worry about the actual numbers used in this example—it's the format that counts. If you work with an investment banker, this type of schedule is mandatory as part of the financial section.

Assumptions:

Original amount of equity investment	$1,000,000
Return required	30%
Payback period	5 years

First two years no excess cash

	Dollars				
	Year 1	*Year 2*	*Year 3*	*Year 4*	*Year 5*
Balance Beginning of Year	1,000	1,300	1,690	1,597	1,076
Return at 30%	300	390	507	479	323
Payment	-0-	-0-	(600)	(1,000)	(1,399)
Balance End of Year	1,300	1,690	1,597	1,076	-0-

The payments in this example are arbitrary. The $600,000 and $1,000,000 payments assume that this was the maximum available cash in those two years. The entrepreneur paid back $3 million over a five year period for the use of $1 million as equity contribution—clearly, a very expensive way to finance a deal. The next two chapters cover financing alternatives in detail; the illustration here is for business plan purposes only.

Historical Data

Financial statements for three years, audited if possible, together with Federal tax returns for the same periods should be included as the final part of the business plan.

Audited financial statements should be included in their entirety as originally prepared by the seller. Additionally, you will probably need to reformat them to be in conformity with your pro formas. This reformatting takes into account the exclusion of seller draws and other compensation. Of course, the reader will want to see a reconciliation between the seller's original format and your new layout. Also try to reconcile the financial statements to the tax returns, at least for any large unusual items. This can often be very difficult and perhaps such reconciliations will need to be done later with help from the seller or his tax advisor.

Once these reconciliations are done, prior years' financial statements, as such, will not contribute to the efficacy of the plan. But rest assured all bankers will want to have them—so don't leave them out.

PRESENTATION

So much for the preparation of the business plan. Following these basic principles should leave you in good shape. There are three final comments about business plans which must be made, however:

1. Unfortunately, many financial people judge the adequacy of business plans not on substance but by size. If there are two competing opportunities for the banker or investment banker with equal or similar security and return criteria, the business plan with the greatest volume of pages will win hands down. So don't be afraid to use paper—it's cheap. Organize your plan for ease of readership and separate each of the sections by

dividers or blank sheets of paper. Make it look bigger than it really is by including charts, diagrams, listings, and tabulations. In the acquisition game, "bigger is better."

2. Remember that looking right is at least as important as being right. Use expensive-looking paper (at least 20-lb. watermark bond). Package the plan in an attractive binder. A hard-cover three-ring notebook facilitates turning the pages as well as allows additional pages to be inserted if required. If it's too thick for a notebook, take it to a professional binder and have it bound properly. It's not necessary to have your name embossed on the cover—in fact, that gets a bit pretentious—but certainly attach a business card inside the front cover. In most cases, there will be only one chance to get the reader's attention, and that's with the business plan. Make the effort to offer the best documented, professionally written and classy looking plan possible. It's well worth the effort and the cost. Many good acquisitions have been lost because of lack of financing and many times it's because the presentation does not have a professional look.

3. If possible, make the presentation in person rather than through the mail. Some bankers insist on reading the plan before a meeting, but if at all possible, try to hand deliver the package so that he can at least see what you look like. The plan could include your photograph if it must be mailed. Also, even with hand delivery, try to get some photographs of the target company from the seller or take polaroids yourself on the facility tour—you'll be miles ahead. Photos of the real estate, some of the shop equipment or vehicles, and a few of the key management personnel are helpful. And by all means, send along the company's sales brochure with pictures of its products or services, even though this is not included in the business plan per se.

Now that we've completed the business plan it's time to begin the search for that elusive banker willing to put up money for the deal. The next chapter examines alternative methods of financing with debt, and Chapter 12 looks at both equity and debt financing through investment banking sources.

11

Where Is All the Money?
Where to Find the Financing

"Working with banks is like dancing on jello."

THEIR BUSINESS PLAN COMPLETE, TED, MARTY, JOEL, AND FRED—OTHERWISE known as Northern Investors Starlight Group (NISG)—began looking for financing for the acquisition of a manufacturing company with a purchase price of $5 million on March 15. On November 1, seven and one-half months later, they finally arranged the last segment of the financing package and the deal closed the following week. What took so long? What mistakes were made along the way? Let's take a look at a classic case of searching for financing without alternative plans.

First some of the facts. Ted was the majority investor in the group and Joel was the financial genius. Marty and Fred were passive investors along for the ride. The target company manufactured products for applications in basic capital goods industries. The economic curve was at the bottom and barely starting up when Ted finished negotiating the price and terms with the seller and executed an Offer to Purchase. There was an abundance of machinery and equipment with a forced liquidation value of over $8 million, so a purchase price of $5 million certainly looked favorable. NISG was prepared to put up approximately 15 percent of the cash purchase price, which was in line with other acquisition deals at that time, and expected to finance the balance as a leveraged buyout.

Joel had excellent contacts in the New York financial markets and immediately called his personal friend, the president of FearNot Capital—an asset-based lender. Joel proposed a complicated scheme whereby NISG would secure the loan with all the business assets of the target and a $2 million trust fund located in Toronto. The trustee lived in Germany, and most of the trust portfolio was invested in Swiss securities. The four investors offered to personally guarantee the entire debt. Then, as Joel confided to his friend, if that wasn't enough, they knew they could also get the personal guarantee of a wealthy friend of Ted's living in Hong Kong.

At first the executive at FearNot was very enthused. This sounded like a no-lose, sure-fire deal. He had known Joel for 10 years and could definitely vouch for his honesty. All they needed was a little more information from NISG—and of course, the personal financial statements of all the group's members, the trustee in Germany, and the personal friend in Hong Kong.

After six weeks of negotiations, several addenda to the business plan, and frequent phone calls and letters to and from Germany and Hong Kong, nothing seemed to be coming to fruition. Joel was finally informed by his friend from FearNot that the deal was just too complicated and the committee had decided to pass.

Their next shot was a large commercial bank in Philadelphia where Ted had been doing business for many years. Believing the advertisements of "your friendly, hungry banker wants to help you," he was certain they would need to go no further. Ted and Joel met with the banker and submitted the business plan. Sixty days and a dozen phone calls later, Ted reached his friend and was informed, "Ted, we would really like to grant you this loan. However, the collateral will be physically located in a city where we don't have a branch and would be unable to monitor the loan. Therefore, the committee has declined your request. I'm sorry, but you understand."

Ted understood all right. He understood that for two months they had been led into believing approval was forthcoming. The banker could easily have told him right up front that his bank wouldn't make a loan outside the region. Another two months wasted.

Next Joel and Ted approached a large commercial bank in the same city as the target company thinking that if a bank wanted to regionalize, then they would go to a bank in the right region. The loan officer was most courteous and welcomed their submission of the business plan. He was sure the loan committee would look favorably upon the application. By this time they were becoming smarter however, and instead of waiting for an answer made simultaneous submissions to a finance company in the same city as well as one on the East Coast with which Ted had previous dealings. A good thing too, because after another 60 days of review and discussions, the local commercial bank turned them down flat. The excuse this time was, "Our portfolio is complete for this type of loan—we just booked the final one last week."

The next week NISG received level of interest letters from both finance companies accepting the loan applications for the deal. Both wanted typically high interest rates but would allow longer amortization schedules than any commercial bank was granting at that time. The group finally settled on one of these sources plus a local commercial bank for the operating line, and the deal closed.

The lesson was learned. If Ted and Joel had originally taken the time to plan a program of alternate sources—commercial banks, finance companies, investment bankers, and perhaps foreign sources—and prepared multiple submissions simultaneously, they could have cut the sourcing time substantially and would probably have had a better chance of choosing from competitive bids.

While preparing the business plan, hopefully research has been started for potential financing sources. There are a myriad of possibilities—some advertise, some do not. The confusing part about searching for these sources is that they continually change. A banker may or may not be receptive to a loan application depending upon the composition of his loan portfolio at the time you make contact. Small financial institutions or specialty houses may not make loans or investments for years at a time and then all of a sudden decide the market timing is right and go after new business.

No hard and fast rules can solve this problem. Certainly word of mouth is still the best source of information, but even here what was true with a given bank yesterday may not be true tomorrow. Those few financial institutions advertising for business in the *Wall Street Journal*, or elsewhere, are usually overburdened with inquiries. Unless you have something truly unique or that happens to fit a specific niche in the bank's portfolio, they probably won't be responsive.

This chapter explores alternative sources of debt financing. Chapter 12 examines equity and special financing through investment banks.

TYPES OF DEBT

It should be obvious already that there are a multitude of different types of financing sources, ranging from commercial finance companies on one extreme to pure venture capital houses on the other, with a host of variations of secured and unsecured, primary, secondary, and mezzanine debt, and equity sources in between. Before going any further, it might be helpful to define what each of these banking terms means.

DEFINITIONS OF FINANCING TERMS
as used in financing an acquisition

Secured Debt—Long-term loans made to a buyer for funding the acquisition using the assets of the business to be acquired as collateral to repay the loan in the event of default. This debt is used extensively in leveraged buyouts.

Leveraged Buyout—Refers to the type of acquisition financing which uses assets of the acquired business as collateral to loans made to the buyer.

Unsecured Debt—Generally short-term loans made without any collateral except the promise to repay, such as a promissory note or vendor trade credit.

Primary Position or First Position or Primary Debt—Refers to the position of the lender in the order of repayment if the assets are liquidated upon default. Lenders with a primary position will be repaid first. Generally, secured lenders are in a primary position on most of the business assets.

Secondary Position or Second Position or Secondary Debt—Refers to the position of the lender in the event of liquidation. Secondary position lenders are paid from the liquidation proceeds after the primary lenders are satisfied.

Mezzanine Debt—Refers to short- (less than one year) or intermediate- (one to five years) term loans repaid after primary position lenders, and secondary position lenders but before unsecured lenders in the event of liquidation upon default. Mezzanine lenders may be in a secondary position, a third position, or be unsecured. As the name implies, mezzanine debt bridges the gap between loans from traditional secured lenders and equity contributors. Often warrants or other equity kickers are attached to mezzanine debt to attract the lender.

Operating Line—Short-term debt used as working capital. Also referred to as working capital debt or revolving credit. Usually secured by accounts receivable or inventory or both. Always in a primary position against short-term assets.

Equity—As the name implies, this refers to an ownership share of the business, usually evidenced by common stock or preferred stock certificates. In a liquidation, proceeds are distributed to equity holders only after all secured and unsecured creditors are satisfied.

Different financial institutions specialize in different types of debt or equity financing. Although the lines between specialty loans are becoming blurred, generally, the traditional lender of secured funds is still the place to go first. Begin with venture capital firms or investment bankers for mezzanine debt or equity.

The choice of financing depends to a large extent on the type of acquisition and the amount of equity contribution from the buyer. Bear in mind that all financing has a cost, ranging from loans against receivables carrying the least cost and no share of ownership, to unsecured equity money with substantial ownership participation, to high-leverage secured loans at high interest rates and stringent operating covenants.

BANKERS ARE HUMAN, TOO

Many beginning entrepreneurs have had little opportunity to apply for bank loans other than a house mortgage or a car loan—both secure from the banker's viewpoint. Borrowing large sums of money to buy a business is a different matter entirely. Before approaching any financial institution for long-term acquisition funding it's wise to keep a few things in mind about both the people who work in banks and the system itself.

Bankers are real people first, and representatives of financial institutions second. Sometimes it's hard to believe this when going toe to toe trying to convince a banker to lend you money at reasonable terms. In the long run, however, you'll get a lot further with financial people by treating them with just as much honesty and compassion as the seller or professional advisors. A smart banker is more interested in you as a person and in your ability to manage the target business than in the market value of the underlying asset collateral—even though he might not admit this. After all, he doesn't look forward to your default and a liquidation of assets. A bank is in business to make a profit, not to liquidate businesses. Therefore, a banker generally wants to get to know the buyer as a person and understand his personal characteristics such as integrity, emotional stability, and family background long before he ever commits to making a loan.

Conversely, the more interest you take in the banker's personal motivations, fears, and apprehensions in committing his company to lend money, the more successful the relationship will be—both before the closing and while running the business. If he knows that you really care about his own business success and pressures, he will more than likely go to bat with his superiors to get you the loan. Bank employees are no different than other employees. The larger the financial institution, the less authority each loan officer has and the more he fears for his job.

I was working for a client, Robert Swannson, trying to get a loan application approved by a very large East Coast bank for a relatively small amount—$1.5 million. There were more than enough hard assets, receivables, and inventory for loan collateral. Robert had over $1 million in personal investments and was willing to sign a personal guarantee for the full amount of the loan. A comprehensive business plan was submitted with the loan application and three meetings were held with the loan officer and others. Robert patiently waited two months for the bank's loan committee to approve the loan, and couldn't understand why it was taking so long. Patience wearing thin, he finally called the loan officer and demanded action. "Either approve the loan or disapprove it, but don't leave me hanging." I had worked with this loan officer before and because we had developed a high level of mutual respect and a good rapport, his call came as no surprise.

"I know your client is upset with the foot-dragging going on here, but doesn't he understand that I have a problem too?" asked the loan officer. "We work under a bonus structure based on the number of solid loans we place before our fiscal year-end. I've done well this year, but don't have much on the agenda for next year. It would be much better for me if we could wait with this loan 30 more days to get it into our next fiscal year. I really think I can get approval, but with your client's attitude, I'm not sure I want to do it.''

Trying to calm him down I suggested we have one more meeting with just himself, Robert, and me, and set it up for two days later. I quickly contacted Robert and told him the problem. ''I would strongly recommend that we take Jack to lunch and while in a relaxed atmosphere, try to show some compassion and concern for his problems. Let him know you want to help him make a mark in his bank and if another month's delay will help, then that's fine with you.''

We had the luncheon meeting. Robert was on his best behavior and convinced Jack that he was as much concerned about the banker's internal political problems as he was in getting the loan. Needless to say, the next month the loan committee approved Robert's loan application. To this day, both he and Jack are good friends. They even try to get in a few fishing days together each year.

Understanding the human element does make a difference. Even though it might hurt your pride—or even your pocket book, at times—try to have patience and understand you banker's problems first. If he knows you care about him, the relationship will be on more solid ground.

SOURCES OF FINANCING

Commercial finance companies usually make acquisition loans on hard-asset security such as real estate or equipment and machinery. More recently they also have been getting into working capital loans taking receivables and inventory as collateral, but they are primarily interested in long-term, hard-asset deals. The term ''asset-based lenders'' is used to describe this type of lender. Usually the term of the loan is five to seven years at an interest rate of prime plus three to five points. Frequently, depending on the profit performance of the company, they also require substantial placement fees and other types of charges. Asset-based lenders require a first position on all hard assets of the business and probably a second position on working capital assets (if another bank has the operating line). The buyer is usually required to sign a personal guarantee for the entire loan balance, and the lender tries very hard to get his spouse to co-sign as well.

The advantage in using asset-based lenders for acquisition funding—assuming the target has the hard assets to offer as collateral—is that they usually require less equity contribution from the buyer and thus are willing to do high-leverage deals.

The disadvantages are the high interest cost and the extreme difficulty in working with these institutions if and when Murphy's Law begins to cause missed forecasts. As soon as signs of financial difficulty start appearing—and all businesses get into trouble at one time or another—a representative from the asset-based lender usually appears on your doorstep with suggestions, advice, and yes, even with orders from the home office, about what should be changed and how to do this and that to improve the company. Some are worse than others, and of course their policies vary over time.

An asset-based lender handled a deal for Jack Moorset. Jack acquired a small manufacturer of metal parts for computers and office equipment with 95 percent leveraged financing. The company had been in severe financial difficulty and Jack purchased it as a turnaround opportunity. The company sub-contracted from major suppliers of IBM, Univac, and other equipment manufacturers. Wide swings in profits left Jack struggling to meet debt service payments. The lender agreed with Jack going in that two to three years to accomplish a turnaround was not unreasonable. But they couldn't wait. Jack missed two monthly interest payments in the first 15 months of ownership and that was too much for the impatient lender. The bank stepped in, forced an auction to liquidate the company, and still held Jack liable under his personal guarantee for the unpaid balance of the loan—even though he had no logical means of settling the liability. The filing of this obligation under the Uniform Commercial Code prohibited Jack from acquiring another company. Four years later, while working as an employee for an Aerospace manufacturer, Jack still struggled to satisfy his old debt.

The moral here is clear: be extremely wary of making a high-leverage acquisition if an asset-based lender is the only available source of funds. The odds are you won't have the business to yourself very long.

On the other hand, they do serve a real purpose. There have been a number of highly leveraged deals financed by asset-based lenders which have turned out very well for all sides. But be careful. As in any industry, there are top-of-the-line companies and those at the bottom of the barrel. If you use one of these lenders, make sure you pick the right one. Check it out with several customers before signing a loan agreement. A current debtor will be quick to reveal whether or not you can work with the lender.

In all fairness to the asset-based lending industry, however, as knowledgeable businessmen, bankers in these companies far outshine traditional commercial bankers. Many have prior experience in the business world outside of the banking fraternity. Their primary mission of making long-term, secured business loans precludes typical banking ignorance of sound business-management principles. If you meet your debt obligations on schedule, a reputable asset-based lender can actually be a source of assistance in some of your operating decisions. Even though we've had our disagreements, I can honestly say that a firm such as Glenfed Financial Corp. has been more of a help than a hindrance, and can endorse using this firm if you decide to go this route.

Commercial Banks

Somewhere in the middle of the financing spectrum lie commercial banks. Since Federal deregulation of the banking industry and continuing liberalization of state banking laws, it has become increasingly difficult to generalize about the services these banks offer in the business financing area. Deregulation has caused banks and other financial institutions to overlap their traditional functions. Most large commercial banks have finance company subsidiaries. Some have set up departments specifically to handle small business loans. Several larger banks also have investment banking divisions. The wave of bank mergers and consolidations left a void in small, local banks and new ones have sprung up to fill this vacuum. A few have concentrated in the area of small business loans. If you're lucky enough to find one of these in your neighborhood, it can be a good possibility for acquisition financing—particularly for small deals. When we get into buying small retail businesses in Chapter 15 we'll see that this is one of the best sources of funding available.

For larger deals, however, commercial banks per se are not interested in long-term secured financing. They regard this type of loan as too risky unless the buyer's equity contribution equals or is greater than the bank's participation. Commercial banks do remain the primary source of working capital funding, however. It is always best to get an operating line from a local bank, so during your planning stage for financing, keep in mind the necessity of establishing banking relations in the location of your new business.

If you happen to have good contacts in a commercial bank through other transactions, however, it can't hurt to explore their willingness to take on the acquisition financing. Don't spend a lot of time trying to convince them of the viability of your deal, though. The odds are much higher with an investment banker, venture capitalist, or reputable finance company—depending on the structure of the deal.

Other Sources

In addition to traditional bank financing, there are a number of other possibilities for locating long-term debt financing. Most are fairly specialized, however. Each source has its own unique criteria for making secured loans. It's easy to say that these sources are not normal avenues to approach, but because no two acquisition deals are ever the same, how can anything be normal in this business? And, as mentioned before, financing conditions and loan portfolios keep changing so what may be out of the question today, might be the best source tomorrow. There are too many possibilities to list them all, but here are four you might consider, depending on the particular deal.

1. Insurance companies. The very large ones such as Prudential or Aetna or those specializing in life insurance such as Northwestern Mutual or

New York Life are the best bet. Although it is difficult to approach these behemoths directly, perhaps your M&A consultant has contacts in one of them or has used one or more in the past. If so, then he can make the contact for you. This is a great source if one does happen to be interested. They have substantial funds to lend, are patient, and generally won't interfere in your business. Many insurance management people are pretty good businesspeople too.

2. Pension Funds. The same difficulty exists in making contact here as with insurance companies. Unless you have a direct line through a third party it's hard to interest a large pension fund. On the other hand, if one is interested in participating in part of the long term debt—or even possibly in the equity funding—they generally leave you alone after the deal closes and won't interfere with management. Preferred stock issues are a favorite of pension funds so you might have to go this route. A word of caution, however. Some pension funds are extremely reputable and easy to work with, but many, particularly some of the union funds, can become overbearing when Murphy strikes. With pension funds, the best bet is to let a commercial bank, asset-based lender, or investment banker be the lead lender with a pension fund participating with them.

3. Foreign sources. Since the development of oil resources in Third World countries in the early '70s and the stabilization of the U.S. economy in the '80s, foreign investors look with glee at opportunities to invest huge sums of ready cash in secure, high return American companies. Several investor groups, principally in New York and Los Angeles, keep surfacing as eager sources of acquisition capital. Your M&A consultant should either know who to contact for information or be able to put you in touch with a third party money broker to source the funds. But once again, use prudence and sound intuition before venturing into these often treacherous waters, as I learned the hard way.

Several years ago, my partner and I identified an outstanding acquisition opportunity with a price tag of $5 million. Neither of us had much equity to invest and we didn't relish the idea of using an asset based lender—for reasons previously mentioned. One day an associate in the M&A business informed me of a financing deal too good to be true. Being a bit naive, we jumped at the possibility. The arrangement was as follows:

- A Belgian money broker had access to several hundreds of millions of U.S. dollars that his principals wanted to invest in American companies— but only in $20 million increments.

- The loan term would be 15 years at a fixed interest rate of slightly over eight percent (prevailing prime was over 10 percent).

- The placement fee of $2.5 million would be discounted off the top of the loan so that a net amount of $17.5 would be available.

- A bank guarantee of repayment must be issued by a recognized U.S. bank to the investor.

- Since we needed only $5 million for our deal, the balance of $12.5 million would be deposited in the guarantor bank as collateral against its guarantee and draw interest at long-term Treasury rates which at that time were about 12 percent. This interest would remain on deposit as additional collateral.

- The assets of our acquired business would also be pledged to the guarantor bank as further collateral.

- The calculations based on these terms showed that over the term of the loan, the differential in interest earned and interest paid to the investor would liquidate the loan at the end of the period with no principal payments from us. In other words, we could buy the company with the investor's money and never pay it back out of our own funds.

When I presented the deal to several major American banks, no one would believe it was real. I couldn't interest any banker to even look into it. It was inconceivable to me why all bankers weren't jumping at this opportunity of such a sure bet.

When I finally prevailed on one of my British friends to investigate this Belgian money broker I learned the reason for their caution. The source of the funds, traced back through three separate front organizations in Switzerland and elsewhere, was not Arab oil money. It was laundered money from illegal activities right here in the States. That was the end of that.

4. Trusts. Several very wealthy families and individuals have allocated part of their fortunes to be invested in a variety of business activities including acquisition funding. Many families of turn-of-the-century railroad and steel—and more recently oil—barons have established independent trusts specifically for this purpose. They do not advertise, are very secretive, and demand confidentiality in their dealings. Don't try to contact one of these trusts yourself unless you have a personal relationship with one of them. The best way to tap these funds is through a well-connected, private, financial advisor. If you're really interested in doing this, try one of the small investment banking houses designated with a star in the appendix listing.

Investment Banks and Venture Capital Firms

Investment banks and venture capitalists are equity players in the financing game. Because of the increasing popularity of these financing sources, the entire next chapter is devoted to various configurations of financing with them.

PROTECT YOUR ASSETS

It always amazes me how many business people ignore the most crucial rule of personal financial planning: protecting personal assets. They seldom consider that unscrupulous lawyers and inequitable courts can very quickly take away everything they own—including their house, car, investments, and bank accounts. Now, when you are about to enter the world of business ownership, pledging assets and personal guarantees to banking institutions, with at least some possibility of a business failure, it makes no sense at all not to do everything possible to safeguard your personal assets. There are steps which can be taken. There are ways to prevent losing everything in a lawsuit. Hard-earned cash, investments, and retirement funds can be protected from unwarranted claims. The time to protect your assets is now—tomorrow may be too late.

Although lawyers can conjure up any number of creative and costly schemes, I have found the following three methods provide adequate protection for most entrepreneurs. Unfortunately, each has its drawbacks.

1. Form a corporation (personal holding company) to hold all of your assets—your house, car, investments, company stock, bank accounts, and so on. Your wife, children, lawyer, accountant, or anyone else you trust can hold the stock in this corporation. Unfortunately, this corporate shield can be pierced by the court if it deems the corporation is merely flim-flam to cheat a plaintiff out of his due process of law. Sounds goofy, but several courts have ruled in just that manner. You should also consider tax consequences of personal holding companies.

2. Establish an irrevocable trust, with your children or spouse as beneficiary, to hold all your assets. Either your attorney or bank officer are usually good trustees. Similar tax considerations and the ultimate ability to pierce the trust also exist here.

3. Transfer everything to your spouse. This is probably the easiest and cleanest way to safeguard your assets. It also makes it difficult, if not impossible, for the plaintiff to touch them. You can put all your bank accounts, your share of the house, the car, even your company's stock and life insurance policy in the hands of your spouse so that you have nothing of your own. The big risk, of course, is if you and your spouse break up. Then the results can be disastrous. If there is a possibility of a divorce and you choose this method to protect your assets, a contract can be executed excluding these transferred assets from any divorce settlement.

These are just a few possibilities. The time is now. Consult a qualified attorney and work out a plan to protect all your assets before it's too late. Personal lawsuits are escalating and the odds are very high that as a business owner you will be sued for something in your life time. If you have no assets, you can't lose anything.

ALTERNATE SOURCING

With this background, it's time to develop an alternate sourcing strategy for the financing package. Every financial institution has its unique advantages and disadvantages. No one source is perfect. That's why, just as in sourcing a variety of potential target companies, a buyer should look at a number of alternate financing sources. He can then weigh one against the other and hopefully, come up with the best option for his specific deal.

Before examining alternative financing options for the Make Money Filter deal, draw the following form on a piece of paper and fill in the blanks with answers relating to your specific organization structure, target candidate, and personal resources. This is how the numbers work for the Make Money deal:

Source of Funding
(in millions)
Loan Value

	Short Term Bank Debt	Long Term Debt	Mezzanine Debt	Equity Outsiders	Equity Yours	Total
Collateral						
Receivables	$1.5		$.6			$2.1
Inventory						
Land and Buildings		$ .7				.7
Machinery and Equipment		2.0				2.0
Other					$ .7	.7
Total	1.8	2.7	.6		.7	5.5

If John can't raise $600,000 in Mezzanine debt, an equity contribution from an outside investor could be another alternative. If he goes that direction, the following calculation must be included in the financing proposal to illustrate how he will pay the investor the required 30 percent return.

Pro Forma Forecast

	Year 1	Year 2	Year 3	Year 4	Year 5
Outside Equity Balance Due	$600,000	$750,000	$775,000	$757,500	$684,750
Fixed % Return	30%	30%	30%	30%	30%
Equity Earnings	180,000	225,000	232,500	227,250	205,425
Dividends Paid	30,000	200,000	250,000	300,000	370,175
Balance Due	750,000	775,000	757,500	684,750	600,000

This calculation assumes the investor will either leave his equity in the company beyond the fifth year, or that a public stock issue in the sixth year will be used to liquidate his holdings.

These two formats can be used to calculate what financing structure a deal should carry. There's no sense going after long-term debt without hard-asset collateral, and it's useless to try for outside equity unless the required return on investment is there. So making these basic calculations is essential before knocking on any banker's door.

There are also a few basic guidelines to assist in getting to the right bank.

GUIDELINES TO FINANCING SOURCES

Use a Commercial Bank

- For short-term debt.
- With receivables and inventory as collateral.
- If the loan amount is less than 85 percent of receivables.
- For long term debt with real estate as collateral.
- If the amount of the loan is under $1 million.

Use an Asset-Based Lender

- For long-term debt.
- With machinery and equipment as collateral.
- With real estate as collateral.
- If the amount of the loan is in excess of $1 million.

Use Mezzanine Debt

- For a loan in excess of that available from the above two sources.
- If payoff is less than two years, or,
- If the debt can be converted to equity in two to five years.

Use Outside Equity

- For excess between total of the above debt sources and the purchase price.
- If return on investment is at least 30 percent per year.
- If either a payoff or a public issue of stock (IPO) can be achieved in five years.
- If you want an operating partner.
- If you plan to make more than one acquisition within five years.

Now let's take a look at some of the alternative financing schemes John E. Joe came up with in his search for a financing package. From Chapter 9 we saw that John proposed the following financing to come up with cash at closing of $4 million and an operating line of $1.5 million.

	Millions
John E. Joe equity	.7
Long-term debt	2.7
Mezzanine debt/Outside equity	.6
Total available at closing	4.0
Operating line minimum	1.5
Total financing package	5.5

In addition, the seller is financing $2 million himself for a total purchase price of $6 million, but there's no need to worry about that here. Right now all John must do is come up with $5.5 million for the close.

Alternative 1

The combination of John's equity and secured long-term debt won't be quite enough to close the deal so the most likely choice for the $600,000 balance is a small investment bank. His first option would then be as follows:

	Millions
John E. Joe equity	.7
Asset-based lender, secured by hard assets	2.7
Investment banker	.6
Commercial bank, secured by receivables and inventory	1.5
Total	5.5

He'll never interest the big investment banking houses in this small amount. A small firm might be just the ticket, however. John started out armed with his list of small investment banking firms, made some telephone calls, and quickly learned that those investment bankers who were interested were not willing to gamble on mezzanine debt. Everyone wanted an equity piece of the action.

Now John was faced with a tough decision. Should he continue trying to extend the debt load with asset-based lenders or give up a percentage of the business—probably 25 percent for this amount? He had already determined early in the game that he wanted to go it alone—didn't want any partner to argue with about operating policies. Now, here was a chance to put the financing to bed in a hurry, but he'd have to take in an investment banker as a partner.

This is not really a bad idea. Chances are the investment banker intends to play a passive role, and at 25 percent he certainly won't have controlling interest. Also, as we saw in Chapter 3, his technical expertise could be of benefit down the road. More important than anything else, with the right one, an investment banker partner makes financing the balance of the purchase price a lot easier. He's a professional and knows where to go to get the best deals on long-term debt as well as an operating line. And with a professional like this on his side, John will be insulated from the long arm of any asset-based lender he teams up with. They think twice before stepping on an investment banker.

Of several small houses John contacted, the best seemed to be TwixBean Corp. of Princeton, NJ. One of the principals had experience in the water business and this was a plus for John. Additionally, he realized that over the long pull such a reputable partner might be a good bargaining chip in relations with the commercial bank and asset-based lender—almost like an insurance policy.

I learned the valuable lesson of buying insurance against lender meddling a few years ago when I helped a client put together a financing package. At dinner one night with a friend who worked in a small investment banking house in New York, I was bemoaning the fact that the deal I was working on seemed ready-made for an asset-based lender but that I had grave concerns about recommending such a source to my client. I had seen too many bad experiences with such institutions and even a few foreclosures.

''Why don't you recommend that your client buy insurance against such a catastrophe?'' Bob suggested.

''Fine, but where do we find that kind of insurance?''

''Very simple. All you need is a third-party professional with an equity interest in the business and I guarantee no bank in the country will harass you. They depend on these people to bring them new business and they are certainly not going to kill the goose who lays the golden egg.''

Bob was right. About 18 months after closing, my client began experiencing difficulties in bringing a new product line to market. Substantial sums had been spent on development work and cash was tight. He knew he had to defer at least six months of debt service payments to give the new line a chance to catch hold in the market and approached his asset-based lender with this deferral request. The response was remarkable. The operating officer informed him that as long as his investment banker supported the program, the bank would defer payment for as long as necessary. My client asked what the response would be if he were in this alone without an equity partner. He was promptly informed that in that case the request would probably be rejected. By bringing in a professional partner, he not only raised much needed acquisition funding, but for a 30 percent ownership interest, purchased an invaluable insurance policy.

Alternative 2

John didn't stop here, however. Just in case he couldn't reach an agreement with TwixBean, he pushed on to investigate a second alternative—an asset-based lender who would handle the entire deal. To accomplish this, the package would be as follows:

	Millions
John E. Joe equity	.7
Asset-based Lender—long-term	2.7
—short term	2.1
Total	5.5

He contacted two national companies and one of these, Blue Moon Capital, was interested enough to look at his business plan. John wasn't very enthused about turning everything over to a finance company but he pushed ahead anyway to hear what the lender would say. In addition to the high interest rate, he was leery of potential interference with his operation later on. On the other hand, he reasoned, if he used diplomacy in dealing with Blue Moon it might not be too bad. At least the Blue Moon loan officer had compatible philosophies about how to run a business. Also, with Blue Moon he wouldn't need to source a separate commercial bank for the operating line.

Some of the larger, more reputable asset-based lenders are listed in the appendix. I can't vouch for their current management philosophies or portfolio policies, but either myself or a consulting associate have worked with them all at one time or another. Although far from complete, this listing should provide a start toward locating a good source for long-term debt. Although going with a finance company carries a high level of risk, it is a way to get long term funding—assuming the target has significant fixed assets and the buyer is short on equity.

Dealing with finance companies is somewhat at variance with commercial banks or investment banking houses. Most finance company officers are accustomed to dealing with high leverage situations and recognize the risk in these deals. Many loan applicants are individuals trying to do a deal on a shoestring rather than experienced business executives. Consequently, loan officers are more distrustful and wary than their counterparts in commercial banks. They are also more attuned to overall business conditions than commercial bankers, however, and therefore can be of assistance after the close. Most reputable asset-based lender executives seem to welcome an honest, openhanded approach from their customers and respond well to intelligent business proposals. They also seem to be more sensitive to human relationships than commercial bankers, as Hal learned from his lender.

Not long after Hal Brokel closed an acquisition for a small machine shop, financing it entirely with a well-known asset-based lender (a subsidiary of a large national commercial bank), he began to have some concerns about the lender's liaison officer. The man kept forgetting appointments and when they were together seemed preoccupied. Hal began to worry that perhaps he was in trouble with the lender even though he hadn't missed any debt service payments. I suggested he ask the officer to lunch and try to find out what was bothering him. If it did have something to do with Hal's business he better find out in a hurry. They met for lunch the next week and later Hal related the following story.

The liaison officer showed up for lunch distraught and worried. "What's the problem Ron? Can I help?" ventured my client.

"I'm sorry, Hal. It's a series of personal problems. Come to think of it though, they do have a bearing on you and your business so I guess you have a right to know."

"Look Ron. We've been friends for a long time. Let's talk about whatever it is that's bothering you and maybe just talking will help," Hal kept probing.

Ron replied anxiously, "Well, OK. Maybe it will help just to let it all hang out. Everything seems to be falling apart at the same time. My boss wants me to take a promotion involving a move to Chicago and he wants to put this junior officer, Sharon Black, in charge of your account. I told him you would never work with her, but he's adamant. Then my wife refused to relocate. Says it'll be too hard on the kids and will take her too far away from her mother. On top of this, an investment I made in the market last month has gone bad, and that takes care of any vacation plans for this year. But the worst is the effect my leaving will have on your relationship with the company. We've gotten along just fine and in this business it's rare to find a customer you can actually talk to and is honest. And I know you are. I hate to see this relationship destroyed."

During this tirade, Ron had downed his second martini and was beginning to feel no pain. Hal put his hand on the liaison officer's arm. "Ron, I appreciate your concern for me and my company, but this isn't the end of the world. Of course I'll work with your replacement, regardless of who it is, and we'll try to develop the same kind of mutual trust you and I have. So don't worry about that. Maybe you can't take a vacation this year. So what? There will be other years to do that. A more important consideration is to work out the differences of opinion between you and your wife. Why don't you bring her over to the house this Saturday for dinner, and Martha and I will try to explain a few tricks to make relocating easier. Even though it's difficult, a new city and new surroundings can be beneficial to a family if approached in the right way. And you know, Martha and I have a lot of experience in relocating."

They did have dinner that Saturday and as Ron and his wife aired their differences openly, Ron became visibly more relaxed. When it came time to leave, Ron took my client aside. "Hal, thanks for being so considerate and concerned about my welfare. I know now that whatever happens, my family will stay together, and that's the most important thing to me. Thanks again for your help."

By the way, the new liaison officer turned out to be very capable and the good relationship between Hal and Sharon has continued to this day. Ron and his family moved to Chicago and his marriage was strengthened by facing new challenges together.

Alternative 3

With two alternative sources of financing under his belt, John E. Joe wanted one more option, just to be safe. This time he contacted a large bank in Chicago, the home of Make Money Filter. The First Farmers and Steelworkers Bank of Chicago wasn't enthusiastic about the long-term portion of John's requirement, but jumped at the opportunity to take the $1.5 million operating line if he could line up the long-term debt with someone else.

Commercial banks don't normally like to get involved in long-term secured loans unless the deal is very small, but they love demand loans with receivables as collateral. The major exceptions are those large regional or national banks having specialized divisions or subsidiaries—venture capital, finance companies, SBIC, or investment banking groups—to pass the deal along to. Almost all large banks have these special divisions and it is highly plausible that one or more would do the financing for your deal, using their own venture capital firm (or SBIC if they have one) to pick up the shortfall in equity funding.

A big advantage in financing with a commercial bank is that you can then consolidate the long-term debt and operating line in one bank making administration of the loans much easier. In any event, it can't hurt to let a commercial banker know about the acquisition and even if he isn't interested in the long term part, he might want the operating line—again saving extra time and search headaches.

There is always the possibility of being turned down by everyone; although, if researching several sources simultaneously doesn't result in at least one taker, something is obviously wrong. It could be with your choice of sources, or with the plan, or with the presentation, or all of the above. In any event, seek professional advice before spending too much time chasing shadows.

So much for debt financing. There is another way to fund an acquisition and that is through the use of equity money. Let's take a look now at the most prolific source of equity financing, investment banking.

12

A New Source of Money
Financing Through
Investment Banks

"An investment banker can make, break, or take."

INVESTMENT BANKING FIRMS HAVE EMERGED DURING THE '80s AS A PRIME source of funds for financing acquisitions large and small. Giant firms such as Goldman Sachs, Merrill Lynch Capital Markets, and Bear Sterns, to mention but a few, as well as a host of smaller investment bankers have been the principal financiers of most acquisition of all sizes. In fact, the investment banking community has been the single most prominent force behind the wave of acquisitions and mergers—including leveraged buyouts—continuing to flow unabated. Billion-dollar deals like the takeover of R.J. Reynolds march alongside acquisitions of small retail and service businesses as opportunities for investment bankers.

As the stock market turned bullish and price/earnings ratios continued to climb, equity participation in an acquisition became a promising investment for these firms. Buyers found that earnings and cash flows were insufficient to service the large amounts of long term debt required to fund astronomical purchase prices. Therefore debt financing from traditional asset-based lenders or commercial banks became unrealistic and equity funding emerged as the only choice. Investment banking firms, willing to provide such funding, have been able to buoy up the acquisition market in the face of these high prices because investors continue to be optimistic about the American economy. How long this will continue is anyone's guess. The tried and true principles of valuing a business as enumerated earlier in this book and the custom of avoiding high P/E ratios have been severely violated by investment banking manipulations. Sooner or later the house of cards must fall just as it did after the wave of high-leverage deals made in the '70s and early '80s. Many entrepreneurs who talked themselves into believing they could buy a company with all debt financing and little or no equity of their own are now out of business.

But let's get back to the mechanics of investment banking. Typically an investment banker is the primary or lead source in putting together a financing package for an acquisition. He finds an appropriate commercial bank to take the working capital loan, a finance company to take a long-term secured position, and sources the mezzanine financing, if required, from his own funds. The balance is his equity contribution to the deal. His share of the company in exchange for this contribution ranges from 15 to 75 percent. He will also probably want a seat on the board or at least be a board advisor.

Many small investment banking houses specialize in particular industries or types of product. These specialty houses, by bringing industry expertise to the table, provide a valuable aid to the small entrepreneur in the often complex world of high finance. There have been several instances where an investment banker on a board has been invaluable in giving professional advice for operating policies in those specialized areas of the industry where he has considerably more expertise than the owner-manager. Don't be afraid to use your investment banker if you go this route. After all, if he requires a share, or even control of your company, the least you can expect in return—in addition to his money—is some sound advice.

Customers of investment banks include public and private operating companies, wealthy individual investors, private trusts, and entrepreneurs. Even though there are no two investment banking firms alike, either in their internal structure or in the services they sell, they all offer at least one, and usually a combination, of the following services:

- They act as financial advisors to individuals and companies in sourcing and putting together financing packages.
- They buy and sell operating companies for their own account.
- They finance deals from their own resources.
- They act as underwriter for initial public stock issues (IPO).

Most investment banks grew out of the early venture capital firms, securities brokerage houses, or small consulting firms. Later on, with deregulation of the banking industry, many large commercial banks formed their own investment banking subsidiaries to compete in this lucrative market.

Small Business Investment Corporations (SBIC), funded by federal government sources and, though privately owned, affiliated with the Small Business Administration, were forerunners of both venture capital firms and investment banks in providing equity financing for small, growth-oriented companies. In the early days of the industry, there was a sharp line of demarcation between investment banks and venture capital firms. The mission of the latter was to serve as a financing source for very small start-up companies with substantial growth possibilities. These start-ups were predominantly in high-tech industries such as computer software developers and electronics manufacturers. Investment bankers concentrated on advising established companies wishing to expand through merger or acquisition or to restructure through divestiture of operating divisions and subsidiaries. As both venture capital firms and investment banks grew in resources, their missions blurred and today, with a few exceptions, the investor, or the operating entrepreneur, can hardly distinguish between the two.

The popularity of investment banking is not surprising. Equity investors have always been hard to find for the operating executive or business buyer. Short of issuing stock to the public, sources of equity funds for companies unable to finance growth through traditional debt channels were usually reserved for those with private connections to wealthy individuals or private trusts. While venture capital firms were formed by these same individuals and trusts to fill this gap, investment bankers sprang up as advisors to operating management in locating this new source of funds. One invested, the other advised. As the demand for private-equity funding grew with the economy, these two service segments also grew. Venture capital firms began providing advisory services, investment banks started providing their own source of funds, and the two industries in effect combined into what today is a single source of financing.

FINANCIAL CONSULTANTS

Some of the smaller investment banks have their roots in selling financial consulting services to individual entrepreneurs, small operating companies, and private investors. In a sense they operate like a money broker, advising clients about where to invest money on one hand, and assisting companies to raise capital on the other. As a financial advisor, the investment banker acts as a pure intermediary between those with money to invest and those wanting investment funds. He brings the two together to form a financial marriage—much like a real estate agent.

For a fee, and in most cases a very substantial fee, an investment banker melds unadvertised, private investors and investment opportunity. This fee is almost always paid by the user of the funds—the expanding operating company or the buyer in an acquisition—and can range from a few hundred thousand dollars for small deals to several million for larger ones. Additionally, an investment banker generally wants future options to share in the profitable growth of the company. The hallmark of using these services from the investors' perspective is a much higher return than he could get in the open market. Demands of 30 to 40 percent per annum are not uncommon.

Why would a business buyer or operating executive agree to such usurious rates when debt money might cost 10 to 12 percent? Equity financing is unsecured by either company assets or individual guarantees. It is risk capital, and the higher the risk to the investor, the higher return he demands and gets. If a developing company needs funds for research or to hire additional personnel and there are no hard assets to secure a loan, the only remaining source is equity funding. Or if the acquisition price of a deal rests on perceived goodwill rather than hard assets, the buyer has no choice but to use equity funding. Additionally, the risk to the buyer becomes much less with equity money. If the business fails and it is financed primarily by debt, the creditor claims possession of business and personal collateral in default. A similar condition under equity funding results in no loss of either personal or business collateral. The buyer can walk away from the deal and the equity holder suffers the loss. So from the buyer's perspective, although far and away the most costly choice, equity financing is the safest and most risk-free way to go. But it is also the most difficult to arrange, and that's why investment bankers play the role of marriage broker.

Most entrepreneurial expertise lies in marketing, manufacturing, engineering, or development. Seldom does someone trained in one of these disciplines have personal contacts in the somewhat esoteric world of private investor finance. As a production-oriented entrepreneur seeking to develop a new product hires a consulting engineer for technical assistance, so must he turn to experts in equity financing to raise debt free capital. Banks and asset-based lenders are readily available for debt financing, but equity investors are not. The investment banker, as an expert in arranging equity deals, fills this niche.

Obviously, the higher the purchase price of an acquisition beyond its asset collateral—that is, the more you pay for goodwill—the greater the demand for equity funding. In the past decade with the Dow Jones averages moving from 600 to 3000 in a long-term prosperous economy, acquisition prices have skyrocketed. And so has the number of investment bankers serving as the prime source of acquisition funding.

As a financial advisor, an investment banker also acts as a financing packager. That is, he brings together equity investors, commercial banks, and asset-based lenders to construct a total financing package. As we saw in Chapter 3, this is one of the real advantages to having an investment banker as a partner going into a deal. His personal contacts in the financing marketplace facilitate structuring the most beneficial financing package available. Whereas an individual entrepreneur probably doesn't have such resources and would have to make cold contacts to raise debt funds, the investment banker can marshal his forces and save a lot of time and headaches for the buyer. Commercial banks and asset-based lenders look more favorably upon a deal recommended by an investment banker than one you try to put together by yourself. And if he is also a partner in the deal, financing is practically assured.

INVESTMENT BANKS AS SHAREHOLDERS

With such a booming demand for equity funds, it's no wonder investment banks have taken the next logical step beyond financial consulting and become investors for their own account. The returns are just too great not to want a piece of the pie. Many entrepreneurs requiring investment banking services find it difficult, if not impossible, to meet the enormous placement fees demanded by these sources. The obvious solution is to give the investment banker a share of the company in exchange for his services. Basic economics of supply and demand generally govern business transactions. Increasing demand for equity funding has pushed the cost of this money to exorbitant heights. The small buyer really has little choice. If he wants to make the deal, he must pay the seller's price, and by paying higher acquisition prices, he forces himself into using equity financing. Because investment bankers are the best, and many times only, source of such funding, they can demand enormous fees for services rendered. A buyer, short of funds to begin with, has but one choice—give up part of the ownership in his company in lieu of cash payments.

By taking an ownership share, the investment banker insinuates himself into a pseudo-management role in the company. True, most will not be party to daily operating decisions. That's too risky. If the company should fail, the entrepreneur merely points to the investment banker and says, "It's your fault, not mine." No banker, whether he be in the commercial or asset-based lending side or the investment banking side wants this type of responsibility. Therefore he'll be careful to structure the deal so that the entrepreneur remains with all the liability in case of failure but the investment banker reaps the benefits in successful operations. The case of Roger and Mary, two entrepreneurs trying to acquire a medical supplies distributor, illustrates the point.

The deal was too good to pass up. Roger and Mary worked together in the lab of a major pharmaceutical manufacturer in Philadelphia. Disillusioned with their lack of progress in the firm, they left the corporation to buy their own business. A consultant friend directed them to a medical supplies distributor doing more than $15 million in sales. The distributor was owned by a competitor of their old employer so Roger and Mary believed they should tread lightly in broadcasting their intentions to acquire it. An asking price of $14 million seemed high but with P/E ratios flirting with the low twenties, the partners proceeded down the acquisition trail.

With few hard assets other than inventory, debt financing was out of the question so their consultant directed them to a small investment banking house in Princeton, NJ, called Exto Partners. A deal was structured by Exto attracting two private, limited partnerships as investors. Financing consisted of two-year mezzanine debt and equity in the form of preferred shares. For their services, Exto charged a flat $200,000 fee plus two percent of the package, for a total of just under $500,000. Roger and Mary, short of cash, agreed to a 20 percent share of the business for Exto.

Everything went well for the first four years. The investors received their dividends on schedule and Exto shared in 20 percent of the profits—amounting to nearly a 50 percent annual return for the investment banker. At the beginning of the fifth year a lawsuit against the company crippled their chances for survival. Roger and Mary begged Exto for a $1 million loan to settle the suit, but were refused. The court penetrated their corporate shield and Roger and Mary faced personal bankruptcy. Their only salvation was to grant Exto another 60 percent of the company in exchange for the $1 million loan, leaving the entrepreneurs with only 20 percent themselves. The lawsuit was settled and the company survives today, but Roger and Mary are bitter and disappointed with their venture into investment banking circles. They are now constantly at odds with their 80 percent partner and their life style is more restrictive and controlled than when they were employees.

I don't mean to imply that all investment bankers are heartless and actively strive to force entrepreneurs out of their own business. On the contrary, most don't want majority control because that makes them responsible for operating results. However, it can happen. Playing the equity markets is a lot tougher than dealing with banks or even asset-based lenders. Equity players demand, and get, ownership where a creditor will not.

INVESTMENT BANKS AS INVESTORS

A third way to finance a deal is from the investment banker himself. Although many of the smaller houses do not have vaults of ready cash to invest, they do have access to some funds for smaller deals. And larger firms can tap sizable cash reserves. Although there are exceptions, an investment banker looks at a deal as a vehicle to earn a sizable return on investment. Whereas a commercial bank or an asset-based lender earn their income by charging interest on loans, investment banks look to dividends and investment appreciation as primary goals. So when an investment banker provides financing from his own resources it must be structured differently than when borrowing money from a bank.

The main difference is that loans are principally in the form of mezzanine debt, which in most cases is fairly short term and may be unsecured or under secured. Mezzanine debt bridges the gap between equity investment and long-term debt to meet the purchase price. Interest rates are usually high, but not usurious. The buyer is expected to liquidate this debt within one or two years—

either through internally generated cash, by additional outside equity investment, or by going public. An investment banker is not interested in loaning
long-term money. He only uses debt to further the return of his equity investment. The loan agreement also usually carries conversion privileges specifying
the lender's right to convert to common stock at a specific time in the future if
the loan isn't paid off or in the event of default. Let's see how Howard Port utilized mezzanine debt direct from an investment banker to close an otherwise difficult deal.

The designer and assembler of telecommunications control devices looked
like a terrific buy to Howard. An electronic engineer by training, Howard could
visualize doubling sales in the next three years by adding a few new products and
modifying others already in production. Everything went smoothly until it came
time to arrange for financing. Then he ran into a serious snag. Howard needed to
raise $1.2 million in addition to his equity of $500,000 to close the deal, but with
virtually no hard assets—a leased building and only a handful of test equipment—
no asset-based lender or commercial bank would even talk to him.

Desperate, he finally asked for advice. "Have you tried the investment
banking fraternity?" was my first question.

"No, I haven't. I thought they were only interested in megabuck deals with
Wall Street companies. Besides, I really don't want a banking partner in this
deal. For the first time in my life I'm going to do something on my own without
someone looking over my shoulder and telling me what to do and how to do it."

"I understand your feeling, but maybe this is the only route. There are a
number of small investment bankers around who like to handle this size deal, and
some are even pretty good businessmen. A passive partner wouldn't be too
onerous. Let me see what I can do."

In about three weeks, after presenting his business plan to three small
investment banking houses I knew from prior deals, a Boston firm agreed to take
a serious look. They proposed the following arrangement.

Equity from Howard	$500,000
Equity from the investment bank	$300,000
Five year debt from a sister commercial bank, secured by receivables, inventory and testing equipment—with a personal guarantee from Howard	700,000
Mezzanine debt from the investment bank	200,000
Total from the investment bank	$1,200,000
Total cash required	$1,700,000

The mezzanine debt was secured by a second position on all assets behind
the commercial bank, bore interest at prime plus three points, and was due and
payable in two years. There were conversion rights allowing the investment

banker to exchange the debt instrument for 15 percent of the common shares after the first year but before the end of year two. Additionally, warrants attached to the note allowed conversion to 25 percent of the common shares after two years if the loan wasn't liquidated. With the equity contribution already netting the investment bank 30 percent of the company, Howard stood to lose control if he defaulted.

Backed against the wall, Howard accepted the offer, closed the deal, and started his entrepreneurial stint. Five years later we met at a trade conference and Howard related that the deal worked out perfectly. Internal cash flow allowed him to liquidate the debt in less than two years and the investment banker turned out to be more of a help than a hindrance. In fact, Howard felt that without the banker's sage advice in financial matters, he could not have made it.

With so many horror stories of banks foreclosing and interfering in a business, it's good to know that a relationship can be cordial and beneficial to both parties.

INVESTMENT BANKS AS UNDERWRITERS

Some investment bankers still make underwriting new stock issues their primary business. Although only in rare cases will this service ever be applicable to buying a business, it's helpful to have someone on board to handle the effort when and if an owner decides to go public. In the book *Getting Out*, the mechanics of an IPO are discussed at length from the perspective of a business owner using a public issue to sell his business, so there's no need to cover the same ground here. It might be helpful, however, to at least understand some of the basic ingredients of an IPO and how an investment banker can lead the way through the maze of SEC regulations and market vagaries. Also, it's important to remember that an investment banker will only get involved in a deal if there is a high probability of major investment appreciation—and a reasonably defined getting out position for him. This usually means that either the company must generate an unusual amount of free cash to buy him out, or be in a position to issue stock to the public and take him out that way.

Let's assume the following financing structure to illustrate how an IPO works:

ABC CORP.
Acquisition Funding

	Millions
Short-term bank debt	$.5
Long-term bank debt	3.5
Equity from buyer	.5
Equity from investment banker	.5
Total Purchase Price	$5.0

Sales and profits have been as follows for the three years prior to the IPO:

	Sales	Profits
Year 1	$ 8 million	$ 800,000
Year 2	10 million	1,200,000
Year 3	12 million	1,500,000

In Year 4, the market is booming and average price/earnings ratios hit multiples of twenty. Long-term bank debt has been paid down to a balance of $2 million. In this year the owner decides to go public with 45 percent of the company. The investment banker, acting as underwriter, recommends an issue of one million shares at a net selling price after commissions of $1.50 per share. Assuming the issue is successful, the company gets $1.3 million in cash, after deducting issue costs of $200,000. It can then buy back the shares from the investment banker for $1.1 million, giving him an average of 40 percent per year return on his money and still leave $300,000 for the company's use.

This IPO worked because three conditions were met:

1. The company showed significantly increasing earnings during the preceding three years.
2. Current stock market averages encouraged a high P/E multiple.
3. The investment banker/underwriter knew where to find the investors.

This is a very simplistic example but it illustrates how an IPO can be used to benefit both the business owner and his investment banker. In real life, the banker usually wants warrants to buy additional stock at favorable prices and the issue might be for more or less shares. It also could be structured to yield enough cash to liquidate the long-term debt holder.

There are truly a myriad of possibilities making most IPO's complex and fraught with danger for the amateur. With an investment banker as either a partner in the original acquisition or a participant in the financing package, the complications of an IPO that an owner must worry about are reduced substantially.

HOW INVESTMENT BANKS ARE STRUCTURED

There are as many variations in the structure of investment banks as there are means of structuring a financing package. Even though they all provide more or less the same activities, the structure of any given firm influences whether it will fit with a particular buyer's criteria. Investment banks might be any of the following:

1. A small group of ex-security analysts who have formed their own company to offer financial consulting and packaging for small deals with equity requirements under $500,000.(TDH Capital, Wissahickon Partners)

2. A division or subsidiary within a large brokerage house.(Bear Sterns, Merrill Lynch)

3. A mid-sized house, either privately owned or the subsidiary of a brokerage house, offering a complete range of services for deals in the $10 to $20 million range. (Golder Thomas & Cressey, Howard Lawson & Co.)

4. Larger firms, private or the subsidiaries of brokerage houses doing deals over $20 million but less than $100 million.(James River Capital, Narragansett Capital, Sprout Capital Group)

5. Giant firms handling deals above $100 million mainly for very large corporate clients. (Smith Barney, Salomon Bros.)

6. Divisions of commercial banks offering a complete range of services and handling deals up to $50 million (Fleet Growth Industries, BNE Associates, Connecticut National Bank)

7. Divisions or subsidiaries of large insurance companies handling deals on their own account up to $1 billion (Allstate Insurance, Pru Capital—part of Prudential Insurance)

8. Wealthy family private trusts (Rothschild, Inc.)

9. Subsidiaries of large foreign banks or trusts offering special industry deals of any size but mainly over $100 million (Charterhouse Group International, Midland Capital)

10. Spin-offs or divisions of pure venture capital firms concentrating in early stage development companies.

The deal size criteria is very fluid and keeps changing depending on portfolios, reputation of buyer, market conditions, and available cash at the moment, but most firms like to work within given ranges. Weighting applied to type of industry, stage of development, growth prospects, and management talent also fluctuates continually. As economic, environmental, and financial conditions change, so does investment criteria by these financial institutions. Venture capital firms are especially fluid, moving rapidly from start-up financing to first, second, and third stage packages. To choose an investment banking house for a specific deal requires a fair amount of research and M&A consultants and other professional advisors can be an enormous help.

It's important to understand the structure of an investment bank because:

- A buyer should choose a firm to fit the deal size.
- Affiliations with banks are best for packaging long term debt and an operating line in one bank.
- Affiliations with brokerage houses work best in underwriting an IPO.
- Private firms offer the most freedom of management actions.

- Small houses are best for overall financial consulting services.
- Small to mid-sized private firms tend to concentrate on industry specialization.

The appendix lists several more investment banking and venture capital firms with a good reputation in the industry and should be sufficient to give you a good start down this road. In the financing business most contacts are by reputation or word of mouth. As sourcing begins, you will automatically learn of new firms that have started up or new divisions formed in large banks or investment banking houses whose portfolios have recently changed and might be good sources. Two or three level of interest letters are ideal so you can choose the best deal.

VENTURE CAPITAL FIRMS

Before going on, a few other distinctions should be made between venture capital firms and investment banking. Both approach acquisition financing from an entirely different perspective than asset-based lenders or commercial banks. At times, however, it's hard to tell the difference between venture capital firms and investment banks because their activities overlap. Generally, a venture capital firm is in business to provide equity, mezzanine, and sometimes secured financing for start-up or first or second stage developing companies. In the '70s, the emergence of high-tech companies in computer software and peripherals, medical diagnostics, and electronic instrumentation commanded the attention of these financial institutions. A true venture capital firm is not particularly interested in a fixed return on its money such as interest, but prefers to take equity positions in anticipation of taking the company public within the foreseeable future and through a public issue recoup substantial investment appreciation.

Venture capital firms tend to stay away from financial consulting. They like to invest their own funds, or be a lead investor for a group of equity participants, in early stage development deals. For this reason, most investments are in very small developing companies.

One of the dangers in using a venture capital firm is that many times they insist on a controlling share of the company. Although many firms never exert control over the operations of the company—restricting their activity to a board seat and participation in major policy decisions—some do, in fact, interfere with operating decisions. No reputable venture capitalist will ever admit to such a sacrilege, however.

Venture capital firms serve a special need in the financing marketplace. With little or no collateral to secure a loan and earnings records that won't support substantial cash flow projections, many small companies cannot raise funds anywhere else. From a financing viewpoint, this type of deal provides the greatest risk for the financier and therefore his reward must be substantial. If you do use a venture capital firm, try to find one whose management has some operating experience fitting the target company's industry. At least its officers should be able to offer helpful operating advice as the company develops.

Having examined both debt and equity as possible means of financing a deal, let's return to the only two steps remaining to reach the final goal of buying a company. The next chapter explores final due diligence procedures and the legal process.

13

Lawyers At Work
Drafting the Closing Documents

"Closing day is a simultaneous glimpse of heaven and hell."

PATIENCE IS ONE OF THE MOST DIFFICULT ATTRIBUTES FOR AN ENTREPRENEUR to master. The driving ambition to accomplish something; the active role of a doer; the incessant need to bring matters to a conclusion, all work against the buyer from this point forward. The search, negotiations, due diligence investigations, preparation of the business plan, and sourcing financing all required him to take an active role in getting things done. The buyer was the prime mover and if he didn't do it, no one else would. John E. Joe is no different from every other entrepreneur making his first acquisition. He is beginning to lose patience. He has been on the run for almost a year now trying to bring the Make Money deal to a conclusion and the last thing he wants to do at this point is sit back and wait.

Yet, that is exactly what must be done. With a few exceptions, from now on most of the responsibility for action rests with others—appraisers, auditors, accountants, lawyers, and bankers. The buyer must coordinate, but there's not much else to do. Patience, patience, and more patience. He must now resignedly rely on others to get the job done.

By this time level of interest letters from his financing sources should be in hand. Only two major areas remain to finally close the deal: final due diligence procedures, and, drafting and negotiating the closing documents. To coordinate these activities the buyer must:

- Obtain updated financial statements, reports, and other current data about the company.
- Get a market value appraisal of all real property.
- Get an appraisal of machinery and equipment.
- Hire a CPA firm to perform an audit review.
- Hire a competent contract attorney to draft the closing documents.

UPDATE DUE DILIGENCE

Getting current financial statements and updating the business plan pro forma forecasts are not particularly difficult steps and they don't take much time but must be done. By this time the seller should be confident the deal will close and be willing to cooperate for the few remaining steps.

Several months have probably lapsed since the business plan was put together, yet it's unlikely that many major operating changes have occurred in that short time period. In fact, there are really only three key questions to resolve:

1. Were the pro forma forecasts for these intervening months reasonably accurate or were they way off base? If you missed it by a mile maybe there's some major element in the business you don't understand?
2. Is the management team still intact and functioning the way it appeared to be during the last facilities tour?
3. Have there been any external occurrences such as lawsuits, strikes, IRS audits or adjustments that might have a major impact on the business now or in the future?

Although many buyers prefer to save money and try to gather data for the update process by phone or letter, this is "penny rich and pound foolish" at this stage of the game. Because of business dynamics, the only certainty about forecasting is that what was supposed to happen, didn't. Actual results might be better or worse—but not the same as forecasted. Because the financial commitments from this point forward become quite substantial—appraisals, audits, legal fees—it only makes sense to make one more trip to the company's offices, gather the data personally, and make sure no major problems have arisen to kill the deal.

Before this final visit, however, try to locate reputable equipment and real estate appraisal companies at the company's location so that appraisal contracts can be negotiated during the visit. The same thing goes for a local CPA firm to do the audit review. But more on appraisals and audits a little later—let's stick with the pro forma update now.

If you can get the updated financial statements by mail first, some time can be saved by developing a question check list before departing. From here on in, time is of the essence. The financing sources won't wait forever, and in fact, their level of interest letters probably have a rapidly approaching expiration date.

The update checklist is substantially shorter than that used for the detailed due diligence investigation. Comparing and contrasting financial data for the current period against the due diligence period is normally the fastest and surest way of spotting any major discrepancies. Also, unless someone was lying the first time around, a few simple comparative statistics out of the marketing department and some pointed questions to the target's legal counsel should provide all the data you need to update the plan. The following checklist provides a handy guide to questions this time around:

UPDATE DUE DILIGENCE CHECKLIST

Since the Detailed Due Diligence Date—

1. What are the monthly sales by product line?
2. What are the changes in inventory?
3. What is the monthly operating profit?
4. Have there been any payments to the pension fund or retirement plan?
5. What are the monthly selling expenses and G&A expenses?
6. Has there been any borrowing against the operating line? If so, how much each month? How much has been paid down each month?
7. What are the manpower additions or deletions each month? Why were people added or laid off?
8. What are the monthly orders received and order cancellations?
9. Have there been any lawsuits started or settled?
10. Have there been any federal or state tax audits completed, started, or scheduled to start?
11. Has there been any change in the union contract?
12. Has the bonus or profit sharing plan been modified?
13. Are there any new or any changes to existing employment contracts or any other contracts?
14. What are the changes in accrued expenses—new accruals and payments?
15. What is the current aging of accounts receivable?
16. What is the current aging of accounts payable?
17. Has there been a physical inventory taken? If so, what were the results?
18. Have any insurance coverages or premiums changed?

19. What have been the fixed-asset additions or retirements?
20. What other changes have occurred that may be relevant to full disclosure?

Management

This visit should be a lot warmer than the last time around. It doesn't take long to judge who is happy to see you buy the company and who isn't. It's important to determine which key employees can be counted on the day you walk in the door after closing. Only rarely will everyone be overjoyed with a new owner. In any organization loyalties built over time tarnish at least some of the employees' enthusiasm for a new boss. By establishing a working rapport with these employees, however, your chances of success immediately after closing are enhanced.

Just as important, try to determine which supervisors are already looking for another job or will be as soon as you close. For example, if the chief engineer plans to leave, the long recruiting process can begin even before the close. Maybe one of the staff engineers could fill his shoes. If so, encourage his participation in the due diligence discussions.

And of course bankers and investors will be very interested in what changes occurred at the supervisory level.

At this stage, the seller should not be adverse to private discussions with his key people. If he balks, probe deeper. Some underlying problems might have developed recently which could be crucial to continuing the acquisition. The seller could have orchestrated a scenario the first time around that he can no longer support. Or he might have known then that the company was heading for a breakdown in labor relations or was about to lose a major customer, but was afraid of losing a viable buyer if he revealed these conditions. You must find out now. This is the last chance to scuttle the deal before committing substantial funds to appraisers, auditors and attorneys.

John E. Joe went through this final due diligence stage at Make Money and fortunately everything turned out to be a go—the actual financial results were very close to his pro formas, key managers continued to be impressive, and there weren't any lawsuits or other external events having a material adverse effect on the operation of Make Money Filters. Now he must arrange for the appraisal and the audit review.

APPRAISALS

Even though the seller might have had real estate and equipment appraisals done a few years ago, bankers, investors, and particularly asset-based lenders want to see current appraisals made by appraisal firms satisfactory to them. A satisfactory real estate appraiser is easy to find. There are appraisers in every major city whose credentials go unchallenged by any banking institution. Additionally, the market for commercial real estate is fairly easy to determine by checking with local real estate firms. As far as the lender is concerned, the loan value of real estate equates to about 75 percent of the market value. It's based on what the property will bring on the open market, not necessarily at a liquidation sale. As long as the commercial real estate market remains healthy, the lender looks to open market rather than auction values.

Machinery and equipment appraisal values are a different matter, however. Here the lender assumes that in a default, he will need to liquidate the equipment as fast as possible—usually at an auction. Therefore, he wants appraised values which realistically—in his mind—reflect these auction values—not what it would cost to replace the equipment or what it could be sold for over a long period of time.

Following are some valuation terms to help in negotiating with an appraisal firm:

Replacement Value—the cost of replacing existing equipment either new or in the used equipment market, including installation costs. This value is generally used for insurance valuations only (although many unsophisticated sellers feel this is what they should get for their business).

Fair Market Value—the sell price possible to obtain from a willing buyer assuming the equipment is in place and operating in a going business.

Orderly Liquidation Value—the sell price possible to obtain from a willing buyer assuming a slow, orderly liquidation sale taking place over time (generally from six to twelve months). This value equates to about 60 percent of the fair market value.

Forced Liquidation Value—the price equipment would bring at an open auction held at one place at one time and conducted by a qualified auctioneer. This value approximates 70 percent to 80 percent of the orderly liquidation value.

Loan Value—most asset-based lenders loan up to approximately 80 percent of forced liquidation value.

These terms change from time to time, but the concepts remain the same. When arranging for the appraisal, agree on a report showing each piece of equipment at its fair market, orderly liquidation, and forced liquidation values. The fair market and orderly liquidation values might come in handy at a later date should you wish to sell off any of the used equipment.

Almost all asset-based lenders have their own favorite appraisers. Many are auction firms hoping to get the job when the debtor defaults. Some are also reputable appraisers. Try to pick your own appraiser if you can, however—maybe with the influential help of your investment banker. If an appraiser works for the buyer—not a finance company—it's likely the job will get done faster, cheaper, and with results favoring the buyer. The appraiser always hopes for additional work from a new owner, or at least a favorable reference. If you don't know who to get, check with a local CPA firm, legal counsel or commercial bank. One of these should be willing to help. If two or more sources come up with the same recommendation, it's probably a safe choice. Just remember to get the lender's approval before engaging an appraiser or there might be a lot of money wasted. Appraisal costs range from about $2,000 for a few pieces of equipment to $20,000, or more, for a full manufacturing shop.

All professional appraisals take time, so get going on this phase right away. A qualified appraiser can come up with a total valuation number within a couple of weeks but it could take 60 days or more to get the final detailed report.

AUDIT REVIEW

Even though most buyers work with their local CPA in preparing the business plan and counsel with him on tax matters relative to the acquisition, the audit review should be performed by an independent CPA firm in the same city as the target company; preferably one of the "Big-5" firms. There are a number of advantages to doing it this way:

- The opinion of a Big-5 firm is more readily acceptable to the banking community.
- It protects the buyer's position in dealing with bankers and the courts if he sues the seller at a later date over misrepresentation.
- A local office will be more accustomed to the peculiar norms of that locale.
- It costs less without travel expenses.
- It's easier for a local office to coordinate with the target company's prior year auditors.
- The seller might be more comfortable with an independent CPA firm probing into his books and tax workpapers than someone closely associated with the buyer and will therefore give the auditor more cooperation.

There are two disadvantages, however:

1. You'll get a better job done with your own CPA (no criticism of the Big-5 intended) simply because he knows you from dealing with other matters.
2. Your own CPA knows what you are looking for whereas a new firm will not.

The audit review consists of a comprehensive look at the business since the last audit with particular emphasis on determining the adequacy of internal controls and internal reports. Additionally, the auditor runs tests to determine the realizable value of both the receivables and inventory. The commercial bank taking the operating line usually wants to do this with their own auditors as well, but by utilizing an independent auditor the bank can be cross-checked. The auditor should also look for consistency between accounting procedures over the past three years and those in effect now. Some entrepreneurs, trying to cut costs, skip this independent audit review completely. Some bankers even let them get by with it—which is astonishing.

Whether it's a stock deal or an asset purchase, a business buyer acquires customer goodwill, product knowledge, vendor sources, tangible assets, and cash equivalents such as inventory and receivables. It's a mystery why a person is willing to trade dollars with the seller—cash in exchange for inventory and receivables—without verifying that these cash equivalents actually exist in the amounts the seller claims—but some do.

You certainly wouldn't pay $300,000 for a house without examining it closely to make sure the roof doesn't leak, the plumbing and electricity work, and the furnace is in good order. Why buy a business for millions of dollars and not be at least as cautious?

The answer is usually ego. After spending weeks, maybe months, performing due diligence investigations, it's natural for a buyer to believe he already knows that the asset values in the books of account are accurate. By the time a buyer gets this close to concluding an acquisition it's difficult to admit that he could have made a mistake. He would almost rather go ahead with the deal, even if the inventory and receivables are misstated, than back off now.

Resist the urge! Both the personal and financial risks are far too great to make a million dollar mistake for the sake of pride.

Bert and Jim had purchased a small manufacturing company two months earlier when Bert came to me with his dilemma. Because of his financial background, he believed he had probed deeply enough into the books and records during the due diligence phase of his investigation and decided not to engage an independent auditor for the pre-closing audit review. He also admitted that his acquisition budget had suffered a significant overrun and that cash reserves were almost gone. Whatever the real reason, pride or lack of cash, he did not order an audit review.

Now that the partners were operating the company and had a chance to take a physical inventory, Bert realized that the book inventory was materially misstated. This fact was bound to come up because their banker required a certified audit at year-end. Bert knew the banker would be more than a bit upset with a million dollar inventory write-down. He would then have to reveal that inventory on the books at the time of closing really didn't represent actual physical goods on the floor.

Bert and Jim were preparing to sue the seller for misrepresenting the financial condition of the company. Their attorney's opinion, however, was that without audit verification at the closing date, he would have a difficult time proving his case in court. What was Bert to do?

Not much he could do after the fact. I did recommend, however, that he hire a Big-5 accounting firm now to audit the inventory records from his current physical count back to the date of purchase and try to prove misstatement through this deductive means. Bert hired an auditor and when the case came to trial, the partners won a small settlement—but nothing compared to what it could have been had they spent the money on an audit review prior to closing.

It's getting down to the wire and if there's anything wrong with the financial condition of the target company it's better to find out about it now rather than later.

That's about it for final due diligence. Now, while waiting for his appraisers and auditors to do their work, the buyer can begin the tedious process of getting the closing documents prepared. But first, it's helpful to understand something about professional advisors—in case you haven't had the opportunity to work with one in the past.

PROFESSIONAL ADVISORS

Appraisers, lawyers, accountants, and consultants hired to assist in the acquisition, all work for the buyer—after all, he's paying them. If he doesn't like their performance he can always fire them just like employees in a company. But management by fear is a dangerous path. The employer/employee relationship is a two-way street. How you treat them determines how well they perform for you.

Qualified professionals almost always do a respectable job—otherwise they wouldn't be professionals very long. But what is true in employee relations is also applicable to professionals. The treatment they get from you determines how far out of the way they will go to help you. By empathizing with their problems, by being compassionate with them when things don't always turn out the way you want them to, and by being openly honest in dealings with them, professionals give back the best they have to offer in advice and service.

Speaking as a management consultant myself, I can bear witness that because these professionals are in the business of dealing with people almost constantly, they are overly sensitive and perceptive when interpreting the words and acts of others. As with everyone else, an honest and open approach and a genuine caring and concern for their problems brings out the best in anyone.

Although an appraiser, lawyer, consultant, or accountant will still do a professional job, it's that extra effort that sometimes makes the difference between success and failure in buying a business. By disregarding a person's human cares and concerns, don't be surprised if you can't reach one of them after five o'clock or on a Sunday morning when a crisis is brewing.

HIRING A LAWYER

"Lawyers are leeches!"
"A good lawyer is worth his weight in gold!"

Two opposing points of view—both probably accurate. As an M&A consultant it seems I have spent at least half my waking hours in lawyers' offices. There are a lot of lawyers out there, some very good, and some grossly incompetent—which, by the way, is also true in any profession. Look at a comparison:

I tried to get Ray to hire a lawyer who was not only a good friend but, in my opinion, one of the most capable acquisition-contract attorneys in Philadelphia. But Ray thought his hourly rate was too steep and instead hired a young, very articulate lawyer, at a modest rate, but with no experience in acquisition work. He drafted the buy/sell agreement and Ray took it immediately to the seller to negotiate some troublesome language. Buyer and seller took two hours to reach an accord, the young lawyer made the corrections and the deal closed two days later on September 30.

By October 15, Ray was in my office trying to figure out how to break the contract. His lawyer had neglected to include either a warranty or an indemnification against federal income tax liabilities for prior years. One week after the close an IRS agent walked in to audit the return from two years earlier and quickly assessed a $200,000 additional tax liability plus penalty and interest for failure to include income from the sale of some heavy equipment. After studying the buy/sell agreement it was evident that Ray had little recourse to the seller and ended up paying the extra assessment.

A similar situation arose with a different client, Aboud Skai, but in this case Aboud had the foresight to hire a competent acquisition contract attorney who drafted and negotiated an iron clad indemnification clause covering everything imaginable. In fact, I couldn't believe the seller had agreed to it, but he had. This also involved an IRS audit for prior years, with a deficiency assessment. In this case, however, Aboud sued the seller and recovered everything, plus court costs and attorneys' fees. Legal fees for drafting the closing documents were $15,000: the savings in the lawsuit totaled $3.7 million.

Which lawyer would you rather hire?

Before getting to the closing documents, a lawyer must be hired. Closing documents are prepared in legal language not readily intelligible to the layman; so you must have a lawyer.

But what are closing documents? As the term implies, they are a series of buy/sell agreements, contracts, and covenants between buyer and seller—prepared by both counsels—together with a set of loan agreements, equity agreements, personal guarantees, filings, and security agreements prepared by lending institutions. These papers must be prepared and then reviewed by all parties for signing at the final closing. If you take all the papers executed for the sale or purchase of a house and multiply them twenty times (at least) you'll get some idea of the volume of papers to be executed at an acquisition closing. For most entrepreneurs without any legal training and unaccustomed to interpreting the fine print in contracts, this process can be a mystifying maze. Add to this the excitement that has been building in recent months when it became clear that you might actually own your own company, and it's understandable why so many buyers have such a terrible time with this phase of the acquisition.

The only thing to do to ease the pain is engage a competent lawyer, in the target's city, with substantial experience in acquisition work. A generalist won't do; nor will a litigation lawyer, nor a labor lawyer, nor a corporate lawyer, nor a tax lawyer. What you want is a lawyer who has drafted and negotiated the language of several buy/sell agreements and hopefully, has actually spent some time in the business world other than as a legal counsel (although the latter is hard to find). The following guidelines and techniques can be useful in choosing such a lawyer:

- Use a large law firm. I have nothing against sole practitioners or small local law firms. Most of the time they give far better service than a larger firm. However, buying a business is such a complex procedure, usually involving several legal specialties—real estate law, pension law, labor law, creditor's rights and banking law, possible litigation, tax law, government regulations, SEC law—as well as business contract law—that in most cases, only a large firm, with specialists available to cover all the bases, can do the job. Looking down the road to possible disputes with banks and bankers, it is extremely beneficial to find a lawyer with a good understanding of the very special "bank and creditor relations" field of law so he won't need to rely on someone else's interpretations.

- Get references from local banks and CPA firms. Don't rely on your own contacts. Ask around for names of contract lawyers used by Big-8 accounting firms and local banks. Try to get at least three different references.

- Interview each of the contract law specialists who will actually write the closing documents.

- Prior experience is most important. Find out if he has ever handled the sale of a company of this size and in this industry. If not, go elsewhere. If he has, get the name of the client's CEO and interview him about the lawyer. Find out if he knows what he's doing.

- Negotiate a fee structure for the entire closing. Most lawyers will charge by the hour, but try to get at least a maximum, not to exceed amount for the engagement.

Either your personal legal counsel or attorney friends can be a good starting point in locating the right lawyer. All law firms have access to lawyer directories all over the country and can at least pinpoint some of the larger firms in the target's city. Other excellent sources are the local offices of Big-8 accounting firms. They always know lawyers. As a last resort try the local office of the State Bar

Association in the target's state, although these people are not usually very helpful. Once you get some names, start the interview process. Yes, interviewing all candidate lawyers is important to be certain you get the best one available—closing documents are that crucial. Most good lawyers welcome a no-fee interview. They want to know who the client is before they accept an engagement as much as you want to know their qualifications to handle the work. Expect to pay a sizable hourly rate for qualified counsel however. Good lawyers don't come cheap and this is no time to begin cutting corners.

During the interview process use the following checklist to be certain to ask the right questions:

CHECKLIST FOR CHOOSING A LAWYER

1. Is there a conflict of interest with the seller or the proposed financial institutions?
2. What are your hourly rates?
3. Will you do the work yourself or delegate to assistants?
4. What experience do your assistants have?
5. What are the hourly rates of your assistants?
6. Are you available at home, in the evening, on weekends?
7. What are the professional profiles of specialists in your firm whom you will draw upon?
8. What personal contacts do you have in local banking circles?
9. What other acquisition deals have you handled?
10. Can I contact these clients for references?
11. During the writing of the buy/sell agreement, will you be dedicated to my engagement or will you also be handling other deals?
12. How well do you know the seller's attorney?

How he answers determines whether to go forward or keep shopping.

There are endless horror stories of entrepreneurs doing the acquisition search, negotiations, and financing with great pains and then trying to shave costs on the legal side. Inevitably they end up with disastrous buy/sell contracts or unworkable loan agreements. Whether you like it or not, once the decision was made to buy a business you also committed to become involved in legal issues. The number of lawsuits escalates each year and many are related to business contract disputes involving labor grievances, bank foreclosures, bankruptcy filings, government compliance, taxes, and acquisitions. So get a good lawyer and don't worry about the cost. Over a period of time he'll save you much more than he charges in fees.

Now let's get on to drafting the closing documents.

THE FINAL STEP

Well, at last John E. Joe arrived at the final phase of his acquisition program. It took 10 months and cost $25,000—so far. Even being ahead of budget on both counts doesn't seem to ease the pain, however. He has related to everyone who would listen that this exercise has been the most wearing experience he's ever been through. And $25,000 is a lot of money.

Closing Documents

Closing documents can be grouped into two categories—those that the buyer brings to the closing and those the financial institutions bring. The buyer's are far more important because banks tend to insist on their own language in their agreements.

In the case of Make Money Filters, John E. Joe needs at least:

- a buy/sell agreement.
- an earn out agreement.
- a promissory note terms and conditions agreement.
- real estate closing papers including title search and title insurance.
- lease assignments.
- employment contracts with his key managers.

Financial institution documents will include:

- an equity agreement with his investment banker.
- note terms and conditions agreements.
- personal guarantees.
- UCC filings.
- collateral agreements.

Because Make Money Filter is a stock-purchase deal with the seller paying off his existing bank debt, it's up to him to bring the appropriate settlement document to the closing. John's attorney will worry about that but John shouldn't. He has enough to worry about with his own contracts and agreements.

Buy/Sell Agreement

The buy/sell agreement is somewhat simplified in a stock purchase deal. There are four main sections:

1. Price, terms, and conditions of sale.
2. Representations and warranties of seller and buyer.

3. Conditions precedent to closing for both seller and buyer.

4. General statements of law.

Price, Terms, and Conditions of Sale. The price and terms section is fairly straightforward. It merely restates what John and the seller have already agreed to. There are paragraphs covering what is being purchased, that the seller will discharge current bank debt, what the total price is, and how the price will be paid (cash at closing, note, and earn out agreement). John doesn't need to concern himself much with this section except to make sure his lawyer thoroughly understands the deal.

Representations and Warranties of Seller and Buyer. About the only representations and warranties that John as a buyer must make are that his parent company, Acquisitions, Inc., is a corporation duly registered and in good standing and that John E. Joe, as an officer of the corporation, is authorized to enter into this contract.

Representations and warranties from the seller, however, are a different story. Here, John must be sure his lawyer includes language for the seller to guarantee that everything he has told John and shown him about Make Money Filters is accurate and complete. If at a later date John determines he was misled during the due diligence process, he will have grounds for a breach of contract suit based on this section of the agreement. His attorney must be very careful to get the right words in place to ensure that John's position will be as strong as possible—and this is where the negotiation process begins, again.

The seller's attorney tries to dilute the warranty language to the point where John wouldn't have a case at all under a breach of contract claim. John, of course, would love to have an iron-clad guarantee from the seller that he knows everything there is to know about the business. The seller points to caveat emptor. John recounts that it was impossible to uncover all the skeletons and he must have some assurance from the seller that nothing was missed. Very often these negotiations take place with buyer and seller, both lawyers, accountants, and all the other advisers from both sides all sitting around a table hammering out acceptable language. It seems absurd, but deals fall apart at this stage even though both parties want to close and the financing is in place—as in the following case.

A small printing company was offered for sale by the single owner-manager. My client, a small group of investors called Jaxton Associates, was very interested in buying. We negotiated a reasonable price and terms and the seller agreed to remain on as the general manager with a lucrative employment contract. We successfully arranged a satisfactory financing package and believed the deal could close in a matter of days, not weeks—and certainly not months. Our attorney was from a large reputable firm and had written many buy/sell agreements. The lawyer representing the seller was a sole practitioner never involved in an acquisition before.

Our attorney wrote the initial draft of the buy/sell agreement and forwarded it to his counterpart. Now remember, both buyer and seller had already negotiated price, terms, and conditions of sale, as well as terms of the employment agreement. We were satisfied that it was a very clean company and that the seller had been extremely cooperative and honest with us. The only representations and warranties language we wanted was boiler plate, with nothing unusual or onerous.

The seller's attorney proceeded to inform his client that this entire section of the agreement should be deleted. If we didn't trust the seller more than that then he should not do business with us. And also, his lawyer argued, the price was too low and the employment agreement wasn't sufficient. We almost walked away at that point, but Jaxton really wanted the business so we tried to negotiate our differences. After more than 60 days of negotiating and drafting and re-drafting the agreement many times, we finally realized that the seller's lawyer was actually causing a larger rift between the parties each re-drafting—and we reluctantly walked away from the table.

As a post script, the seller never did sell his business and within a year auctioned off his equipment and locked the doors.

A very good deal for both parties was wasted simply because we could not agree on contract language. This also points out the importance of choosing professional advisors carefully. A lawyer, a CPA, and yes, even an M&A consultant can ruin an opportunity for his client if he doesn't know what he is doing. None of us like to admit that we are not infallible—our egos keep getting in the way. But don't believe everything you hear from your professional advisors. Check them out before hiring them—it's your money—and then, once hired, try to understand where they are coming from when they give advice. Don't accept everything an advisor says, just because he is presumably an expert.

Conditions Precedent to Closing. Conditions precedent to closing is lawyer's terminology which means very simply, that this section of the agreement lists all those items which must be completed by both buyer and seller before the close. For example, in an asset sale (rather than a stock sale), the seller must comply with the state's Bulk Sales Act. Even though a state law, most have fairly standard provisions. What it really means is that, in order to transfer title to assets free and clear of any liens, the seller must inform all his creditors, in writing, that such a sale will take place. Any creditor then has a fixed time period to respond with notice of a lien and if he does not assert such a claim, cannot come back against the new owner after the sale.

Other examples may be that the buyer would like to continue the same insurance policies, in which case the seller must deliver the policies prior to closing. Or if there are leases to be assigned, it's the seller's responsibility to deliver such assignments. Or the buyer may want a listing of all customers or open-purchase orders, or he may want an updated version of the union contract, or the pension plan. Any document or clearance from government agencies, creditors, and banks which must be in hand before title can transfer at closing, whether a stock or an asset sale, is enumerated in the conditions precedent section of the agreement.

Not much disagreement arises about the language in this section, unless one or the other makes an unreasonable demand for production of documents. If that occurs, it's customary to reach resolution by covering the concerned party in the representations and warranties section. Few deals fall apart because of disagreement on conditions precedent to close.

General Statements of Law. General statements of law are up to the lawyer. Items such as governing state laws, arbitration procedures, and notification of parties are covered here. Don't spend time worrying about this section. Most of us don't have the legal background to know what is preferable in these areas and a good contract lawyer should insert whatever he deems reasonable.

Coordination with Financing Parties

While John and his lawyer have been busy drafting and negotiating the buy/sell agreement, employment agreement, and other buyer/seller documents, the investment banker, asset-based lender, and the commercial bank handling the operating line have been preparing their closing documents. But John doesn't dare leave this to chance. Financial institutions always seem to be overloaded with work and unless he continues to follow-up and coordinate with them, chances are they will not meet the closing deadline.

One thing for sure—John must make time to coordinate the drafting of the equity agreement with his investment banker. Language in this agreement could be crucial to the well-being of the business for years to come. As discussed earlier, John's investment banker gets 25 percent of the company for his contribution. The banker also wants an agreement with John to either take the company public at the appropriate time or to have him buy back the banker's share at an agreed upon price. He also wants a seat on the board of Acquisitions, Inc., and a hand in making major policy decisions. These conditions must all be covered in an equity agreement executed at the closing so that there can be no dispute later on about each party's rights.

The language in the agreement can be tricky and most likely the banker will want to have his counsel do the drafting. That's OK, but John wants to be sure his counsel explains any language they insert which he doesn't understand.

I can't emphasize enough—don't agree to anything you do not thoroughly understand and don't sign a document if anything is confusing or contradictory. It will only lead to disaster later on.

Only one more point relative to the equity agreement. Even though John's investment banker has made the financing of the acquisition possible, this does not mean John has to agree to everything he wants. The buyer always has the right to negotiate language and terms he can live with. After all, John and his investment banker are going to be partners for several years to come and he might just as well get off on the right foot in the beginning.

The asset-based lender and commercial bank loan agreements, filings, and so on are another matter. John doesn't have much say here. Most of these documents use boiler plate language dictated by the bank for all its deals. He might be able to modify some language in the personal guarantee—but not necessarily. The buyer's caveat here is that under no circumstances can he allow a joint personal guarantee with his spouse. That's taboo no matter what the loan officer may say. If push comes to shove, even at this late date, and the banker insists on a joint guarantee, walk away from the deal. Easier said than done, I know, but if you agree to such a document, it's almost a sure bet you will live to regret it sometime down the line.

Even though a buyer won't have much input to the bank closing documents, it's important he continues the follow-up process to make sure the banks are moving with diligence toward the closing date. Most bankers are in no hurry to do anything and more than one closing date has slipped because of some errant bank closing document.

Both of John's lending banks wanted to make an audit review with their own people. Because their main concern was the condition of receivables and inventory at closing the audit was done the week before. John's own audit had been completed previously, so the Make Money Filter books and records were in good shape and the bank review didn't take long. John made sure he coordinated it, though. He wasn't about to leave anything to chance at this late date.

One final comment in this area. John has gone to the expense of doing his own audit review and it's just common sense to ask to have a sit-down meeting with both his auditor and the bank's auditor to compare audit results. One or the other may have missed something, and this is almost his last chance to walk away.

The audit review was completed. John kept all the lawyers under control; no one walked away from the deal over contract language, and the bank auditors didn't turn up any surprises. At last he is ready for the closing—that day he has been shooting at for almost a year now. The day the keys to Make Money Filter get turned over and John's life-long dream is fulfilled.

CLOSING

The closing will be at John's lawyer's office and the two of them have spent the last two days going over all the last minute details. He has also coordinated with the seller to determine the best way to announce to the Make Money employees, customers, and vendors that he is the new owner—the day after all the papers are executed and cash deposited in the seller's account.

There is a mood of anticipation, of excitement, and even—if the truth be known—of fear. Of all the events which take place in the business world, nothing can match an acquisition closing for pure excitement and thrill. The lawyers are always very tense; and each side, including the bank lawyers, are afraid they have forgotten something. The seller is on pins and needles worried that, even now, the deal won't go through.

But John is in seventh heaven: this is his first closing. The feeling is similar—but much more exciting—to the time you purchased your first house after saving for years for the down payment. Or graduation day from college, or even your wedding day, or the birth of your first child. But none of these events can match the glamour, excitement, exhilaration, and throat-tightening fear of the first acquisition closing. After all, this is something John has wanted and waited for all his life, and never really believed could happen. But here he is, ready to sign! His wife is probably anxiously waiting for his phone call to hear that it's finally over so she can hop a plane and join him in celebration.

Second only to his first appearance in court, the first acquisition closing will be the most frightening experience of a buyer's life. The old adage, "it's never over 'til it's over," continues to run through John's mind. What if something happens to kill the deal after spending almost a full year and a significant part of his savings getting this far? What will he then do to earn a living? How can he face his friends to whom he has boasted of his new business life? How can he face his wife, who stood by through all this turmoil, but still worries incessantly about earning a stream of income? All these fears and a great many more race through John's mind almost non-stop. The lawyers seem to be busy, but he has nothing to do and the inactivity is nerve-racking.

Everyone has finally gathered for the signing and cash transfer: John's lawyer, his consultant, his CPA; the seller, his lawyers, his advisors; the asset based lender's loan officer and his attorney; the investment bank officer and his attorney; the commercial bank loan officer, his lawyer and a host of typists (for last-minute changes); a secretary; and last, but certainly not least, John.

If all the documents are in order, the actual signing won't take more than an hour; however, there are always last-minute changes or corrections or some piece of paper gets lost and has to be duplicated or somebody can't get there on time, so in reality, a closing takes most of the day. The seller wants his money in the form of a wire transfer so John made arrangements ahead of time with his investment banker to have someone standing by at the office to make the transfer immediately upon execution of the sale documents.

John can't concern himself with what he's signing now. He must trust his lawyer that everything has been reviewed and clearly understood during the dry run. Let him run the meeting and call the shots. By this time John is too tired to function properly anyway. And the investment banker will be very careful that everything is handled properly. All John really has to do is sign his name where he is told to do so. Let the rest of the people do their thing now. He has done everything he can to make the deal and now it's up to the lawyers and bankers, all of whom want the deal to close as much as he does.

Wait. Someone seems to have forgotten something. What was that? You don't have proof of liability and casualty insurance coverage? The banks won't close without it?

Back to the telephone—get hold of the insurance agent—have him quickly draw up some binders—bring them over to the lawyers' office. Three hours later he shows up, and it looks like the deal is on again.

What now! Someone forgot to notify the seller's bank that a wire transfer is coming—and it's nearing the time of the bank's wire transfer department deadline. Quickly the seller gets on the phone to his bank—hold the lines open, the money will be coming momentarily—don't let the wire transfer clerk go home yet. The investment banker gets on the phone to his contact and notifies the sender that the deal is done: transfer the funds.

At last, John E. Joe made it. He now owns a company. Quickly, still shaking, he gets on the phone, calls his wife and tells her to hop the first plane out. He is now truly an entrepreneur. Tomorrow John will worry about greeting his new employees.

14

After The Dance Is Over
Transition of Ownership

"The first day is exciting, the first week traumatic, the first month frightening."

THE GLAMOUR OF MAKING AN ACQUISITION IS OVER. IN FACT, THE DAY HE WALKS into his office for the first time, the new business owner realizes that now the work really begins. Now it's time to get to know his new company, his employees and customers, and begin making command decisions. After all the effort and frustrations, the aspiring entrepreneur finally owns a company. He can now implement those operating plans he's been dreaming about for so long—the new computer system, more efficient expediting procedures, new sales incentives, the ad campaign, and improved cash management systems.

But there's a right way and a wrong way to take over the management of a company. The first day, the first week, and the first month are critical periods when certain tasks must be accomplished, fears laid to rest, and goodwill infused.

THE PERSONAL TOUCH

Changes and improvements only work if people want them to work, and goodwill can only be nourished if the new owner is viewed as a capable and caring boss. It's human nature to resist change. Employees find hundreds of reasons for resisting new procedures and policies. Small groups ban together to protect the status quo. And right now you, the new owner, are threatening that status quo.

You are the intruder and the antagonist. It is you whom the employees must protect each other against. No matter that you sign the payroll checks, the fear of job security will predominate. To begin operating his new company efficiently, the business owner must first put to rest the debilitating fear of losing jobs and win the respect and confidence of his people.

Supervisory personnel are the backbone of any organization and it's crucial to get them on your side as rapidly as possible. A staff meeting immediately upon entering the offices that first day is a good beginning. Before leaving the closing, alert the seller what time you would like to hold the meeting and ask him to alert the key personnel to be ready.

THE FIRST DAY

Several years ago, Don and I purchased a manufacturing company with 100 percent leveraged financing. Both of us were M&A consultants and before that stretched a lifetime of managerial experience. No question that we could find the right company to buy or that we could negotiate and finance the deal without too much difficulty. And, with our combined wealth of experience in managing companies profitably, there could be no question of our ability to manage this small enterprise—or so we thought. After all, the company had sales of only $15 million and we were both accustomed to managing companies much larger than that.

The first day after closing, my partner and I went to the plant to announce to the employees that we were the new owners. Word spreads fast, and our entrance was expected. Rumor was rampant that these two very wealthy investors from the East had purchased the company, were prepared to invest hundreds of thousands of dollars in new equipment and inventory, and planned to increase the work force by at least 100 people. It wasn't until much later that we understood the implications of this prevalent, but false, ''deep pockets'' rumor.

We didn't have the opportunity to meet everyone during our due diligence visits, so the first step was to call the supervisory group together and introduce ourselves. I explained that, although we had uncovered several minor operating problems during our due diligence phase, nothing seemed insurmountable and we looked to this group to initiate ideas for improvements. Don talked about a new, very lucrative, management incentive bonus program to be implemented within the next month.

We immediately launched a request for their help. Being the newcomers we realized these key employees had the experience and knowledge of the MSM business that we lacked. My partner asked each of them to prepare a brief personal profile so we could get to know them faster, and then I asked for a memo from each listing what he saw as the major strengths, weaknesses, and problems of his own functional area. I also asked for suggestions for improvements in personnel and operating policies.

Later that morning, while trying to sort out my new office, I was approached by the marketing manager, the controller, and the chief engineer with concern written all over their faces.

"Mr. Tuller," Martin, the marketing manager began, "we appreciate you taking the time to meet with us this morning, but we're confused. Since you asked for suggestions, may we make some now?"

"Of course," I responded, somewhat surprised.

"Well, to begin with, Bob (the production manager) has a wife in the hospital awaiting an operation and needs to be with her today. He was afraid to ask for the afternoon off, knowing you want to meet with his people. Second, although you asked for suggestions, neither you nor Don said what you expected from us. And lastly, our major customer was on the phone not five minutes ago asking, and I quote, 'What's going on over there? Who are these highfalutin' Easterners coming here and telling you how to run your business?' I really need to meet with him for lunch and soothe his feathers."

During the due diligence investigation I had been skeptical of this man's ability but now he turned out to be far more perceptive and sensitive to people problems than we were. He was totally correct. Don and I had missed two of the most important items in that first meeting:

1. Before worrying about the business, be concerned for the personal problems of your people. Show compassion and understanding for their problems before you worry about your own, and,

2. Be forthright and honest right from the beginning in telling everyone exactly what the ground rules are for the conduct of the business.

It always helps to have some notes to follow when starting something new so here's an outline to follow during that first day on the job to help prevent what happened to us. Since my experience at MSM, I have used it several times in structuring the first day program for other entrepreneurs and it seems to do the trick.

AGENDA FOR THE FIRST DAY

Supervision
- Conduct a staff meeting with the key supervisors.
  - Introduce yourself with a brief background of the experiences which qualify you to run this company. (Remember, at this point the group is evaluating you more than the other way around.)
  - Ask for the following from each of the staff:
    - Personal profiles of background both with the company and elsewhere.
    - Memo of strengths and weaknesses in his functional department.
    - Functional organization chart for his department.
    - Personnel evaluation of each person in his department.

- Set up a schedule for fireside chats over the next two days with each of the group.
- Ask for suggestions for new personnel policies, operating policies, and operating systems and procedures.
- Ask for their help!
- Explain what they can expect from you:
  - Honesty and loyalty will be a two-way street.
  - Open door policy.
  - Objectives for improved profitability and growth.
  - Incentive program for management personnel and others.
  - Management performance evaluation standards.
- Tell the staff how you purchased the company with debt financing and silent equity partners (if any). If it's a high-leverage deal, tell them. Don't hold back any secrets about the financing.
- Conduct an open question-and-answer period.

The Hourly Employees
- Conduct a group meeting of all hourly employees.
  - Introduce yourself with a brief background of technical experience in similar businesses. (They want to judge the new boss just like the supervisors did.)
  - Ask the group for written, constructive criticisms of existing conditions and suggestions for improvements.
- Explain what the employees can expect from you.
  - Honesty and loyalty.
  - Open door policy.
  - Objectives for improved profitability and growth.
  - Incentive program for all employees.
  - State your intentions to work with their union representative (if any) and shop committee to improve working conditions.
- Tell the group how you purchased the company. Try to convince them there are no "deep pockets" around to fund additional equipment or higher wages. (Not the same depth as with the supervisors, however. Word will spread quickly enough about the details.)
- Conduct an open question-and-answer period.

The Salaried Employees
- Conduct a group meeting of all salaried employees.
  - Introduce yourself with a brief background of managerial and technical experiences which qualify you to run this company.
  - Ask the group for written constructive criticisms of existing conditions and suggestions for improvements.

- Explain what the employees can expect from you.
  - Honesty and loyalty.
  - Open door policy.
  - Objectives for improved profitability and growth.
  - Incentive program for all employees.
- Tell the group how you purchased the company. Emphasize that there are no "deep pockets" around. (About the same depth as with the hourly personnel.)
- Conduct an open question-and-answer period.

In following this outline, four areas should be stressed. They apply not only in dealing with supervisory personnel, but also with the rest of the employees:

1. Show humility. Everyone already knows the deal has closed and you're the new boss. It doesn't help to emphasize your power—that can only alienate people. If you approach employees with the attitude that you want to learn from them; that you want them to continue to do the good job they are doing; and that you recognize that each of them has problems of his own that you will willingly listen to and help solve, the odds are very high that you'll be off to a flying start in inter-personal relations.

2. Using your best sales approach—but with honesty—explain how you were able to buy the company. Most people have never tried to make an acquisition themselves, but have read articles about this Wall Street tycoon or that oil billionaire buying up companies right and left. From media coverage, they naturally assume that anyone buying a company must be wealthy and have very "deep pockets." I missed this point at MSM and to this day, several years after we sold the company, many employees still believe we were extremely wealthy to be able to buy MSM and are even wealthier now that we have sold it. Nothing could be further from the truth but after that first day it was too late to convince anyone.

   If the employees do not fully understand that a good part of the cash flow must be used to pay acquisition debt service, they will always think you are milking the company instead of buying them the equipment they think they need or giving them the salaries and wages they believe they have earned. And with this misunderstanding underlying all human inter-relationships, it's impossible to enlist their active cooperation and support. So be honest about your financial capabilities. It certainly can't hurt, and you will gain respect for your willingness to take the risk.

3. Be open and caring in personal relationships. Convince the employees, both with words and actions, that their problems and concerns are vitally important to you. Show them that you understand how crucial their jobs

are to their well-being and will do everything you can to make them secure. An open-door policy of encouraging anyone to come to your office to talk about their problems—at any time during or after working hours—is a good start toward convincing them of your sincerity. Maybe you can't solve all the problems, but at least listen to what they have to say with a sympathetic ear. Many times this is all anyone really wants. A little compassion and empathy go a long way. You were probably once an employee yourself and remember how you felt toward your boss?

4. Set forth in clear terms what your objectives are in buying the business and what you expect of the employees to help meet these objectives. Most people are not mind readers and cannot know what you want unless you tell them. Everyone has experienced at one time or another the frustrations of trying to do what the boss wants without knowing precisely what he does want. In my early years as a struggling controller, I took a new job with a company in Chicago. I was a bright-eyed and bushy-tailed kid eager to do a good job. I soon learned, however, that my subordinates didn't seem to need a supervisor, my peers sullenly guarded their own domains, and my boss was never around to tell me what he wanted. I lasted 12 months and quit, never understanding what was expected of me.

Set forth clear standards of performance from the first day for the supervisors, and as soon as possible during the first week for the rest of the employees. Explain the honesty and loyalty you expect (and will reciprocate in return); what the profit and growth objectives are; how you expect supervisors to treat their subordinates; and finally, what type of rewards can be expected if goals and objectives are achieved.

Nothing is more difficult for a person to cope with than not knowing what is expected of him—from employers, clients, parents, or spouses. Few of us are completely anti-social and therefore, we need to know what is expected of us in our jobs, our friendships, and our home life. Corporate manuals and formal policies might work in a large corporate structure—although I'm not sure they do—but in a small company it's the personal touch that makes people feel wanted and needed. It's the personal touch that demonstrates to employees what is expected of them.

THE FIRST WEEK

Once the first day becomes history, a new owner begins to feel that maybe everything will turn out all right after all. If there weren't too many barbs, if the tension wasn't too thick, and no key employees gave notice, you're probably on safe ground. The next get-over is the balance of the first week. Difficult situations always seem easier if there is a written plan to follow—something to fall back on when situations get sticky. Nothing complicated, just one or two sheets of paper to provide a guideline for getting things accomplished. I've used this technique religiously in my own companies. It's a technique you could also use in the first week as boss.

PLAN FOR THE FIRST WEEK

- First Day
  - Meet with all employees for introductions, clarification of goals and objectives, and question-and-answer sessions. (This has been done.)
- Balance of the Week
  - Hold daily staff meetings the first thing in the morning.
  - Establish cash-control procedures.
  - Meet with key customers and vendors.
  - Meet with bank.
  - Meet with union representative and shop committee or employee group leaders.

Daily Staff Meetings

Some people say that daily staff meetings are unproductive and time consuming and that supervisors could put their time to better use in managing their own activities. I wholeheartedly agree. During the first week, however, supervisory personnel are the best source of information. They can tell you what's going on in the company—and this you need to know, right now. Also, the more you're with the key people the better and faster you'll get to know each other. And this is even more important than the information flow. Establish open lines of communication as soon as possible so that a constant interplay of ideas, recommendations, and problem-solving can evolve. To make these meetings productive and not bull sessions lasting for hours, a short printed agenda can be utilized.

During this first week, continue to emphasize the need to develop good people relationships. The mechanics can come later, but the first week should be used to convince the supervisors—and teach them if necessary—your strong belief in good human relations as the cornerstone of meeting goals and objectives. They will respond with a myriad of ideas for improvements. Everyone thinks he's an expert in personnel matters—and that's good. Encourage it, and open lines of communication with these managers will rapidly unfold.

Establish Cash Control Procedures

Establishing cash control procedures is such an obvious necessity why even discuss it? Or is it?

Bart Rikell had just closed a deal and taken over a small chain of plumbing distributors. Because of his financial background he looked very closely at the internal control procedures covering cash management during his due diligence investigation. He assured himself the controller was competent and managing cash effectively.

The first week was hectic. Two key executives resigned and Bart was left with direct supervision of the warehousing and shipping functions until he could find replacements. By the third day he was ragged, and although faithfully holding staff meetings every morning and managing to either meet or set up appointments with his major customers, Bart just didn't have time to scrutinize the cash. He still felt secure, however, knowing he had done a thorough job during the due diligence. He was convinced adequate controls existed.

At the end of the first month the controller handed in his resignation and left the next day. Now Bart was forced to handle the cash receipts, sign the checks, and make the bank deposits himself. When he closed the books at month end, he found $10,000 in cash was missing. The only explanation possible was that the controller had been lapping the receivables and stealing cash over the past four months—ever since the ex-owner announced his intention to sell the company.

Bart could not have saved the entire $10,000, but certainly, by establishing new cash controls that first week, he could have uncovered the misappropriation, stopped it for the rest of the month, and maybe collected restitution from the controller.

Meet with Key Customers and Vendors

In most companies there aren't many large vendors so the big problem is usually meeting the key customers. Local customers are easy. Set up breakfast or luncheon meetings and have the sales manager in attendance. Out-of-town customers take some scheduling. There is never time to meet them all the first week, but at least get the meetings scheduled for the future so they'll know you care. Some introductions may be handled by telephone and those should be done the first week.

Meet with the Bank

Meet with the bank as soon as possible. This is really part of establishing good cash control procedures. One of the first requirements should be new signature cards. If you're using the same bank, get your own signature in place of the seller's, and order new facsimile plates if needed.

Be sure to meet the account executive responsible for your account. Work out the procedures for draw downs on the operating line; cash transfers between accounts; authorizations for wire transfers (this authorization should be a numeric code known only to you and the bank wire transfer department); deposit procedures; bank statement formats if there is a choice; the use of lock boxes for receipts; duration and format of reports to be submitted to the bank for the security to the operating line (receivables and inventory); and finally, a schedule with the audit department for periodic reviews.

Meet with the Union Representative and the Shop Committee

It's generally best to meet with the business agent separate from the shop committee. If that's not possible then a joint meeting will do. The importance of meeting with the union in the first week is to show that you are sensitive to labor relations and recognize the union as the bargaining agent. You may not like unions but if the company comes with one in place, it's wise to acknowledge its importance right up front. Creating a good working relationship with union leadership, can solve many problems which otherwise could take up valuable time. Without a union, hold the same type of meeting with the employee group leader(s).

THE FIRST MONTH

After introductions are completed and cash control procedures in place, it's time to settle in and begin running the business. In addition to normal daily decisions, there are three activities to be completed in the first month of ownership:

1. With key employees, put together a monthly operating plan for the next 12 months.
2. Design and put in place internal operations reports needed to control the business.
3. Reassess current marketing strategy and begin changes where necessary.

The Operating Plan

With the original business plan as a guide, preparing the operating plan will be easy. Simply dig out the pro forma forecasts for the next six months and update them from current data. Well, not quite that easy. Unfortunately, the operating plan is substantially different from the business plan.

The operating plan should include income statements, balance sheets and cash flow statements by month for the next 12 months. If the accounting records segregate revenues and costs by product line or service categories, try to do the forecasts by these same groupings. The smaller the increment to deal with, the easier and more accurate income and cash forecasts become.

The first week we owned MSM, Don asked the department heads to put together just such an operating plan. The objectives were to provide a tool to measure performance on a monthly basis and to plan for cash requirements as far out as possible. Each manager was assigned the task of compiling those elements of the plan for which he would be responsible; such as manpower projections, orders received and sales forecasts, a purchasing plan, a new product development program, new systems implementation and requested capital expenditures.

The controller was to assimilate all data in a comprehensible format. We were the new kids on the block and other than from due diligence investigations, knew very little of the inter-relationships of costs, pricing, and volume peculiar to MSM. Remember, the controller is the analyst in the organization structure and should be capable of calculating various "what if" results so that the components of the plan can be manipulated into the optimum configuration.

To get the attention and cooperation of the supervisors, we earlier announced a management incentive program, tied to the operating plan, so that if the sales growth, profitability and defined return on investment at the end of the year were at least equal to the operating plan, each of the key employees would receive a check amounting to 50 percent of his base salary. That got their attention in a hurry.

We knew there were two potential dangers, however:

1. A department manager will invariably submit a very conservative forecast to be sure he achieves it.

2. To gather the data and massage each element can take a long period of time during which the manager is not performing his operating responsibilities.

To get around these problems we set up three rules: (1) a tight, one-week time schedule for submission, (2) certain financial ratios had to be maintained (profit percent to sales, inventory turns, receivables' days sales), and, (3) maximum funding available for capital expenditures was stipulated.

Even though it was a struggle, all managers except one submitted his plan on schedule. Now the controller took over to shuffle the numbers. A couple of revisions and two weeks later we had an operating plan structured by the operating management.

There was only one catch. The plan didn't provide sufficient cash flow to meet the debt service obligations. So back to the drawing boards, and a month later a more aggressive plan emerged, satisfactory to the bankers, but a stretch for the employees.

The final segment in this chapter of the MSM saga is that by structuring our salaries at 20 percent of what we thought we should get and proving to management that as owners, we were making a far bigger sacrifice than they, both Don and I thought we had their support for the plan. What we didn't realize at the time, was that because the employees believed we were deep-pockets entrepreneurs, they saw no urgency in making the plan happen—the new owners would always bail them out with cash infusions. In fact, the company never did come close to our goals—but that's another story.

Internal Reports

There's no need to wait for the completion of the operating plan to design internal reports needed to operate and control the business, although the format of the plan, at least, should be done first to determine what information is available. Internal management reports are very personal—every business manager looks for different signs to signal opportunities or problems. But there is one report hardly anyone can get along without—a report showing the daily cash receipts and disbursements against forecast. It might take some trial and error to finally determine the exact format, but starting on Day Two you should be receiving a report of cash receipts and disbursements from the controller.

The bank will also dictate certain reports: receivables' aging, inventory turns, cash balances, loan balances, and so on.

Some other types of internal reports most new owners find valuable are:

- Weekly manpower counts by department.
- Weekly orders received and order backlog.
- Daily and weekly shipments.
- Monthly customer delivery promises kept.
- Monthly vendor purchase orders placed and open purchase orders.
- Monthly sales by territory/region.
- Monthly gross profit analysis by product line.

It goes without saying that every new owner should design his own format for the monthly financial statements—income statement, balance sheet, cash flow.

Market Strategy

No matter how busy you may be meeting people, preparing the operating plan, or developing internal reports—and regardless of how big or small your company may be—market strategy must be reviewed and redefined, if necessary, as soon as possible. After all, without sales you don't have a business. You can't afford to wait until things quiet down before being certain the sales force is going down the right road. The entire marketing plan can't be revamped in a matter of hours or days. But it's important, right in the beginning, to make an effort to understand what the sales people are trying to do and whether or not you agree with their program. Maybe some low-margin products should be purged, or changes in the pricing structure need to be implemented, or the cost estimating procedures might need revision, or new and larger discounts should be offered to move slow moving items. Again, these are long-term decisions and cannot be made lightly, but at least try to grasp the questionable areas and begin dealing with them as quickly as possible.

The first week at MSM we tackled the marketing strategy relating to pricing procedures. All products at MSM were made to customer specification and priced on cost estimates. The procedure called for a customer inquiry with engineering sketches, then an estimate of the total cost of the order, then an offer to the customer to deliver certain quantities at requested times and at specified fixed prices. The entire pricing structure was predicated on the estimate of total costs to produce and sell, including overhead and profit.

When I asked the question, "How do you develop the detailed cost build-ups in the manufacturing area?" I was aghast at the answer from the marketing manager.

"That's simple," Martin replied. "We figure out what machines the product requires and then estimate the value of each machine to the customer. From that we apply predetermined factors to these machine values to price the products."

I had never heard of such a haphazard pricing strategy. Quickly the meeting adjourned and I called Martin to my office. "How did you ever arrive at that pricing policy?" I asked.

"We didn't have any choice really. We've had so many customer inquiries the past year that with only one pricing analyst, we couldn't handle the volume any other way."

"In other words, you're overworked and understaffed. Without a computer you had to do something fast to get the pricing done. So you devised a simple system to give the customer what he wanted. Does that about sum it up?"

Still tight as a watchspring Martin replied, "Yeah, that's it—and I don't think anyone could have done any better!"

"Look," I told him, "as I said at our first staff meeting, my job is to help you do yours, not to beat you over the head because you don't have the tools. I've been in your position and I know that you can't change a tire without a jack. How would you like to go to a computer store this afternoon and pick out a personal computer for your pricing analyst? Will that solve the problem?"

"Hell yes! Then we can do the job right."

By applying a very small amount of understanding and caring about his problems, a disastrous pricing strategy was converted to a workable system which eventually won overwhelming approval from our customers. Compassion, caring, and common sense really did work. Martin went on to become a leader in the company responsible for a significant increase in sales over the next two years, and without additional pricing analysts.

The path to survival during the first month requires getting the people on your side, controlling cash expenditures, and plenty of planning. Understand the human element, follow the rules of good planning and control, and the odds are high you'll be a success. Ignore these basic tenets at your peril.

As a footnote to the MSM story, we managed to get through the first month all right—in spite of all the mistakes. As time went on, however, an even more serious problem arose. Don and I had acquired MSM with an equal partnership—that is, each of us owned 50 percent of the company. Even though we gave ourselves different titles, the fact that neither of us had the final word in a dispute began to cause an irreconcilable rift. As in any business, many decisions requiring judgment calls needed to be made. In the beginning, with the glow of entrepreneurship shining brightly, we both managed to swallow our opinions when they differed. But as time wore on, differences between Don's judgments and my methodology for running a business widened. Employees soon realized that there wasn't one boss—there were two—and they began to play one of us against the other. Customers used the same ploy. Even the lender banks realized they could get their way faster by encouraging internal political strife. The partnership finally ended when we sold the company. Since then, we have remained friends but will never again do business in an equal partnership.

The only reason for mentioning this personal story is to alert all potential entrepreneurs considering partnership arrangements that only one person can be the boss. When you establish the buying entity, be sure all partners realize that the committee approach won't work. Everyone must agree—right in the beginning—who is the boss.

ON YOUR OWN

Those are the major areas to take a look at the first day, the first week, and the first month. There will inevitably be many more problems needing immediate attention. Each company is different—simply because people are different. A complete, foolproof checklist of how to run a company is impossible. Besides, as an egotistical entrepreneur, you wouldn't look at it anyway.

When you walk through the door that first day, you are the intruder—owner or not. Major obstacles will be thrown in your path. Actions and results planned for the first six months almost certainly will not happen. Employees will quit, customers will go elsewhere, a vendor or two will go out of business or be sold, new state and federal laws will require unplanned expenditures, and, of course, the roof will leak. Profits will be less than expected and all of a sudden the cash flow will dry up and you'll need to draw down on the operating line you hadn't planned on using until next year. But don't worry, it's just Murphy raising his head. If you have the courage to stick to your convictions and are adept at getting the support of your people, right will prevail. Practice merciful management, keep one eye to the sky, and have faith. The first six months are the worst. Beyond that the waters get smoother. And if you have an investment banker-partner, lean on him in emergencies. Two heads are usually better than one.

Put people first. Be kind and considerate of others. Let it be known, quickly, how much you value the rights and human dignity of all employees. Extend these human principles to customers, vendors, government officials, community peers, and everyone else over whom you exert power. The merciful exercise of this power begets success; abdication of responsibility leads to failure. Spend the first week in your new company getting to know the people—their names, faces, positions, needs, and desires. If they really believe you have their best interests at heart, there will be little resistance to change. Let customers, suppliers, and bankers know as soon as possible that you are a person who is honest and above board: that you really do care about them and they are not just numbers in an computer data bank.

Trying to run a company alone is a fearsome task. It is far less difficult and frustrating if you ask for help from employees, partners, or in some cases even bankers. People love to help other people, contrary to the way many of them behave. By practicing merciful management you can count on others to help you in difficult times.

The transition period when buying a small retail business can be just as trying and the same principles should be employed. Without several key employees to rely on, however, and with far less complete financial records, the new owner must depend more on the seller and his own ingenuity to survive. The next chapter deals with this problem as well as the other major differences in buying a small retail business.

15

Small Is Beautiful
Tricks in Buying a Small Business

"Who says you can't make money selling paper clips?"

AS DIRECTOR OF PROCUREMENT FOR A LARGE PAPER COMPANY IN WISCONSIN, SI Smith was very familiar with the intricacies of buying raw materials and supplies for large production runs, but buying a box of paper or a carton of paper clips was another story. When his company merged and his job became redundant, Si took early retirement. He and Rose decided to become entrepreneurs. They didn't have a lot of cash, and at their age, they certainly were not ready to relocate. When the office supplies store in their neighborhood came on the market, they jumped at the opportunity.

The store had been profitable for many years. It had the reputation as the place to go for any and all office and school supplies. Other services such as copying, Western Union, and facsimile telecommunications were also provided. Their local banker was willing to lend Si and Rose enough to close the deal and within three months from start to finish the couple were entrepreneurs.

Two years later, Si was beside himself with worry. Rose developed a heart condition and had to stop working in the store; volume dipped, and there wasn't enough money to pay the bank and still draw a living wage. A year later, Si sold out and the couple retired on his meager pension and social security.

What went wrong? About everything that could:

- Demanding volume discounts, pressuring suppliers for quick deliveries, replacing soiled or damaged materials, forcing 90-day payment terms—all the tricks Si had used when buying materials and supplies for a giant corporation, didn't work for small quantities.

- The eight-hour days and five-day work weeks Si tried to maintain wouldn't fly in the highly competitive office supplies business.

- By offering an additional one-half percent discount, competitors stole his largest business accounts.

- Walk-in business at four competitors within a five-mile radius of his store increased because of higher stocking levels of computer supplies and greeting cards.

- Monthly debt service payments strangled the business during slow periods and Si and Rose were trying to live on less than $10,000 a year income.

- Two key employees related to the seller resigned when he sold the business. Four large commercial accounts followed these employees to a new store they opened just down the street.

- The banker who seemed friendly enough all those years Si deposited money increased the pressure to pay down the operating line.

- The myriad of taxes were more than Si had bargained for. With no tax advice during the buying stage, Si ignored many of the state and local taxes in forecasting cash expenditures and now they drained what cash remained.

- A lawsuit against Si personally by a major supplier left the couple emotionally and financially drained.

And on and on and on.

THE BASIC INGREDIENTS

Buying a small business may look like a piece of cake but in reality can be just as tricky and fraught with just as many unforeseen problems as acquiring a multimillion dollar manufacturing company. Although the same sequence of steps are valid, much of the emphasis and many of the mechanics differ, starting with the mental attitude of the potential buyer.

It's difficult for an employee accustomed to the luxuries and clout of a large corporation to grasp the radical differences in running a small business. To change from a narrow, structured environment with talented specialists compensating for each other's weaknesses to the chaotic, broad-based, centralized decision-making of an owner-managed small retail business, requires a dramatic shift in priorities and effort. By retail I mean any small business selling goods or services to the general public or to a broad commercial market.

To effectively manage a small retail business an entrepreneur must:

1. Be self-sufficient and enjoy doing everything himself. There won't be any staff people to help with details. He must be the salesman, purchasing agent, controller, chief engineer, stock boy, secretary, file clerk, and computer expert.

2. Be willing to work long hours. Most small businesses do not operate nine to five, five days a week. Many are open seven days. Many more conduct business from eight or nine to six or seven or even later.

3. Be satisfied with a reasonable income without trying to reach for the stars. Although some small businesses can yield income in the hundreds of thousands, most provide a living wage—but no more.

4. Be content with stable sales and profits without striving for rapid growth. Assuming they survive the first three years, most small businesses maintain a fairly even sales volume year to year.

5. Be able to survive in highly competitive markets allowing little room for product or service specialization.

6. Be willing to accept only a modicum of power. The small businessman with only a few employees will not attain the broad power base realized by the owner of a larger business.

The huge doses of power, vast sums of money, and substantial freedom of choice and action possible in a larger company won't happen in a small retail business. So there must be other reasons for buying one of these. And there are.

Most people acquiring a small business do so because they want to be their own master, lead their own life style, and achieve at least some financial independence without incurring the enormous risks and costs of buying a larger company. And many don't have the cash reserves to acquire a larger business even if they wanted to. The case of George and Janice Chin is a perfect example.

George was a successful aerospace engineer with Lockheed Corp. for nearly 14 years. Expecting their second child in six months, the couple made a cataclysmic decision. George could see his job becoming more and more oppressive and time away from his beloved family stretched for longer and longer periods. Both he and Janice longed for the good old days when George was just starting out and they had plenty of time to do things together. When their first child arrived, George had already begun the traveling treadmill and never seemed to be home when Janice needed him. They decided not to make the same mistake a second time. So George resigned, took count of his investments and savings, and decided to buy a company.

With meager savings, he knew it had to be a small business. Also, George wanted to run it himself without the responsibility for employees. Janice certainly wouldn't have any free time—at least for a while. And it must be located in the neighborhood so he could get home for emergencies. Neither George nor Janice aspired to great riches—they just wanted to get by, raise their kids, and along the way provide retirement reserves.

George began the search and soon located a small restaurant and bar for sale in a neighborhood shopping center. The deal closed quickly with seller financing and the couple became entrepreneurs. Once again they began to lead a happy and full life—even though George worked harder and more hours than he ever did as an employee. In Chapter 17 we'll see what happened five years later.

There are enormous advantages to buying a small business—not the least of which is reduced financial risk. A larger acquisition with layers of bank debt, convertible provisions in case of default, and personal guarantees, can easily result in financial ruin if the business falters. Potential loss of personal assets added to continued liability for unpaid debts is a greater risk than many are willing to bear. At least if a small business does go belly up, the owner loses only the business, not his personal assets. But more on financing aspects a little later.

A small business also offers the opportunity to remain close to home, have more free time for the family, and reduce stress and anxiety—although the latter is not always the case. It was stress that caused Marcia to leave her corporate administrative assistant job and buy an interior decorating business. At 46, she grew tired of the continual headaches and irritability and opted to trade in the corporate rat race for a quiet neighborhood business. Within a year, however, she found herself worried about collecting receivables and satisfying demanding, wealthy customers. She had less and less time to create new and unusual designs. The stress returned, and Marcia sold out within two years. She is now happily living on a Caribbean island as manager of a small resort—with no headaches, few worries and content for the first time in many years. So buying a small business is not always the solution to excessive stress.

Timing factors are less crucial, however. Prices of video stores, flower shops, photography studios, and barber shops have little to do with stock market ratios or industry business cycles. True, in a deep, general recession prices tend to be lower than when the economy booms and disposable incomes soar, but not by very much. External timing conditions affect start-ups far more than established small businesses. If a pharmacy has been operating profitably for several years, chances are it will continue at about the same level whether the Dow Jones average hits 600 or 2600 and whether the pharmaceutical industry is in an upward cycle or a downward spiral.

So if you want to get into your own business, close to home, with minimal financial risk and stress, and becoming a millionaire is not your main goal, buying a small retail or service business might be the answer. But then the first question to ask is, ''Where do I find a business for sale that matches my experience and knowledge?''

LOCATING A SMALL BUSINESS

There are four common ways to find the right small business:

1. Cold calls.
2. Word of mouth.
3. Local newspaper business opportunity advertisements.
4. Business brokers.

If you live in a smaller community where the number of businesses in your chosen market is limited, the best and fastest way to find something is to ask. Granted, a business owner will most likely over-value his business if approached directly—after all, everything is for sale at the right price—but it can't hurt to try. Even if the starting price is outrageous, many times by the time you get done negotiating, the price comes into line with reasonable standards. Asking the question directly gives an owner the opportunity to sell his business rather than merely close the doors when it's time to get out. Surprisingly, many small business owners never think of their business as having a market value and when they are ready to get out, they just liquidate assets and walk away. Such was the case with Nini Cott.

Nini owned a specialty boutique selling imported Scandinavian clothes and bolts of material to tourists. After 15 years she was ready to get out. She told me she planned to close the doors and hold a liquidation sale. When I asked why she didn't sell the business intact, her answer was, "Why would anyone buy this business? All I've got is inventory, a few store fixtures and a five year lease."

Trying to convince her to give me time to find a buyer before locking up was useless. A liquidation sale provided cash to pay off debts and a small amount left for her. Less than 60 days later, a tourist, looking for just such a business to acquire on the island, was disheartened that he hadn't known that Nini wanted to get out.

As pointed out in the book *Getting Out*, every business has some value over and above its hard assets. No matter how small, every business making a profit—and even those temporarily operating at a loss—enjoy some amount of customer goodwill. And it's this goodwill that a buyer values. It is much less expensive and less risky to buy a going concern than to start one from scratch. At least it has an established location, inventory, operating procedures, and a customer base. So it can't hurt to knock on doors for a while. Identify the type of business you want, research who owns such businesses in your locale and ask the big question, "Will you sell?"

Newspaper business opportunity ads and business brokers are also good sources—especially in large cities where the business community is more formal than in a rural setting. Many times brokers also advertise in the paper so by answering ads you'll very likely come across them as well as selling owners. As we saw in Chapter 5, business brokers are like real estate agents; they list businesses for sale and advertise for buyers. If you don't like the cold approach of knocking on doors or soliciting through direct mailings, a reputable broker can be a good source of businesses already on the market. Most brokers won't be of much help in providing detailed information about a business, or in helping to negotiate a deal, or in sourcing financing—but they do know which companies are for sale. They can save a buyer a great deal of time. It certainly can't hurt to use brokers as well as cold calls.

Business brokers are also listed in the telephone yellow pages. Pick out two or three in your neighborhood, give them a call, and if one or more sounds like he knows what he's doing, set up an interview. Before spending much time with a broker, however, be sure he is not one of the many charlatans in this business. The fastest way to ascertain this is to use the questionnaire presented in Chapter 5 while conducting a personal interview. Business brokers usually specialize by geographic area rather than industry or type of business, so the starting point is to decide where you want to locate, then contact brokers in that area.

Once a reputable broker starts providing targets, be certain to look at more than one. Just like buying a home, you seldom decide to buy the first house you look at. Comparisons are necessary to get a feel for prevailing prices, neighborhoods, structural characteristics, and relative values. The same holds true for buying a small business. If a broker only has one business fitting your criteria, take a look at that one but also go to other brokers to examine two or three or four different businesses. Don't let anyone tell you that a specific company is the only one of its kind available. As mentioned earlier, everything is for sale at the right price. So be sure to get comparisons before choosing.

BUYING A FRANCHISE

Franchising has become a way of life in the small business community. With the enormous number of franchised retail businesses, chances are high you will probably encounter one or more for sale during a search. Before jumping at the opportunity to buy one of these, however, you should have some understanding of the rules of franchising.

Franchises have become a very popular mechanism for the entrepreneur with little or no practical experience in a specific industry to start up a business of his own. There are literally thousands of different types of franchise businesses. Usually, one thinks of franchising in terms of starting a business from scratch, and indeed this can be a very viable alternative to buying a going business.

There are some distinct advantages provided by the franchiser:

- Training programs to teach the entrepreneur how to run the business.

- Lump-sum acquisition of new machinery and equipment required to run a complete business.
- Franchiser advertising programs to introduce the new business to its local markets.
- Franchiser financing of equipment—either through purchase or lease.
- Continued on-site guidance until the business is operating normally.

There are also some disadvantages that many find intolerable:

- Initial start-up franchise fee can be substantial. Even for a small print shop it can run between $25,000 and $50,000.
- Rigid compliance with franchiser rules for operating the business.
- Costly monthly, quarterly, or annual royalties—normally running up to 10 percent of gross sales, payable off the top before deducting any operating expenses.
- Restrictions on geographic territory the business can service.
- Continued requirement for participation in franchiser advertising and promotion programs.

If you're interested in the possibility of starting a franchise from scratch, check with the local library for one of the many books available offering guidance in this area.

But what about buying a franchised business already in existence and operating? There are plenty available, ranging from large hotels like Holiday Inn and other national chains, to fast-food restaurants, to car washes and quick-print shops. The advantages listed above for starting a franchise business don't usually apply to a buyer of an existing franchise—except for a brief training period offered by franchisers at the buyer's expense. On the other hand, most of the disadvantages—except for the initial start-up fee—do still apply.

There are other disadvantages depending on the particular business, but these seem to be the broadest and most onerous.

The buyer of a franchise business is saddled with the same compliance and royalty provisions as the original franchisee. Additionally, the franchiser usually insists on approving any potential buyer before a deal can be closed. This means submission of personal financial statements, reference checks, and other invasions of privacy. Although franchisers always promise to keep this information confidential, one has to wonder. Somehow a person's name keeps appearing on strange and obnoxious mailing lists.

The compliance feature is the most difficult to handle for many entrepreneurs. In many respects, operating a franchise can be just as restrictive as being an employee. You have your own business—but you really don't. You have all the liabilities and the risk of failure, but are severely restricted in choosing location, sales incentives, ad campaigns, product or service modifications, expansion or combination with other businesses, and on and on. Many franchisers also restrict the choice of suppliers for materials, inventory, and fixtures and equipment. The freedom of choice associated with owning a business just doesn't come with franchises.

Also, it's customary in the sale of many franchises for the buyer to assume the continuing leases and debts of the seller—a very risky and limiting proposition. Buying a franchise might look appealing, and indeed it might be a very good deal, but better to be safe than sorry. If you locate a viable target which happens to be a franchise, insist on reviewing the franchise agreement first, before taking another step. And have your legal counsel interpret any confusing clauses. Even if that checks out all right, step back, take a second look, and remember—you'll never be your own boss.

Other than passing muster with the franchiser and arranging for the liquidation or transfer of the seller's original debt—which can get sticky—the steps in buying a franchise are no different than for any other business.

VALUING THE BUSINESS AND NEGOTIATING THE DEAL

Once a likely target is chosen, and a level of interest letter executed, the next step—just as in a bigger deal—is to calculate the value of the business. No sense wasting time negotiating with the seller if his asking price is so far out of line as to preclude reaching an accord.

But how does one calculate a value for a business without unique products or services and poor bookkeeping records? The quality of financial records is normally poor in small businesses. In spite of the emphasis by the IRS placed on accurate record keeping for tax purposes, most small business people don't have the time nor the inclination to worry about formal accounting systems. Receipts are recorded on cash register tapes, disbursements made from the same cash register or the petty cash box, and bills paid from the checkbook recorded on check stubs. Few small businesses worry about such accounting niceties as journals and ledgers. The bookkeeper or tax accountant prepares tax returns by sorting through cigar boxes of receipts and register tapes. Interim financial statements are unheard of and unless required by a bank, so are annual statements.

Sales are usually fairly well-documented—either from register tapes or bank deposits. But when you try to ascertain what the cost structure is or what the trends in costs or profits have been, it's almost impossible. Many, if not most, small businesses account for sales and expenses on a cash basis so any attempt to calculate true profits is really meaningless. Measurement criteria is limited to cash receipts versus cash disbursements and how much remains left over for the owner to take home.

Additionally, personal expenses of the owner are often intermingled with business transactions. If it's a food store, restaurant, or small hotel, the owner probably feeds his family from purchases made by the business. In real-estate agencies, insurance agencies, pharmacies, and computer stores, the owner's automobiles and related expenses, insurance premiums, and personal entertainment expenditures are frequently paid by the business. It's not uncommon in a hardware store or lumber yard to find the owner's home repairs, remodeling costs, and appliances—even the kitchen sink—expensed by the store. The IRS has a fit, but nevertheless, most small business owners do these things as an entrepreneurial fringe benefit.

A potential buyer has a real problem trying to sort out this hodge-podge of expenses to determine how much cash the business is really generating and therefore how much he should pay for it. There is no accurate way to do it. He can always ask the seller how much he takes home, but seldom will the answer be truthful. Being pragmatic, he must work with the available records—tax returns and bank deposits—to ascertain sales, and apply his own judgment to the expenses. If the business is incorporated, he can use the corporate tax returns. If not, then Schedule C from the owner's personal return will have to do. Even tax records, however, probably won't reflect the true income of the business. It's always a mystery how a retail business owner showing profits of $20,000 on his Schedule C can afford to drive a Cadillac and live in a $300,000 house.

Using tax returns, bank statements, and common sense, the only two commonly used methods for valuing a small business with inadequate records are the reconstructed cash flow method and fair market value of hard assets and inventory.

Reconstructed Cash Flow

Using hypothetical numbers, the following calculations show how to reconstruct annual cash flow for a delicatessen and specialty food store.

Cash Sales	
Bank deposits less loan proceeds and owner's loan paybacks matched against register tapes and tax return sales	$200,000
Cash Expenditures	
Food and other resale purchases—	
From major supplier invoices plus tax return cost of sales	100,000
Rent—from lease	7,500
Electric, gas, fuel oil—from utility bills	15,000

Payroll—from payroll tax returns	30,000
Sales tax, use tax, payroll taxes and licenses— from tax returns filed	10,000
Miscellaneous expenses—estimate	5,000
Total Expenditures	67,500
Net Cash Flow	32,500
Multiple	× 2
Cash Value	65,000

The multiple of two is arbitrary and one of the negotiating points with the seller. Common multiples range from one to five, depending on the product or service sold, growth prospects, competitive environment, and location. Most buyers are not willing to go beyond a two to three year payback for goodwill and asset value combined so the factor used for cash flow might be no more than one. Note that nothing is included in the calculation for owner's draw or fringes. The buyer really doesn't care what the seller has taken out—he wouldn't believe him anyway. He is only interested in what cash the business can provide for himself.

The calculated goodwill must be added to the value of inventory, equipment, and fixtures. The definition of value is always negotiable but customarily inventory is valued at actual cost and fixed assets at depreciated value. Using the following numbers in our hypothetical company, the asset value calculation results in the following:

Inventory cost—from most recent purchase invoices matched against tax returns. For older merchandise, factor down by 20 percent for each year's inventory	$25,000
Store fixtures, net book value—from tax return depreciation schedules	10,000
Equipment, such as freezers, scales, computer— net book value from tax returns	10,000
Total Asset Value	45,000

It's entirely possible there won't be any detailed depreciation schedules in the tax return to derive the asset costs or book value of specific assets. Current depreciation methods permit lumping of assets and most small businesses do not keep detailed asset records. In that case, you'll just have to estimate the value of the fixed assets included in the deal if different from the tax return. Inventory records can also be inadequate. Industry gross profit ratios or mark-up ratios weighed against annual purchases can yield a usable inventory value if necessary.

In this example, the total valuation would then be:

Two years' cash flow	$65,000
Asset value	45,000
Total business valuation	110,000

This is about where a seller starts for this size business. With an annual cash flow of $32,000 it will take a buyer three years to pay off at this price—with no salary to himself. For a super location, no competition, outstanding growth opportunities, a favorable lease, and fairly new fixtures, this might not be too bad. But most businesses aren't that fortunate and therefore, a buyer must want the business a great deal to pay this much.

After looking at the competition and sales levels, a smart buyer should estimate how much it would cost him to start up a similar business next door and how long it would take him to reach these sales levels. If the answers are more than $100,000 and more than three years, then obviously he's better off making this deal—even if he has to pay the seller's price. In most cases, however, unless it's a franchise operation with guaranteed territorial rights, his estimates should be less than the asking price and therefore he'll want to negotiate downward.

Nearly all small business deals are asset rather than stock sales, and therefore current cost of replacing inventory and fixed assets influences how far the seller will go. Chapter 4 highlighted tax considerations in an asset deal from the buyer's perspective. As we saw, current built-in gains provisions increase the tax bill to the seller and this gives him further impetus to hold fast on his price.

As a last resort, if you can't get much movement on price, and a three-year payout is just too long, creative financing arrangements might still make the deal feasible.

FINANCING A SMALL BUSINESS PURCHASE

Not only are search and valuation techniques different for small retail businesses, the approach to financing is vastly dissimilar. In a larger deal the buyer must worry about sourcing long-term debt or equity through asset-based lenders and investment bankers. Here, the seller will have to carry whatever financing can't be done through a local commercial bank.

Because of the size of the business and the lack of hard assets, commercial banks are usually the only external medium for raising acquisition funds—and then only for an operating line secured by inventory (and receivables if there are any). That means the seller must carry any long-term debt required to close the deal. Most are willing to do this because the sums aren't that great. The same three forms of seller financing covered in Chapter 11 apply here: buyer paper, earn outs, and contingency payments. Generally, however, contingency payments are rare.

The most commonly used seller financing is buyer paper, usually evidenced by a promissory note with either monthly, or quarterly payments of interest and principal. Terms can vary, but most sellers prefer three years with a maximum of five.

In the above hypothetical example, if the negotiated price ended at $90,000 and the buyer put in $25,000 of his own equity, buyer paper would support the difference of $65,000. With quarterly payment terms for three years at 12 percent interest, annual debt service would run approximately $26,000, leaving only $6,000 remaining for the new owner—obviously not satisfactory.

Another approach might be to negotiate a balloon payment at the end of three years for $35,000, leaving $30,000 to be amortized quarterly. This would yield annual debt service of approximately $12,000, leaving $20,000 for the buyer. Still not much to live on but better than the first alternative. Of course, he must then worry about raising $35,000 at the end of the third year. Perhaps this could be done with a short-term bank loan secured by inventory.

A third approach would be to structure the debt as an earn out over, say, five years, with a guaranteed minimum payment of perhaps $5,000 per year and a note for $25,000 at 12 percent interest payable at the end of five years. Assuming the same profitability and an earn out split of 25 percent to the seller, the calculation yields payments of $8,000 per year, leaving $24,000 for the buyer. Of course at the end of five years he must come up with about $44,000 ($25,000 plus compounded interest at 12 percent) which is more than the loan value of business assets. No matter how you look at it, a buyer investing $25,000 cannot afford to pay a multiple of three times cash flow.

The purpose in this illustration is to explore alternative calculations to determine how much you can really afford to pay for a business—regardless of what the seller wants. One of the advantages in buying a small business is that the calculations of value are relatively easy to make—even by using estimated numbers. It doesn't take long to figure out how much you can afford, regardless of sophisticated or mathematically accurate valuation procedures. If you can't negotiate what you can afford to pay, there is no deal.

DUE DILIGENCE INVESTIGATION

If buyer and seller do arrive at a negotiated price and terms, an offer to purchase should be executed—just as in a larger deal—and then the due diligence investigation. The same procedures apply here as well:

- Visit the location.
- Meet with seller and employees (if any).
- Appraise the capabilities of supervisory personnel (if any).
- Gather tax returns for three years and any financial statements available, along with supporting cost and sales data.

- Obtain copies of all contracts and leases.

The due diligence checklist used here, however, is slightly different than that presented in Chapter 8.

CHECKLIST FOR DUE DILIGENCE

For Small Retail or Service Businesses

Financial

- Federal income tax returns for three years—Schedule C and accompanying schedules if not a corporation.
- Annual financial statements for three years or most recent financial statement for bank.
- Summaries of daily sales for last year.
- Vendor invoices to support purchases of goods for resale for last year.
- Listing of orders received for each month for the past three years and current year-to-date, if different from sales.
- Listing of expenses for last year.
- For any charge sales, a schedule of aged accounts receivable by customer as of each quarter for the past year and as of current month end.
- Physical inventory summary or detailed breakdown as of each year-end for past three years.

Personnel

- Payroll register for last year.
- Payroll tax returns for last year.
- Copies of employee resumes.
- Listing and description of all outside salesmen, representatives or agents, including agreements and commission schedules for each.
- All employment contracts or agreements, oral or written, including any severance or termination compensation arrangements with employees.
- All bonus, deferred compensation, profit sharing, or retirement programs or plans covering employees.
- If there is a pension plan, all documentation, including actuarial reports, tax returns, trustee reports, population census reports, funding requirements, unfunded liabilities, and so on.
- If more than three employees, an organization chart showing function responsibility, tenure, age, salary, name, and title.
- All documentation relating to employee insurance coverages—health, life, AD & D, dental.

- A description of mechanics of transferring any Union contract.

Facilities
- All recent (within three years) appraisals of real estate (if any) and equipment.
- Listing of equipment, fixtures, and furniture.
- Legal descriptions of all real estate including deeds, title reports, title insurance documentation, together with documentation of any lien thereon.

Legal and General
- Copies of supplier contracts.
- Copies of sales contracts.
- Copy of lease for building space.
- Copies of all equipment leases.
- All contracts or agreements with vendors and customers.
- All contracts or agreements with employees.
- All contracts or agreements with collective bargaining units.
- All contracts or agreements with other third parties.
- All insurance claims outstanding.
- All patents, copyrights, or license agreements.
- All non-compete covenant agreements.
- Listing and description of all outstanding litigation or anticipated litigation.

Performing the due diligence investigation in a small company can be a real headache. The owner is usually on the floor or out on calls and not available to sit with the buyer and lead him through the records and other data. Data is seldom accumulated before the buyer's arrival so he almost always has to gather it himself. Rarely will an employee have either the time or the knowledge to assist. Records are a mess, files are disheveled, and half of what you need is missing. There is seldom an office to work in. To top it off, the seller can't see the need to dig into all these matters and many times is not cooperative at all.

Unfortunately, no one has discovered a way around this problem. The best approach is to get whatever you can, bring it back to your office for analysis, and then return it. Keep going back until you get everything—although this may require many trips. A serious buyer must do a thorough due diligence, however. Even in a small company, a buy/sell agreement is necessary and the seller will balk at sweeping representations and warranties just like he would in a bigger deal. So somehow, all the data must be gathered and analyzed.

THE BUSINESS PLAN

About the only shortcut a buyer can make is in the preparation of the business plan. But this is only true if he doesn't need bank financing. With bank financing the same type of business plan as covered in Chapters 9 and 10 is necessary. It won't be quite as long, though, for several reasons:

- There isn't that much to say about the business, its products, markets, and competition.
- The organization is small or even non-existent, and the personnel section can be reduced substantially.
- Without significant growth plans or major changes to the business, the pro forma forecasts are much easier and shorter. Also, with probably few if any financial statements from prior years, this entire sub-section can be deleted.

Nevertheless, with bank financing a business plan must be prepared, and the presentation should look just as good as with a bigger deal. But it won't be as thick, that's for sure.

Even if you don't need a business plan for outside financing and might never show it to anyone, it won't hurt to go ahead and prepare one anyway. Remember, the other reason for doing it is to help you get a thorough grasp of the business. Even in very small businesses, each one is different, and until you do the due diligence and compile the results in an orderly format, it's difficult to get a total picture of what you're buying.

AGREEMENT TO PURCHASE AND SELL

Large or small—retail, manufacturing, or service—buying a company in any industry of any size requires legal contracts. So you can't get away from lawyers merely by going to a smaller company. And all the arguments for choosing the right one, with experience in drafting closing documents for similar businesses, are equally applicable. But there are a few differences, mostly as a result of buying assets rather than stock.

Let's take a look at a simple buy/sell agreement which can be used for most small business asset sales.

AGREEMENT TO PURCHASE AND SELL

THIS AGREEMENT, made this _____ day of _____ , 19 ____ , by and between xxxx (''Seller'') and xxxxx (''Buyer''):

WITNESSETH:

WHEREAS, Seller is the owner of a Widget business located at _____ in the city of _____ and State of _____ , and,

WHEREAS, Seller desires to sell and Buyer desires to purchase all of Seller's rights, title, and interest in and to the said business under certain terms and conditions more hereinafter fully set forth;

NOW THEREFORE, in consideration of the mutual promises and good and valuable consideration and intending to be legally bound thereby, the parties hereto agree as follows:

1. Sale

Seller shall sell and Buyer shall purchase free and clear of all liens, encumbrances, and liabilities the Seller's business owned by Seller and operated at the premises above described, including inventory, furniture, trade fixtures, equipment, customer lists, and other assets of the Seller's business more fully described in Schedule "A" and attached hereto; *(This is different from buying stock. Now the seller must list each piece of equipment or other assets included in the deal and he must be certain all assets are free from any creditor's claim. If he has a bank loan secured by the inventory or other assets it must be paid off prior to closing or if he owes trade payables he must get assurances from all creditors they will not place claims on these assets at a later date—bulk sales laws cover this area.)*

2. Price

Buyer shall pay Seller a purchase price or consideration for the purchase of said business the sum of FIFTY THOUSAND ($50,000) DOLLARS payable as follows:

(a) THIRTY-FIVE THOUSAND ($35,000) DOLLARS at the closing of sale pursuant to this agreement.

(b) FIVE THOUSAND ($5,000) DOLLARS ninety days after the closing; and,

(c) TEN THOUSAND ($10,000) DOLLARS thirty six-months after closing.

(Notice the hold-back of $5,000 for three months. This is to allow the buyer's auditors time to verify the exact amount of inventory and other assets as of the date of closing. If you're buying assets you want to be sure that you actually receive what the agreement lists.)

3. Allocation

The purchase price shall be allocable as follows:

Inventory	$ 7,000
Furniture	1,000
Equipment	20,000
Covenant not to compete	15,000
Customer list	7,000
Total	$50,000

(This allocation is primarily for tax purposes. The allocation to Customer list is really goodwill. Amounts allocated to each of the assets are part of the negotiation.)

4. Closing
Closing and transfer of all assets shall be on or before the 31st day of January 19xx, at _____ .

5. Employment Agreement
(No need to cover this now. A standard one to three year employment contract is the norm if you want the seller to remain as an employee, or a simple consulting contract if he stays in that capacity.)

6. Accounts Receivable
Seller shall be entitled to collect and receive all accounts receivable due as of the closing date. *(No need to trade cash for receivables. Let the seller struggle with his own collections.)*

7. Lease
It is understood and agreed that Seller shall secure and present to Buyer at closing an assignment of Seller's presently existing lease covering the premises, dated _____ .

8. Documents at Closing
At settlement Seller shall deliver to Buyer all keys to the business premises, a Bill of Sale, assigned Lease, an Affidavit that there are no creditors of said business at time of closing *(this means the seller must either pay off or get a written agreement that he will be responsible for all liabilities to suppliers, taxing authorities and banks)*, and any and all other documents necessary for the transfer of Seller's business and assets to Buyer.

9. Casualty Loss
(Standard format.)

10. Seller's Covenants
Seller covenants and represents:
> (a) That he has received no notice from any government authority of any violation of any law;
> (b) That he is the owner of said business and the assets agreed to be sold and conveyed herein;
> (c) That he and the business have complied with all the laws, rules, and regulations of state, local, and federal governments;
> (d) That there are no judgments, liens, attachments, or actions now pending against Seller in any Court;
> (e) He has not contracted to sell, pledge, or mortgage all or any part of the business;
> (f) He has paid or will pay before closing, all state, local and federal taxes;
> (g) That there are no outstanding contracts or services, supplies, or materials otherwise relative to Seller's business that will extend beyond the date of closing or settlement.
> (h) That he has told, relayed, or otherwise communicated all relevant data,

information, conditions, and other matters currently applicable to the business to Buyer;

(i) That there is nothing Buyer does not know about the business.

12. Bulk Transfer Requirements

Seller shall comply with all notices and other requirements of the laws of the State of _____, including but not limited to, the bulk transfer requirements.

13. Covenant Not to Compete

Seller agrees that for a period of five (5) years from the date of closing or settlement, he shall not either directly or indirectly as a principal, agent, manager, owner, partner, employee, officer, director, or stockholder of any company or corporation engage in or become interested financially or otherwise in any business similar to the business being sold within a fifty-mile radius of the business being sold.

14. Time

15. Survival

(Both standard clauses.)

16. Personal Guarantee of Seller

Seller warrants and represents that he is the current owner of the business being sold and that he personally guarantees that he is and will be responsible for settlement of all debts outstanding against the business as of the date of closing.

17. Indemnification

Seller agrees to hold Buyer harmless and indemnify Buyer from any and all claims, demands, liabilities, actions, or causes of action asserted against Buyer arising out of any transaction or by virtue of any act, deed, or omission of Seller, its agents or employees. *(This is an additional assurance to the buyer that he has been told everything about the business. Just one more section to claim breach of contract under if anything goes wrong.)*

IN WITNESS WHEREOF, the parties (. . . etc. The Agreement goes on to quote General Statements of Law and has room for signatures.)

The main points to remember in drafting the buy/sell agreement for the purchase of business assets, other than standard representation and warranty clauses are:

- A hold-back portion of the purchase price to give your auditor time to verify account balances.
- Clauses to ensure that the assets are free and clear of any liens.
- Hold harmless and indemnification clauses in the event of breach of contract.
- Assurance that bulk sale laws have been complied with and all taxes are paid.

- A non-compete covenant to ensure an opportunity to build your own goodwill.
- Allocation of purchase price between the balance sheet assets, a covenant not to compete, and goodwill.

THE TRANSITION

When a buyer takes over a company with supervisory personnel, he can rely to a large extent on their expertise and knowledge of the customers and business to carry him over until he becomes familiar with the operation. In a small business, he doesn't have that luxury. When he walks in the door, other than a handful of employees, he is on his own. Because most small deals are financed at least in part by the seller, it behooves him to be certain the buyer knows how to run the business before he begins his vacation. And a buyer certainly wants all the help he can get in the beginning—from the seller or anyone else.

For these reasons, it's usually a good policy to work out a side agreement with the seller to compensate him a small amount for staying with you for the first week or two. It won't cost much, but can save a bundle later on. Most sellers are willing to go along with such an arrangement and many will not even want to be compensated. But whatever it costs, if the seller will stay on for a short period and teach you the ropes, it will make life a lot easier.

Summary

If you are interested in becoming an entrepreneur in your own business but need a stream of income right from the beginning, it makes a lot more sense to buy an established business than to start one from scratch. Unless you have $100,000 or more to invest in this venture, it also makes more sense to buy a small business rather than a larger one with a heavy debt load. And finally, unless you yearn for far-reaching power and the opportunity to make large amounts of money, a small business can provide a very satisfactory living and significantly more freedom than a larger company.

Let's summarize the eight main differences:

1. Personal Attributes. The buyer of a larger company must be a heavy risk-taker, an effective manager of people, a combination thinker, doer, and analyst, and thrive on delegating work to others. A small business entrepreneur takes significantly less risk, is willing to do all the jobs himself, and need not worry about motivating and otherwise managing many people. Generally, there also is less stress in owning a small business.

2. Timing. The acquisition of a larger business must be done at the right time relative to macro economic conditions, the stock market, and indus-

try cycles. A small business may be purchased almost any time assuming the market it serves is local or regional.

3. The Search. Locating a small business is much easier. Cold calls, newspaper ads, and business brokers are relatively easy methods compared to using M&A consultants, massive direct mailings, and answering wide-flung *Journal* ads.

4. Valuation and Negotiation. Because of inadequate record keeping, the number of techniques for establishing a price for a small company are very limited. Negotiations are normally straightforward and fast. Success in closing a deal is very often dependent on the seller's willingness to do the financing. On the other hand, complex valuation techniques and difficult, drawn out negotiations often characterize a larger deal.

5. Financing. A larger acquisition almost always involves outside financing—either debt, equity, or both. Debt service and dividend returns take a large amount of the cash flow and can strangle an otherwise profitable business. Outside financing is also difficult and time consuming to arrange. Seller financing for a small acquisition can hasten the process and can be structured more to the means of the business. On the other hand, there is less cash to manipulate in a small company and therefore, unless the seller is willing to take an earn out or vastly extended payment terms, there might not be enough cash to pay him and make a living wage at the same time.

6. Due Diligence Investigation. Whereas a larger company usually maintains fairly good records, a small business often keeps track of transaction through cash registers and a checkbook. Reconstructing the real profitability of a small business can be extremely difficult and often impossible. Many small businesses use the cash basis to account for transactions. Decisions to proceed are often made by judgment calls rather than hard facts.

7. Buy/Sell Agreement. Most small business deals are asset sales rather than stock transactions. Special provisions in the buy/sell agreement must take account of payment holdbacks to verify account balances, indemnification for missing data, and compliance with the bulk sales laws. A larger deal is normally a sale of stock and the representations and warranties are mush easier to negotiate.

8. Transition. A larger company, with qualified supervisory personnel to manage the day-to-day routine, can be transferred without assistance from the seller. Because a small business usually doesn't have personnel to carry the ball, a buyer must get some help from the seller during the initial transition period.

Those are the dissimilarities in a small versus a mid-sized acquisition. Although reference has been made to small retail businesses as the basis for the comparison, the term "small business" actually refers to any business with few or no employees—except professional practices which will be covered in the next chapter.

16

All Together
or One at a Time
Tricks in Buying a
Professional Practice

"They don't teach debits and credits in medical school."

MANY DOCTORS WORKING IN HOSPITALS, LAWYERS EMPLOYED BY GIANT LAW firms, accountants in Big-8 firms, dentists in assembly-line clinics, and other such professionals long for the day they can get into a practice of their own. Their problem, however, is that they have been so intent on learning their trade that they haven't had time to learn the techniques of surviving in the business world. Certainly no time to absorb the tricks of entrepreneurship.

Claire graduated from medical school and after her internship, opted to stay on with the hospital as a resident physician. Five years later, tired, disillusioned with internal politicking, and convinced the medical staff was more interested in collecting fees and improving their golf scores than helping patients, she pondered her next move. "I'd sure like to try it on my own. I know I can give better care in my own practice than I'll ever be allowed to do here at the hospital. The problem is, I'm a bit frightened at the prospect of starting a practice from scratch and I don't know a thing about buying an existing one."

"Maybe I can help," I suggested. "Are you interested in practicing on your own, or would you prefer to buy into a partnership?"

"I haven't any idea. I don't know much about either way."

I invited Claire to come over to my house that weekend to hear a short course on buying professional practices. The following is a synopsis of our meeting.

A PROFESSIONAL PRACTICE IS A UNIQUE BUSINESS

There are several features of a professional practice making it different from any other business. These characteristics hold for nearly any type of profession—medicine, law, dentistry, accounting, consulting, architecture, or engineering. Following are 11 unique characteristics that make buying a practice different from acquiring any other type of small or large business:

1. The services sold to the public are performed by the owner himself, not employees.
2. Extensive training and professional standards establish operating guidelines making technical knowledge fairly uniform between practices within each profession.
3. Client loyalty flows to the individual practitioner, not the business.
4. Individual skills of the practitioner make one practice unique from others in the same profession.
5. A practice may be a one-man business or a group of partners.
6. The geographic area served is normally quite restricted.
7. Advertising and promotion are minimal and most new business comes from referrals.
8. Few, if any, hard assets are required to run the business.
9. Most are on a cash basis, or close to a cash basis.
10. There are many small clients, so billings are voluminous, but each has little value.
11. Inventory is normally restricted to operating supplies.

There are essentially three ways to buy a professional practice:

1. Buy into a partnership with several partners
2. Join a sole practitioner in a successor partnership
3. Buy out a sole practitioner.

There are pros and cons to each of these methods. Buying into a large practice with two, three or more partners—such as a clinic—has all the advantages of buying a minority interest in any operating business:

- The business is established.
- Other partners are available for consultation and guidance.

- The risk of failure is lessened.
- The cost of office space and other overhead can be shared.
- A getting out position is assured with no successor problems.

Disadvantages are also present:

- Freedom of action is restricted by the wishes of the group.
- Profits and cash are split between the partners and this allocation might might not be in proportion to effort or hours expended.
- Operating decisions made by committee are less timely.
- Differences of opinion are overruled by the majority.

Buying into a multi-partner practice is not for everyone. If working as an employee in a hospital, clinic, large firm, or private industry creates disappointments, frustrations, and the longing to be on your own, a member of a large partnership can produce exactly the same results. On the other hand, some professionals prefer the security and camaraderie associated with a shared partnership, and if this appeals to you, then by all means give it a shot. Techniques of buying into such a group are much easier than for the other two alternatives. The group itself places a value on a partnership share, that in most cases is not subject to negotiation. Financing is almost always carried by the partnership itself, after a small down payment, and deferred payments are made out of your share of the partnership earnings—just like an earn out agreement. The legal work is boiler plate and again not subject to negotiation. So all you really have to worry about is raising the down payment and whether your personality traits and goals are compatible with the other partners. If the answer to both questions is affirmative, you have yourself a deal.

The other two alternatives—buying into a one person practice as a successor, and buying out a sole practitioner at one time, are a bit trickier. Because of the complexities of these two arrangements, the balance of this chapter will deal with the process and alternatives in coping with them—not with buying a minority share in a multi-partner firm.

From an acquisition perspective, the two alternatives are similar except in the following areas:

- The partnership and buy/sell agreements.
- Financing the deal.
- Transition management.

But let's cover the common elements first.

LOCATING A PRACTICE TO ACQUIRE

Finding a practice to either buy into or buy out completely can be a nerve-racking experience. Occasionally an accounting practice, dental practice, or other professional business will be listed in your local newspaper or the *Wall Street Journal* Business Opportunities section. But these are few and far between. Also, the quality of most of those advertised is inferior. Either they are located in some out of the way place, or they specialize in a very small market niche, or they have a very few number of clients, or something else is wrong.

The same can be said of practices listed with business brokers. Although occasionally a quality one shows up, most are not worth bothering with.

If ads and brokers don't work, where do you turn?

The first step is to pick a location. With the exception of some consulting and engineering practices, most professionals conduct their business within fairly narrow geographic constraints. A physician draws patients from within an easy commute of his office. With the exception of a few specialties, lawyers draw clients from the city in which they practice. Accountants tend to restrict their client base to an accessible commute. Some consulting and engineering practices specialize in activities which apply universally throughout the country—such as M&A consultants—and in these cases location becomes irrelevant.

So let's assume you have chosen a location. What next? There are four methods that seem to work pretty well for locating available practices—although each will have varying degrees of success depending on location, type of profession, size, and specialty:

1. Trade journal ads. All professions have their trade magazines. Many of these include listings of practices for sale or partners wanted.

2. Word of mouth. Questioning professional associates often turns up leads otherwise obscured.

3. An M&A consultant. Although not usually specializing in professional practices, some consultants perform a search here the same way they do for a commercial business.

4. Direct mail solicitations.

Reggie Thomassen had worked for a dental clinic in Milwaukee for three years. Although enjoying his job, he longed to return to his hometown in northern Wisconsin—but this time with his own practice. He began answering ads from the state dental association journal. One, located only 20 miles from his hometown, specifically caught his attention. The seller was becoming desperate because no one seemed interested in such a remote location. When the two met it was a perfect fit and within two weeks the practice belonged to Reggie.

Simply asking the question can also bring surprising results. Bill was a young attorney, two years out of law school, working for a three-partner firm in center city Philadelphia. Getting the entrepreneurial itch, he mentioned to one of the partners his desire to eventually practice on his own. The partner understood perfectly—in his younger days he had done the same thing—and put Bill in contact with the alumni office of his law school. This in turn led to an introduction to

Mark, a 70-year-old sole practitioner eager to find a young man to train as a successor and eventually buy him out.

When all else fails, cold solicitations asking the big question, "Do you want to sell?" can bring amazing results. Although I already owned a small CPA practice in Minnesota, I wanted to expand beyond the small community I serviced. Being a bit impatient and not willing to go through the normal state CPA society grapevine, I compiled a mailing list of all sole practitioners within a 100-mile radius and mailed each a brief letter, on my professional letterhead, asking the big question. Of the 200 or so inquiries, 15 responded in the affirmative, and within three months my expansion was complete.

I suggest using an M&A consultant only if you don't have the time, resources, or inclination to do the search yourself. Chances are he won't take any different actions than you could—unless he happens to have a friend or knows someone in your profession who just happens to want to sell now, which can happen. Also, a consultant costs money. For an engagement like this, a good one will probably want a monthly retainer of $3,000 to $5,000. That's a lot of money for a one-man business.

If none of the above ideas bear fruit, try putting your own ad in a state professional journal stating that you are interested in buying or joining an existing practitioner. This often brings better results than a direct mailing because the seller can keep his identity confidential until you reveal who you are. Dentists and architects seem to have pretty good luck with this method, although I don't know of any other professionals striking pay dirt. But that doesn't mean it isn't possible.

Timing

As we've seen, national and industry economic factors can have a major influence on the proper time to acquire an industrial or commercial business. Although impossible to generalize—there are too many different professions—this does not seem to be the case for most professional practices. Again, there are exceptions depending on the profession, but people always need doctors, dentists, lawyers, accountants, psychologists, and many other professionals whether the economics of the moment are good or bad. Some consulting professions do feel the impact of national economics more than others, however, such as engineers, architects, and business consultants. In recessionary times, companies are less likely to engage consultants to improve their operation—but again, there are exceptions.

If it's possible to generalize at all, these economic fluctuations tend to have a reverse effect on the demand for professionals. With a bear market on Wall Street, unemployment skyrocketing, interest rates going through the roof, and inflation out of control, more people seem to get in legal trouble, try extra hard to reduce the tax burden, seem to have more accidents, and appear to suffer more distress—certainly higher stress levels. Discretionary expenditures will be down so perhaps the orthodontist might suffer, but mental illness goes up and psychologists prosper. In total, however, contrary to industrial and commercial businesses, there doesn't seem to be any way to generalize about how timing influences buying a professional practice.

TAX IMPLICATIONS

Structuring a deal to minimize taxes is very straightforward. All small practices are structured as asset sales, and with very few hard assets available for price allocation, negotiations really come down to how much should be allocated to goodwill and how much to a non-compete covenant. The buyer naturally wants everything charged to an amortizable non-compete covenant. The seller argues for goodwill to take advantage of capital gains provisions—assuming he has capital losses to use as offsets. If he doesn't, then the debate is moot. Allocate most of the price to the covenant and go on to other matters.

If you intend to incorporate, double taxation of cash draws results in the same problem here as discussed in Chapter 4 for any other business. Limited partnerships don't apply to small professional practices so the practitioner usually relies on an S corporation to accomplish the pass through of cash. Of course, if you don't incorporate, then there is no problem and all draws are taxable to you as ordinary income.

One thing to keep in mind that distinguishes the professional practice from a retail or service company. In a strictly personal service business only the individual can perform the service—a corporation cannot. From a tax perspective, this means the IRS will probably treat a corporation consisting of one individual as if it didn't exist and tax rules applying to individuals, not corporations, invoked. You might still want to incorporate for non-tax reasons, but don't expect any benefits from the IRS. Any occupation generating service income from the activities of one person has the same problem, including athletes, artists, writers, actors, and musicians.

It should be mentioned that all professionals—or any business person for that matter—operating as a proprietorship are considered as self-employed by the IRS. Because a self-employed taxpayer does not have an employer to share the cost of Social Security taxes (FICA), he is always obligated to pay the self-employment tax in lieu of FICA.

One tax haven for a professional not customarily available to other entrepreneurs is a deduction for expenses of maintaining an office in his home. Many professionals find it more economical and convenient to use a portion of their personal residence as a permanent office rather than leasing outside space or buying real estate. When this is done, all expenses of maintaining your house are proportionately deductible as business expenses. The amount deducted is calculated as the same percentage of total expenses as your office space bears to the total square footage of the house. For example, if an office occupies two rooms out of a ten-room house, 20 percent of all expenses are deductible as business expenses—whether you operate as a proprietorship or a corporation. This can be extremely beneficial because expenses such as utilities, trash removal, yard maintenance, and house insurance—not otherwise deductible—are included as expenses of maintaining the office. And all expenses directly attributable to the office space—such as remodeling—are deductible in full.

The biggest deductible expense—which is never allowed as a personal deduction—is depreciation of your house. This can amount to several thousand dollars of tax savings each year and all by itself can determine the advisability of working at home rather than renting space.

Following is a list of expenses normally associated with keeping an office in your home—all of which are deductible as business expenses.

DEDUCTIBLE EXPENSES FOR AN OFFICE IN THE HOME

- Expenses Deductible in Total:
  - Advertising
  - Bad debts
  - Bank service charges on business accounts
  - Car and truck expenses
  - Commissions
  - Dues and subscriptions
  - Business liability insurance
  - Cleaning
  - Legal and accounting
  - Repairs of office furniture and equipment
  - Office supplies
  - Travel and entertainment
  - Wages pay to outside help
  - Telephone (if separate phone line for business)
  - Decorating and maintenance of office space
  - Depreciation of office furniture and equipment

- Expenses Relating to the House Deductible as an Allocation:
  - Electricity
  - Oil and gas heat
  - Water
  - Telephone (if no separate business phone)
  - Yard maintenance
  - Trash removal
  - Snow clearing
  - Repairs to house, including painting
  - House insurance
  - Real estate taxes

Mortgage interest
Depreciation of house

Any other expense of maintaining the house—without which you could not have an office—is also deductible as a shared expense.

VALUING A PROFESSIONAL PRACTICE

Valuation techniques for most businesses are fairly well defined. Records are orderly and historic cash flow is easily determined. Book value of receivables, inventory, and hard assets can be readily obtained. Future prospects can be analyzed through market share, competition, and product development factors. From this, future cash flow can be calculated without difficulty. Industry norms for multiples of profit or cash flow are well known.

Even in a small retail or service business without adequate bookkeeping records, known sales and expenses can be used to reconstruct cash flow. Appraisals can substantiate hard assets if necessary.

But with a professional practice conditions are different. Regardless of the form of doing business—proprietorship or corporation—professionals are probably the worst bookkeepers around. Ledgers and journals are almost always nonexistent. Cash registers are not used to record receipts. Offices are frequently in the home or shared with other businesses. Most use a hybrid system of cash and accrual accounting—cash for receipts and expenditures, accrual for billings. And finally, I have never known a professional, regardless of his specialty, who prepares financial statements. Even if they did, very few if any, would be willing to show them to an outsider—even a potential buyer.

So what is available? Bank statements—which most never let you see. Tax returns—either Schedule C for proprietorships or corporate returns for professional corporations. Client lists with annual or monthly billings (if this isn't available it can be compiled). And perhaps some records of the original cost of equipment, reference libraries, furniture, and small tools of the trade. Very few ever tell you how much cash they pocketed last year so there's not much sense even asking. This is the data you'll have to work with, and it's almost always the same whether the profession is medicine, law, psychology, dentistry, consulting, or engineering.

Customarily, a professional practice is valued at a multiple of annual gross billings plus any equipment, tools, supplies, or real estate included in the sale. The reason is simple: expenses such as office costs, payroll, transportation, travel, and so on are totally under the control of the owner. A buyer will operate the practice differently than the seller. Perhaps even in a different location. So historical expenses are not really germane to the calculation of what cash flow the practice can produce after the sale. About the only financial statistic worth using is annual gross billings. From this are deducted all the expenses you expect to incur to run the business. The remainder is discretionary cash. Even if the seller's client base changes year to year, an historical three-year average of gross billings should provide a good indication of what you can do.

Multiples of one to two times gross billings are applicable for most professional practices, although this is always negotiable. This calculation represents the goodwill of the practice being sold. The rationale behind a multiple of one to two is that by the end of the first year—and certainly by the end of year two—the buyer will have established his own client loyalties and the goodwill built up by the seller will no longer be valuable. Out of sight, out of mind. With a personal services business the loyalty is to the person performing the service—not his predecessor.

To the calculated goodwill must be added the fair market value of any equipment, supplies, references works, and so on. With no magic formula for getting this value, sellers usually argue for replacement cost. Buyers respond with tax basis value. Negotiations result in a compromise and that's that.

A buyer's major concern should be whether he can retain the existing client base until he has time to establish new clients of his own. After all, the only reason for buying a practice rather than starting one from scratch is to generate income during the period of building a client base; although hopefully most of the seller's clients can be retained permanently. This fear of transferring clients, both by the buyer and the seller—if he is financing the deal—encourages partial sales and temporary partnerships until client loyalties are established. The mechanics of structuring a deal this way will be covered a little later. Whatever structure might be negotiated, however, the valuation technique is the same.

Those are the common elements, whether you buy out a sole practitioner at one time or whether you enter into a temporary partnership for eventual takeover.

By this time Claire, my young doctor friend, was becoming a bit bleary-eyed. The session had gone on long enough. "I think I get the idea, Larry. Let me think about it and see which way I want to go. Although, right now I'm leaning toward finding an elderly physician to bring me in for a while before I buy him out—the same way your attorney friend Bill did it. That certainly sounds like the least-risk arrangement."

Claire went on her way and eventually did find her patriarch mentor. The deal they negotiated will be used a little later to illustrate a very workable succession partnership arrangement. Now let's look at some of the peculiarities of each of the two options.

A COMPLETE BUYOUT

Of the two possibilities for buying a total practice, a complete buyout carries the greatest risk to the buyer. Individual practices can be categorized two ways:

1. Those which rely on the personality of the practitioner to maintain the client base.

2. Those which rely on the technical knowledge of the practitioner to maintain the client base.

The former, which are strictly personal services practices, such as psychotherapy, marriage counseling, or private investment advisory services, rely on the personality and character of the practitioner rather than purely on his technical knowledge. A buyer is not likely to retain the patient/client base simply by taking the place of the seller and exhibiting technical credentials. These practices are not usually salable through a complete buyout.

On the other hand, those practices based on technical knowledge rather than personal services can more easily be transferred to a new buyer without undo risk. Clients use a tax advisor not so much because of any personal relationship with the practitioner but rather because the tax returns he has prepared over the years seem to have been creative and accurate, acceptable to the IRS, and he charges reasonable fees. If he recommends that a client use the services of a successor to whom he sells the practice, chances are good the client will continue. Bankruptcy law is another specialty where technical knowledge seems to be more important to the client than personality. So is general-practice dentistry.

There are strong economic reasons for buying a practice in total. If the income a practice generates makes it a one-family business it probably could never support a partnership. The only way to transfer ownership is all at one time.

A buyer acquiring a one-family professional practice faces the same transition dilemma as the small retail or service company purchaser, only worse. His biggest challenge is to build the confidence of his clients or patients and convince them that he is as technically competent as his predecessor. This requires an adeptness in human relations practices and a mastery of professional sales techniques. It's not easy, but with a caring attitude and patient nurturing it can be achieved.

When I expanded my Midwest CPA practice several years ago, one of the steps was to acquire a thriving practice in northern Wisconsin—150 miles from my home office. The seller had built the practice to over 200 clients but because of failing health had to get out. An immediate move to warmer climates precluded helping me in the transition and I was left with the task of meeting—and selling—his clients on the idea that I was as qualified as their ex-CPA. Having acquired two practices earlier, I knew the type of sales pitch required. It consisted of a three step program:

1. The first week, I sent a mailing to all clients introducing myself and including a personal profile describing my background and experience, a recent photo, a fee structure, and an invitation to attend an open house three weeks hence with their spouses and children. Free food, free beer, free punch, and door prizes.

2. At the open house I made it a point to spend most of the time with the spouses and other family members, knowing there would be time at a later date to promote the clients themselves.

3. Two days after the open house I made a second mailing which included my brochure, a calendar with tax deadlines, a brief newsletter covering new tax changes, and a warm cover letter expressing my appreciation for their time and the opportunity to meet their families.

This system might not work for everyone or in every setting, but it sure did for me. Not one client left, and over the next two months 28 new clients walked in the door.

Financing a Total Buyout

Financing the acquisition of a professional practice must usually be done by the seller. With no hard assets, few receivables, and little or no inventory, banks of any type are not interested in taking the risk. Most smart sellers know this and are ready to carry some form of buyer paper—although many will want at least one-third to one-half as a down payment.

In those practices with a repeat client base—such as a medical, accounting, or business consulting practice—the best arrangement from the buyer's perspective is a contingency payout. Because you are buying the right to do business with the seller's clients, if these same clients don't come back, you haven't purchased anything. Therefore, it's best to negotiate a deal with deferred payments over a three-year period. The amount to be paid each year should be equal to one-third of the gross receipts of the seller's clients. This arrangement accomplishes three things:

1. It minimizes the risk that the seller's clients will go elsewhere for their work. If they don't show up, you don't pay for them.

2. It eliminates the need for stringent representations and warranties in the buy/sell agreement. The seller doesn't need to warrant any matters relative to clients or client activities.

3. It enforces the non-compete covenant. If the seller starts up a competing business and takes your clients, you don't pay him for them.

In those practices without a repeat client base, such as a bankruptcy law practice, about the best you can do is structure a deferred payout over three years based on total gross receipts. The goodwill you're buying here is primarily the reputation of the firm epitomized by the name of the practice. If the name doesn't attract new clients, the goodwill isn't worth anything. On the other hand, if there really is goodwill built on reputation, then the seller should be willing to agree to this type of arrangement. As added incentive, you could secure part of these payments—say one-fourth—with a promissory note. But don't agree to this unless forced into it.

Again, with the seller financing most of the purchase price on a contingency payout, the buy/sell agreement is very simple and the non-compete covenant easily enforced.

THE TRANSITION

Under the best of conditions, transition management is difficult without the presence of the seller—at least for a while. Unless you buy the practice from an estate, or the seller is physically incapacitated—such as with my Wisconsin practice—part of the buy/sell agreement should include the seller's assistance during the transition period. If the seller personally introduces you to his clients/patients—as in the case of repeat business—or if he actively participates in public relations activities, as in the case of non-repeat business, the transition will go much smoother.

You won't need him for an extended period—just long enough to meet the clients and get your feet on the ground. If he won't do it gratis, it's worth agreeing to a short-term consulting contract and paying him for his services. If you've negotiated a contingent payout plan, however, he should be more than willing to ensure a smooth transition. The better you do, the more he gets.

As in any other business, showmanship is important. With the seller present for a period of time, the sale can be made to look like a partnership rather than a buyout and this makes the clients a lot happier and feel more secure. It doesn't take long. Usually, in a few months you'll be comfortable with the practice and won't want him any more. So don't sign any long-term consulting contract. Then you really have a partnership—except you take all the risk.

A SUCCESSION PARTNERSHIP

Forming a temporary partnership with the seller and gradually buying him out over three to five years is far and away the best method to buy a professional practice.

- The risk to the buyer is minimal. By working with the seller over a period of time you get to know his clients and they develop confidence in you. When he does leave, you should be well established.
- If for some reason a buyer decides not to proceed with the deal he can back out anytime during the buyout period with a minimum loss.
- Payment can be made out of earnings, just like an earn out contract.
- Non-compete provisions in the sale contract are not needed.
- The buyer has a chance to develop his own client base while earning a living from the seller's client base.

- There are virtually no problems in transition management.

The seller also gains:

- He gets to know the buyer and can be sure he can do the job before turning over the practice.

- Deferred payments are secure because his presence ensures buyer performance.

- Psychologically, a phase-out is much less traumatic than an abrupt departure.

There are some real dangers in any partnership, however, and one formed for the purpose of eventual buy-out is no different than any other. The partners must be congenial, honest, and technically competent. They must have the same personal values and objectives. And they must be willing to share management responsibilities. Before agreeing to any succession partnership, be sure the following seven rules of succession partnership describe the relationship.

1. Reputation—Check character references with other practitioners in the area and with the state licensing agency. If there is any question about his honesty, don't go forward.

2. Background—Choose a partner with similar moral values and personal objectives. Be sure you like each other. If you can't work together, the partnership will collapse.

3. Escape Clause—Leave the door open to break the partnership if, for any reason, you become dissatisfied with the arrangement.

4. Price—Right in the beginning, agree to a fixed price for the practice as it exists at that time. Also agree on the price paid for additional business brought in by the seller up to the time of complete takeover.

5. Time—Establish a fixed date for the complete buyout and fixed intervals for incremental shares of ownership.

6. Early Buyout—Have a buyout clause in the partnership agreement in the event you should die or become disabled prior to completing the full takeover. The price of the buyout should be at least what you have paid in plus a value for new clients brought to the practice.

7. Responsibility—Define what responsibilities each partner will have in matters of joint interest such as additions or changes in overhead costs and professional judgment calls with clients/patients. Who will decide if there is a dispute? What voice will you have in decisions affecting clients you bring in?

The number of ways to structure a succession partnership is limited only by the imagination of the two parties. It's impossible to list even a meaningful representative sample. So probably the clearest way to see how such an arrangement might work is to use an actual case history to illustrate one way of doing it. My young doctor friend, Claire, located just such an opportunity so let's use her case as an example.

The Case of the Cautious Physician

About two weeks after leaving the house that Saturday, bleary-eyed and confused from my lecture on acquiring professional practices, Claire decided to investigate partnership buyout opportunities. Personal contacts didn't get her very far, but a mailing to local family practitioners resulted in several good leads. Of the three most promising she selected a Dr. Brown.

Dr. Brown had practiced family medicine from his small office in the suburbs for 40 years. Approaching 70, he was thrilled to hear from Claire. It was the solution he had been looking for as a way to finally retire, fulfill what he felt was his continuing obligation to provide medical care to his patients, and still get a few dollars out of the deal. After a few meetings, the two parties negotiated the following arrangement for Claire to buy the practice over a three-year period at a total purchase price of $200,000.

- Claire began practicing with Dr. Brown immediately. Dr Brown paid her a monthly consulting fee of $3,000 for her services.
- She made a down payment of $40,000 in exchange for a 20 percent share of the practice.
- If at the end of the first year either Claire or Dr. Brown felt that the arrangement would not work out, Claire would get half of her $40,000 back, but no share of that year's profits, and go on her way.
- If, at the end of one year, both Claire and Dr. Brown agreed that the partnership/succession should go forward, her consulting contract would be voided and the following takeover schedule put into effect.
  - At the end of that first year, Claire would purchase another 15 percent of the practice for $30,000.
  - At the end of the second year, she would buy another 15 percent for $30,000 assuming the annual gross billings remained at least constant. If total annual billings from a combination of her clients and Dr. Brown's exceeded the base year, this increment would be priced at an amount equal to 15 percent of one-half the incremental billings.
  - At the end of the third year, the balance of the practice would be purchased for $100,000 plus 50 percent of one-half the incremental billings for that year. The practice would then be hers and Dr. Brown would retire to Southern California.

The calculation for the deal worked out as follows:

- **As a Down Payment**
  Claire paid down payment from savings $25,000

  She borrowed against the cash surrender
  value of her life insurance policy for
  the balance of the down payment   15,000

     Total Cash Paid Down   40,000

- **At the End of First Year**
  Cash profit from the practice was $144,000
  of which Claire was entitled to 20% or   28,800

  Dr. Brown took back a note from Claire at
  10% interest, payable in two years for $1,200   _____

     Total For Year One   28,800

- **At the End of Second Year**
  Cash profits on base year billings were
  $140,000 of which Claire was entitled
  to 35% or $49,000. She kept $30,000 for
  her own draw and paid the difference   19,000

  Billings increased by a $50,000 increment,
  of which Claire was entitled to 35% or
  $17,500. She used part of this as the
  excess payment—$50,000- $\times$ -1/2- $\times$ -15%   3,750

  Claire used another $11,000 of this
  incremental income to pay the balance
  of her 15% due   11,000

     Total For Year Two   33,750

- **At the End of Third Year**
  Cash profits on base year billings were
  $152,000, of which Claire was entitled
  to 50% or $76,000. She kept $40,000 for
  her own draw and paid the balance   36,000

  Billings increased by another $60,000
  this year, of which Claire was entitled to
  50% or $30,000. She used part of this as
  the excess payment of $60,000- $\times$ 1/2- $\times$ -50%   15,000

  The balance was used to pay against the base
  price   15,000

She used her share of the incremental billings from the second year ($50,000-$ $\times$ -35%) to pay first against her note from the first year (plus interest)	1,440
For the balance due against the base price, Dr. Brown took another note at 10% interest payable in two years, secured by her entire interest in the practice	49,000
Total For Year Three	116,440

Now the practice belonged to Claire and Dr. Brown left town. She still owed the doctor a note for $49,000, though. The next year, her first year of full ownership, she grossed about $250,000 (when Dr. Brown left several of his long-term patients also departed), and netted about $175,000. After paying off the notes to Dr. Brown and her insurance company she still pocketed almost $111,000.

Over the course of the four years, Claire purchased a $200,000 practice for $25,000 out of her own pocket. She lived frugally for three years with take-home pay of only $36,000, $31,300, and $40,000, respectively. But now in the fourth year, even after paying off the two notes, she netted over $100,000, and next year was close to $200,000. Not bad for a young physician. Dr. Brown, on the other hand, found a way to retire without deserting his patients and pocketed nearly $220,000 for the practice. Clearly, a win-win situation for both parties.

It's no wonder succession partnerships are popular with professionals. Assuming the integrity of both parties to the transaction, it's hard to conceive of a cleaner, easier, or more profitable way to buy or sell a business. Financial risk is minimal for both parties, financing the deal is not a problem, and transition is smooth. About the only serious flaw in a succession partnership occurs when one or the other party either wants to withdraw or is forced to withdraw from the deal before it culminates. To safeguard both parties in such a case, a comprehensive partnership agreement with buy-back clauses must be executed. A buy-back clause is a provision for one partner to buy out the other upon death, disability, or major disputes, causing the dissolution of the partnership. The appendix includes a sample of a partnership agreement incorporating buy-back clauses.

This is only one example of many different ways to structure a partnership buyout. Each situation is different and must be structured to meet the needs of both parties. Although the possibility always exists of teaming up with someone who turns out to have different characteristics than you believed in the beginning, careful adherence to the seven rules of succession partnership, competent legal counsel, and plenty of common sense can put you into your own business easier and faster than almost any other method.

Specific techniques of acquiring a professional practice vary from those used in buying a commercial business, as we have seen. Yet the acquisition process remains the same: locating, valuing, negotiating, financing, investigation, contracts, and transition management. The differences lie in the application of techniques to resolve each step in the process. The tendency of many professionals seeking entrepreneurship is to rely on their own abilities and acumen for managing the acquisition process. In nearly every case, this is a major mistake. It's too easy not to see the forest for the trees. Even a lawyer, an accountant, or a consultant should seek and follow outside advice in the acquisition process. Most people only make one acquisition in their lifetime, and with no experience to rely on, it's easy to make mistakes. So take the time and spend the money for professional assistance.

On the other hand, even some professionals get the urge to expand beyond their first acquisition. The next chapter focuses on the risks and methods of going beyond the first purchase and what to look for the second time around.

17

The Next Time Around
Making the Second Acquisition

"If I could do one, I can do more. The sky's the limit."

THROUGHOUT THIS BOOK, THE ANECDOTES, EXAMPLES, AND CASE HISTORIES
are true. Real people said, thought, and took the actions described. Of the 49
deals, nine fell through and were never closed. Forty entrepreneurs actually
made acquisitions and went on to become active business owners. Since buying
a business, some have failed. There have been three bankruptcies, two liquida-
tions, and two entrepreneurs have died. Three have sold their businesses and
either retired, entered political or social services work, or gone back to working
as employees. One CPA and one lawyer merged their acquired practices into
larger firms and rejoined the ranks of addictive organizations. The 28 remaining
are still active business owners—some successful beyond their wildest dreams,
others barely surviving.

At least 12 of these entrepreneurs have tried to expand their businesses
with additional acquisitions—either producing the same products and services or
diversifying into new industries and markets.

No book about buying businesses would be complete without at least a brief
analysis of some of the pros and cons, pitfalls and advantages, joys and heart-
aches of making subsequent acquisitions. In addition to losing the naivete and
star-struck dreams of the new entrepreneur, the experienced business owner
traversing the acquisition trail for a second time learns that the process takes on
significantly different characteristics than the first trip.

MOTIVATION

One difference is the owner's basic motivations for pushing ahead. As a beginning entrepreneur the challenges of power and money coupled with a perceived freedom of action and thought provided driving forces to overcome whatever obstacles may be in the way. Financial risks, excessive stress, and the need for complete dedication were but a few more stones barring the path and needing to be pushed aside. The vision of fulfilling a life-long dream spurred the would-be entrepreneur to accomplish what few have tried and even fewer have succeeded in attaining.

But once you become a business owner or once you are established in your own professional practice, the star-filled dreams begin to fade. Faced with the daily, and in many cases, hourly trauma of making decisions affecting not only your life but the lives of those who depend on your success, it's easy to lose track of original value systems and personal goals. Particularly in a thriving business—when the owner sees his bank account rising even faster than expected—greed can easily take the place of merciful management. Decisions can become tainted with the desire for even more accumulation of wealth. Power addiction can profoundly influence rational decisions and cause the entrepreneur to begin believing the myth that if he can do it once, he can do it again—only this time more easily. Such was the case with Jackie Jones.

A financial consultant bitten by the acquisition bug, Jackie put his consulting business on hold and acquired a mid-sized manufacturing company. The company had been losing money steadily for three years, but with his experience, Jackie was confident he could turn it around. He made the acquisition at the bottom of the business cycle and shortly after closing, the industry began its upward climb. He rode the economic curve successfully and within six months customer orders were flowing in with very little effort by the sales department. Jackie was elated. Cash rolled in far in excess of his projections. Intoxicated with newly found power and money, he began to think that cautious warnings about recognizing the needs and feelings of people were just conservative pessimism. He really believed improvements in the company's fortune were of his own making. He convinced himself that success was merely a result of his clever manipulation of employees, customers, and the banks. Jackie had everyone eating out of his hand and felt infallible.

Armed with euphoric conceit, Jackie decided to look in Florida for the next acquisition to add to his growing empire—he had always preferred warm climates anyway. If he could bring off one acquisition using the bank's money, he could certainly do it again. In a six-month period the newly found power and money had corrupted this entrepreneur into believing he could do anything he wanted— he didn't need anyone's assistance—not from employees, advisors, banks, or me.

Against my advice, Jack went ahead and acquired a small northern Florida plumbing products distributor. He immediately laid off nearly half the work force to cut costs and deliberately ignored all warnings about dealing with the human element. In less than 12 months the company was out of business. Jackie auctioned the equipment and locked the doors, absorbing the additional acquisition debt in his first company, placing additional cash strains on this profitable business. Finally forced to acknowledge he had made a serious mistake, Jackie became disillusioned and morose. Without the unwarranted assistance of several key employees he would surely have lost his other company as well.

Greed can destroy, and if the motivation in making a second acquisition—or a third, or a fourth—is to make more money and to achieve more power be wary of the self-serving trap of avarice. Money breeds greed, greed enhances power, and power leads to addictive behavior. The entrepreneur who fails to recognize that his success is largely due to the willing support and efforts of other people will surely fail the second time around. And the higher one goes, the more companies a person buys, the longer and harder the fall when it comes.

Jack persevered with his one company against some very substantial odds. Because of the cash strain of additional debt service, his profitable company began to falter. The Garden of Eden turned into a nightmare. Foreclosure was threatened by the bank, a labor strike stopped production for two months, the market for his products collapsed, and employee turnover reached serious proportions. But he learned to keep striving and have faith in his people and himself. He is no longer the cocky, self-assured entrepreneur who went to Florida to make his fortune. He now recognizes that power and money can blind; and has vowed never to repeat his self-indulgent adventure in the sun.

I certainly don't mean to imply that greed is the only motivator for expansion—nor that it is even the major impetus. But greed is pervasive. When you see how simple it really is to buy a business with someone else's money; when an operating line enables you to draw hundreds of thousands or even millions of dollars into your own coffers with the stroke of a pen; when employees and customers begin treating you with deference; when your garage now houses a Mercedes and a Jag; when month-long vacations to Europe become a normal occurrence, it is very tempting to become egotistical and fantasize that if one is good, two or three must be even better. But don't be fooled. It isn't just your doing that made the first deal successful. Many other people had a hand in it. You were the beginner, the newcomer, with great odds against making it. Everyone loves to help the underdog. But now, once you're responsible for everything entailed in owning and operating a business, these same people treat you not as the new kid on the block, but as an experienced businessowner expected to compete in the marketplace along with everyone else. In making a second acquisition, optimism and forecasting errors attributed to inexperience the first time around will not be tolerated again—either by the banks, employees, competitors, or customers. This is the second major difference: this time around you will be expected to know what you are doing.

EXPERIENCE

Accomplishing his first acquisition and managing his first company provides the entrepreneur with an experience base the novice lacks. This time he should know the acquisition process fairly well and avoid much of the trial and error characteristic of his first venture.

When Rick and Mary, whom we met in Chapter 4, closed the deal on the country inn near the Finger Lakes, they had already decided that their long-range objective was to acquire at least two additional inns, one in their home state of West Virginia and hopefully, one in New England. The West Virginia acquisition came first. Previously owning the Midwest motel and now success-fully buying The Crossed Fingers Inn, they knew exactly what to look for and how to search out what was available. This time it took only six months to locate and negotiate a deal for The Brown Bear Inn, a small pub with a six-room guest house. After hiring their son and daughter-in-law to manage the Crossed Fin-gers, Rick and Mary moved back to West Virginia to manage their newly acquired inn.

The couple knew that this time around they wanted an inn catering to year-round trade rather than seasonal, in a location near other relatives and friends, small enough to manage on a part-time basis, and sufficiently profitable to even-tually provide retirement income. Experience had taught them the type and size of inn to look for; what market niche they wanted to fill; how to structure the deal to minimize taxes and maximize long-term income flow; what to look for in competition; and most importantly, how to manage the establishment.

The reputation Rick and Mary established as honest entrepreneurs, good managers, and prudent business people earned them the confidence of the finan-cial community. Financing The Brown Bear went off without a hitch. Of course, putting in 50 percent of the purchase price as equity didn't hurt either.

Two years ago Rick and Mary turned The Crossed Fingers Inn—and a third guest house acquired in Vermont—over to their son and his wife and now live a comfortable, secure retirement life at The Brown Bear.

Here was a couple without visions of grandeur who parlayed their experi-ence as entrepreneurs into businesses providing them with financial security as well as a retirement lifestyle. They never expected to be so successful after their initial financial disaster with the Midwest motel. However, by persevering with a merciful management style and sound financial planning, they achieved their ultimate retirement goal.

RESOURCES

In addition to different motivations and proven experience, an owner also has more resources to draw upon than in the beginning. People resources, financial resources, and a reputation in financial and business communities provide a stable business base for expansion. No longer dependent on unproven supervisory or technical talent in the newly acquired business, you can draw upon existing employees to provide the management base. Earnings left in the company form an equity base. Proven earning power and management abilities create confidence in banking circles. Delivery, quality, and competitive pricing establish customer confidence and loyalty. In other words, with one operating company securely in tow, you can parlay a second acquisition from a base of strength rather than as an untried and unproven entrepreneur.

The risk is also greater in a second acquisition, however. In the beginning, all you could lose was your personal savings and assets. Now, failure could wipe out your savings as well as endanger the livelihood of all the employees, and wreak havoc among your customers. The bigger you are, the more damage if you fail.

The following 12 caveats form a framework to help determine if you are ready for expansion and how to structure the deal.

ACQUISITION GUIDELINES

Don't

1. Expand unless the existing business is profitable and cash-positive.
2. Expand unless there is adequate management in the existing business to run it independently.
3. Expand within the first three years of acquiring the first business. It takes this long to shake out all the operations bugs and establish a reputation in the financial community.
4. Pick an expansion location too far removed from the existing business.
5. Make a subsequent acquisition with high-leverage debt.
6. Expand for diversification reasons.

Do

1. Raise equity capital to make the deal—either through internally generated cash or an IPO.
2. Establish an administrative function and office for yourself.
3. Implement daily, weekly, and monthly financial reporting systems.
4. Train or hire a general manager for the existing business.
5. Budget to fund all acquisition costs out of the existing business.
6. Clean up all short-term debt before expanding.

FINANCING THE ACQUISITION

Before jumping into a second acquisition it's important to structure your existing company to take advantage of the resources you have. The starting point is to pay down the operating line so that no short-term debt remains on the books. You'll need all the short-term cash you can get during the acquisition process—a lesson learned during the first purchase. The first time around, this cash came from your own pocket—this time it should come from the company.

Additionally, if it makes sense to raise equity capital by making an initial public stock offering, expenses can be paid from the existing operating line. The one temptation to be avoided at all costs, however, is to use operating line funds for the equity contribution in a second leveraged buyout. This has been tried over and over again and never works. You can't use short-term borrowings for a long-term purchase. Though often violated, the principle makes sense. A loan should be repaid from proceeds generated by the asset acquired with the borrowed funds. For example, a working-capital loan used to build inventory and carry receivables should be paid back out of these same receivables. A long-term loan to buy a piece of equipment should be repaid from new business generated by this equipment. And an acquisition loan to buy a company should be repaid from cash generated by this new company—over and above what is necessary to pay back working capital loans.

Try to use a bank other than the one financing the present business for the operating line of the new company. The time may come when you'll need more cash or better terms than originally negotiated with one or the other. And two competing banks create more negotiating leverage in dealing with each.

Though many business owners yearn to make a second leveraged acquisition, this can be a very dangerous decision. Most asset-based lenders insist on cross-collateral between the target's assets and those of the existing operating company. This means that if the new acquisition fails, they can collect against the assets of both companies. Instead of gambling on the success of only one company, you're now placing both at risk. Far better to make the second acquisition with your own equity, or an IPO, and avoid debt completely. Or, if you must use debt as a minor portion of the financing package, negotiate a single collateral agreement for the new company.

Equity can be raised in the same manner as during the first acquisition—by personal contributions from your own savings (or cash reserves in the existing company) or by outside investment from a new partner—either private funding or an investment banker. Investment bankers usually give a warm reception to the idea of expanding an already profitable operation.

If the company is in the right industry, has a profitable history, and is big enough, an initial public stock offering, commonly referred to as an IPO, can generate equity capital. Chapter 12 touched on an IPO as a method used to pay back the investment banker for the first acquisition. A more common use is to raise capital for long-term investments such as buying a second company.

Though not feasible for very small retail, wholesale, or service businesses, and certainly not for professional practices or other small personal services companies, (the company should have sales of at least $10 million or be in a rapidly expanding, high-tech industry to attract investor interest), given the right type of business and the right economic environment, a public offering is far and away the easiest, and cheapest, way to raise equity capital.

To make a successful IPO a company should:

- Be large enough to have at least some professional management, such as a controller, sales manager, and production manager.
- Sell a product or service with a potential for significant sales growth over the next five years.
- Have three years of continually increasing sales and profits and be able to project a continuation of this growth.

Additionally, the economy should be in a bullish mood. Some stock offerings can be successful in a downturn market, but by and large, an optimistic business environment enhances the likelihood of a successful issue.

An IPO requires planning. It's not something to be done on the spur of the moment—but then neither is an acquisition. Depending on the size of the offering, planning should begin either two or three years in advance to meet SEC and underwriting requirements, which are:

1. The company must have audited financial statements for at least two years, three if the offering is for more than $7.5 million. The audits should be performed by a nationally recognized CPA firm.

2. The company should be able to show a steady growth in both sales and profits during the preceding two or three years.

3. The management organization must be in place with credentials recognizable to the public, such as education, experience, and product or service notoriety.

4. There must be a strategic operating plan for five years out showing continued growth and market penetration to be included in the offering prospectus.

5. There should be at least one or two new products or services on the drawing board having snappy sounding applications.

6. Ideally, the company should be visible to the public eye, either through national advertising campaigns, the development of new products or technology, or some unusual public relations achievement.

7. Outside directors with public recognition sitting on the Board can be invaluable.

In addition to these specific company criteria, there are a few other considerations affecting an IPO:

1. The company's market is especially relevant. A mundane industry such as ball bearings or plumbing fixtures is far less attractive to the investor

than bio-genetics, holographic lasers, or space communications. Products or services in a basic industry can still qualify, it just makes the selling job more difficult for the underwriter.

2. Current status and trends in the stock market are also crucial determinants to a successful issue. Generally, a bull market and prognostications for a continued upward climb is the best time for an IPO. A market trough can also encourage investment because of expected improvements. The worst time is during a falling market when Wall Street tycoons see a recession on the horizon.

3. Whenever you decide to issue public stock, the SEC regulates what can and cannot be done from the legal side. These regulations are extremely complex and require expert interpretation by qualified legal, financial, and tax counsel.

4. The selling tool for a public stock issue is the offering prospectus. Many of the features of the original business plan are incorporated in this document but there are also some major differences. Again, the specific sections of the prospectus, what to include or not include, how to formulate the words, and cautious disclaimers and warnings to the investor are all controlled by SEC regulations. This is not something you as an entrepreneur can undertake by yourself. You must have competent legal, accounting, and underwriting guidance.

5. There is no law that says you must use an underwriter to sell the stock. But if you don't want to spend needless hours and huge sums of money for an issue that won't sell, it's better to use one. A qualified underwriter has the marketing expertise to know what stock will sell and what an acceptable price per share would be at any given time. They are in the business and should know how and where to market the issue.

6. Any public stock issue is expensive to put together—either an initial issue or subsequent offerings. Annual audit fees from a Big-5 firm can run the gamut from $10,000 to $100,000, or more, depending on the size of the company and complexity of the audit. Attorney's fees can run from $75,000 to $100,000 or more. Underwriters generally charge a commission of seven percent to ten percent of the offering price. Most firms will also want some kind of kicker—warrants or options—to give them the opportunity to buy your stock at a favorable price. Then there are printing costs, filing fees, and a host of other expenses easily totaling over $250,000. The cost alone is enough to discourage smaller companies from trying an IPO.

In spite of all the drawbacks and the high initial cost, given the right circumstances, an IPO can be the best way to raise equity capital for the next acquisition. Obviously, the corner grocery or video store are not large enough to use this means, but any business doing over $5 million sales should seriously look at the possibility. Certainly, it's feasible if the business does more than $10 million.

Regardless of how you raise the equity capital, and even though it might not be needed for the purchase, as a further insurance policy, it's a good idea to get your original asset-based lender to loan at least something on the new deal. Perhaps a mortgage on the real estate, or an expansion loan for more land. The more money a banker has committed, the more he has to lose, and the greater your bargaining power—assuming of course, a reasonable level of equity investment on your part.

STRUCTURING FOR A NEW ACQUISITION

There are two organizational matters to attend to in getting ready for the next acquisition:

1. Become an administrator.
2. Organize a corporate office function.

When purchasing the first company, the buyer himself becomes the manager of the newly acquired business. On the premises, he directs the day-to-day activities of employees. He makes decisions on the spot. He deals with production problems, customer idiosyncrasies, supplier coordination, and most important, he personally controls the cash. The business rises or falls on the capabilities and effort of the owner-manager.

But with a second acquisition, a new set of operating rules ensue. A business owner can't be in two places at one time. He can't worry about production, marketing, supplier, and financial matters simultaneously in both companies. In fact, he no longer enjoys the luxury of autocratic control. Suddenly he gets thrust into the role of an administrator rather than a manager. He must free himself from routine operating decisions. He must administer the affairs of two businesses now and let others manage the day-to-day affairs of each.

This requires two organizational changes before beginning the acquisition search:

1. The original company must be organized to run independently of the owner. That means someone must be appointed general manager. It also means there must be competent supervisory personnel to support the new GM.
2. There must be some type of corporate office for the owner. This may be just a desk in a room, but it should be physically separated from the general manager to allow him breathing space in performing his duties. If not, employees will continually ask the owner for direction rather than the GM. Eventually, after closing the second acquisition, there will probably be a need for a formal corporate office with perhaps one or two staff

people or a secretary. There will certainly be additional overhead expenses of some type—even if only the owner's travel expenses and acquisition costs.

3. Part of the administrative activity is to monitor results of the operating unit(s). This requires a financial reporting system to provide daily and monthly data for the owner to exercise proper controls.

These organization and operating changes all cost money. They are costs incurred because of the expansion to a second business that wouldn't be necessary with only one operating entity. The money to fund these costs must come from the operating business, which means that all of a sudden an additional cash burden is placed on the company. Before starting out, make sure the company can afford this extra cost, and budget accordingly.

MATCHING CRITERIA

In addition to a strong cash flow and adequate management talent, a subsequent acquisition should:

- Have synergistic characteristics with the first business—products, marketing, distribution, advertising—to provide vertical or horizontal integration or expanded regional market penetration.

- Be located in close proximity either to markets of the first company or to new markets if the industry is regionalized, and easily accessible by the owner.

When you make a successful acquisition and see that the company is performing at or near original expectations, the temptation to diversify is great. Arguments abound for protecting against economic downturns in one industry by diversifying into other markets with counter cyclical characteristics. Corporate giants personify this philosophy. Tobacco companies buy pharmaceuticals. Food companies branch out into the toy industry. Telecommunications giants diversify into hotels and insurance. And on and on.

This may work for the giants—although such wisdom certainly bears scrutiny in recent years—but it most assuredly does not work for private entrepreneurial companies. The biggest mistake a small or mid-sized company can make is to expand into industries or markets so diverse from the existing business that cross-fertilization of resources cannot be achieved. The major purposes in expansion should be to take advantage of existing management talent and technical background, to complement existing product lines, to provide additional production capability, or to open new markets. If the new acquisition is either remotely located or in a different industry, such cross-fertilization becomes impossible. You're far better off staying with one profitable company than moving in this direction.

EXPANDING A SMALL RETAIL OR SERVICE BUSINESS

It might seem that the above steps and principles apply only to larger companies. In some cases, such as using an IPO to raise equity capital, there is a definite size limit to the business below which such a maneuver becomes uneconomical. But the rest of the guidelines apply to any size business. In fact, let's take a look at how George Chin used these same principles to expand his restaurant and bar business. Remember George Chin, the ex-aerospace engineer, and his wife Janice from Chapter 15?

Business at George Chin's restaurant, The Purple Rose, burgeoned when he introduced live music on Fridays and Saturdays. George was so successful in the first three years that he paid off the balance of his note to the seller 18 months earlier than scheduled. As the children grew, Janice was able to spend more and more time with the business and quadrupled food sales through innovative menus. Both George and Janice began thinking about expanding. If The Purple Rose was so successful, why not another restaurant patterned along the same lines? With a broader business base, any economic or demographic changes should have less impact than with a single restaurant. Because neither George nor Janice had time to search out the right opportunity, they asked if I would help find another acquisition and structure a deal for them.

I agreed, but only on two conditions. One, that the couple reorganize The Purple Rose to run independent of their constant supervision, and two, that they establish a command post—not at The Purple Rose—which could be used as their headquarters when the next deal finalized. Although hesitant to spend the money, within a month George hired a manager, agreed to set up an office in his house at the appropriate time, and I was off and running. While the couple trained the new manager, I located two target possibilities within an easy drive of The Purple Rose: a restaurant specializing in Greek food and a deli bar catering to luncheon crowds from the nearby industrial park.

George and Janice opted for the Greek restaurant—The Olympic—however, the price of $1 million was substantially more than the $200,000 George could muster from his savings and $400,000 in the bank account of The Purple Rose. The owner of The Olympic had recently died and the estate was anxious to peddle it at a fair price, but would not carry any of the financing. "Now what do we do, Larry?" asked a disappointed George Chin.

One choice was to try for bank financing, but I hesitated, knowing the added stress this would put on George and Janice. Instead, I contacted an old acquaintance who had owned restaurants several years ago but was now enjoying his retirement in the Virgin Islands. "Orly, I know you're comfortably retired and living off the fat of the land, but how would you like to invest $400,000 in a Greek restaurant? My client will structure the deal any way you like and I'm sure a 25 percent guaranteed return is in the cards."

"Normally no," Orly responded. "But if you say it's a good deal, count me in."

This gave us the equity, now all George needed was a way to manage The Olympic. He searched for a manager but couldn't locate the right one soon enough. The deal closed and George took over the management, against my advice. Janice set up her financial and cash controls for The Purple Rose and the couple proceeded with two restaurants.

A few months later I checked with George to see how things were going. "Great. The Olympic is beginning to pick up and the remodeling is almost completed. There's only one problem. I was spending ten hours a day at The Purple Rose. Now it's fifteen to eighteen hours plus full time for Janice. This is way too much."

"Well, you better get that manager we talked about," I suggested. Within another three months George found the manager he wanted and two years later the couple finally took their first vacation—seven years to the day since leaving Lockheed.

THE NORTHERN INVESTORS
STARLIGHT GROUP (NISG) EXPANSION

A different approach to subsequent acquisitions was employed by NISG—remember them from Chapter 11? After struggling for months trying to raise debt financing for a $5 million, 85 percent leveraged buyout, the NISG group eventually settled on an asset-based lender holding $4.250 million in seven-year debt and a local bank for an operating line of $1 million. The active partners, Ted and Joel, and the two passive investors, Marty and Fred, had contributed $750,000 as equity. The St. Louis company manufactured precision bearings and other machined parts for the machine tool and aerospace markets. Sales of $12 million and a near-loss position when they purchased the company had been improved to $14 million and a small profit two years later. The original plan in acquiring MyChor was to turn the company around financially and then use it as the flagship for several regional bearings manufacturers throughout the country.

By the end of the second year, even though the profitability of MyChor hadn't reached planned levels, Ted and Joel became restless and decided to begin the expansion program. They still owed the asset-based lender nearly $3.5 million of original debt, but that didn't deter them. Although earnings weren't sufficient to generate much cash to use as equity, they reasoned that an equity contribution of $200,000 could be raised by drawing down the MyChor operating line. They also judged that the principal pay-down on the long-term debt plus any hard assets in the new acquisition would be enough to interest their current asset base lender in leveraging another deal just like Mychor.

NISG rented office space in downtown St. Louis as the corporate headquarters and Joel and Ted moved in. No one at MyChor had proven general management capabilities, but Ted believed he could continue to manage Mychor and a second operating company without too much difficulty. Joel had implemented a few monthly financial reports at MyChor and even though he wasn't totally confident of his ability to exercise needed financial control over an additional acquisition, acquiesced to Ted's enthusiasm. Also, he wanted to hire an old friend to be financial vice president of NISG to reduce his own workload. He realized that a second acquisition would justify such an action to the rest of the partners and to the banks.

A small assembly company was soon located in Los Angeles, and although this meant extensive travel for both Ted and Joel they justified the deal on the basis of establishing a presence in the West Coast markets—plus they both liked the warmer climate California offered. The deal closed for $2.5 million of which NISG contributed the $200,000 equity (borrowed on the operating line) and the asset-based lender provided the balance. Of course a cross-collateral agreement with NISG was required.

The new acquisition, Techaero, Inc., had been managed by the seller. When Ted and Joel took over, they recognized that Techaero was too small to justify the hiring of a qualified general manager, so they would somehow have to run this company as well as MyChor. In the first six months, Techaero lost two major contracts and sales plummeted. Losses mounted and with just enough cash to meet payrolls and buy materials, debt-service payments were foisted on MyChor. Conditions continued to deteriorate and soon Ted and Joel realized there was little prospect of recovery for at least three years. Mychor would just have to continue funding Techaero. The partners were forced to remain on the commuter run to manage both companies.

Eventually, the MyChor business cycle turned downward and, saddled with double debt-service payments, the company began suffering a severe cash drain. Debt-service payments were missed and the asset-based lender started turning the screws. Within another six months, the bank forced NISG to liquidate the assets of Techaero, consolidate activities, and reduce the labor force at MyChor. In wasn't long before Ted and Joel faced the ugly choice of filing for protection under Chapter XI of the Bankruptcy Code or closing the doors at MyChor. A highly leveraged acquisition which originally was very profitable and cash rich was decimated by the decision to go after a second acquisition without following the basic ground rules.

George and Janice Chin, unsophisticated in entrepreneurial techniques, made a successful second acquisition because they listened to sound professional advice. The NISG group, laden with management talent and financial savvy, failed in their attempt with a much larger business. Why the difference?

Let's compare how each performed against the fundamental criteria for a second acquisition.

	The Chins	NISG
1. Waited a full three years after the first acquisition.	Yes	No
2. The first acquisition was running profitably before trying a second.	Yes	No
3. General management in place before making a second deal.	Yes	No
4. Established independent corporate office.	Yes	Yes
5. Synergistic products/services.	Yes	No
6. Accessible location.	Yes	No
7. Implemented effective financial reporting system.	Yes	No
8. Financed predominantly with equity money avoiding high leverage debt financing.	Yes	No
9. Avoided cross-collateral provisions.	Yes	No
10. Acquisition costs financed from existing company.	Yes	Yes
11. Pay off all short term debt before making the second acquisition.	Yes	No

SOCIAL RESPONSIBILITY

George and Janice Chin, as well as innkeepers Rick and Mary, expanded through a second acquisition for sound economic reasons. They paid attention to the human element in dealing with employees and customers. They expanded only when their first business was on a sound financial footing and they followed professional advice rather than their own instincts.

The NISG group, just like Jackie Jones, expanded because greed and power addiction took the upper hand. Little consideration was given to developing a sound management base. The effect their management and expansion moves would have on other people was totally ignored. In both cases, fundamental acquisition criteria was disregarded. And the results of the expansions of both Jackie Jones and the NISG group were predictable.

By the time an optimistic entrepreneur becomes a business owner and faces the hard-core problems of successfully managing a going concern, he should have learned the rules of the game. Unfortunately, many do not, and that is the dilemma. Although it's possible to achieve the first acquisition even by ignoring the human element, sound financial planning, and proven management techniques, seldom will a second one be successful if these basic tenets continue to be violated. A person can ignore good nutritional practices and exercise for a while, but sooner or later the body rebels and falls apart. It is the same thing with acquiring and running a business. Ignore sound financial management and human relations practices at your peril.

The social cost of power addiction, greed, high leverage deals, and flagrant disregard for other people on the part of the business owner playing the acquisition game is beginning to be felt. Bankruptcy courts are overflowing. Workers secure in jobs with small companies find themselves out of work when debt payments and dividends absorb much needed cash. The cost to the taxpayer of public welfare programs to aid the disinherited and to cover the mistakes of incompetent and uncaring business moguls is escalating. Only you, the business owner, can put a stop to this social waste. Be wise, be caring, be prudent. Don't put yourself at the mercy of the banking system. And don't succumb to power addiction. We can all contribute to the improvement of the free enterprise system—if we care. However, if we are not willing to place human welfare and social needs above our own greed, we will surely fail: and society will pay the cost.

Epilogue

As long as the free enterprise system exists, optimistic business and professional men and women will feel the urge to become their own bosses. And as long as they are willing to pay exorbitant interest rates and dividends, bankers and investors stand ready to loan the money. Throughout this book I have attempted to point out the inherent dangers of plunging into an acquisition with inordinate amounts of debt. Commercial bankers, asset-based lenders, and investment bankers remain eager to lead the unwary down this dangerous trail. They tempt entrepreneurs into buying businesses with little or no equity. Nearly all fail. And the reason remains clear: operating a business with exorbitant amounts of debt precludes the possibility of socially conscious management.

Except in very unusual cases, to employ high-leverage debt financing or disproportionately large amounts of investor funding to buy a business can only lead to heartache and misery for the entrepreneur and his family. Committed to pay back high interest loans or outrageous dividends, the business owner usually does not have sufficient cash flow to manage the business for the welfare of himself, his family, employees, and customers. Cash which could be used for education, social reforms, or improved working conditions instead lines the pockets of bankers and non-productive investors. Money which could be spent on higher wages, employee benefits, or productive facilities to improve the quality of products and services goes to reimburse the money lenders. Funds which could be used to improve the life styles of millions of people, both in America and abroad are squandered on high interest rates, financing fees, and outrageous dividend returns.

We have all been suckered into believing that credit is money. That the more we borrow the better we'll live. That we must have everything today because tomorrow may never come. That our primary responsibility is not to family, employees, or customers but to keep our credit ratings clean so we can get more credit and sink deeper into debt. Eighty percent of new businesses or purchased businesses declaring bankruptcy do so because of undercapitalization—too much debt and too little owner's equity. If this vicious cycle continues, the end result can only be filling the welfare ranks with ex-entrepreneurs and the eventual demise of the private enterprise system.

In the thriving economic environment experienced by American business for the past 40 years, there should be more than enough money to provide food and shelter for all the homeless; to provide a high-school education to every one of our young people; to provide medical care and comfortable surroundings for all our aging citizens; to protect and preserve all our natural resources; and still have plenty left over to maintain a secure national defense policy, research funding for space exploration, and other potentially beneficial long-range programs. But the facts show just the opposite. And one must ask the all-important questions: *Why? Where has all the money gone?*

The only reasonable explanation is that there has been a consistent and unrelenting movement of cash out of productive private businesses into the nonproductive sphere of the financial establishment. The greater the amount of borrowed money throughout the country, the more money flows into repayments of loans and usurious interest and fees and away from higher wages, new production facilities, and socially beneficial programs. As businesses continue to burden themselves with debt payments, the cost of this money gets passed on to consumers in the form of higher prices. The cost of money has driven the inflation monster during the past decade, not higher wages. And unfortunately, the greatest obligations for repayment of funds during this period have been incurred through the vehicle of business acquisitions. Of the more than $11 trillion in total outstanding debt in this country, the business community is responsible for $2.5 trillion—more than the total debt of the federal government. No wonder there isn't enough money to feed the homeless or care for the aged. And financial institutions continue to encourage consumers and businesses to increase the debt burden even more. As the Citibank TV commercial states, ''Americans want to succeed, not just survive.'' And the implied definition of success has evolved from being a reward for effort and achievement to the ability to accumulate vast sums of wealth and power through the use of credit, regardless of who gets hurt, and irrespective of social disparities.

What can be done to stop this horrendous prostitution of the American system? Plenty. The small businessman or professional practitioner, the entrepreneur, has it within his power to change what is happening in the world around him. It's time for the little guy, you and me, to stand up and be counted. But to do this we must invoke major changes in our own value systems. We must stop playing into the hands of the greedy power addicts. We must return to sound financial management of our own affairs. We must fight the evils of greed and envy and begin to conduct our businesses not only for our own gain but for the benefit of our employees and customers. We must stop believing the "something for nothing" philosophy and tear up our credit cards, stop borrowing money at outrageous rates, force honesty and integrity back into business deals, and begin the climb out of the grip of the money lenders. When values such as family responsibility, social consciousness, and a sense of moral commitment replace greed for money and power, we will be heard. When we begin to value caring and compassion for fellow human beings above the beatification of wealth and material possessions, the corrupted part of the world of high finance will be left to feed upon itself and eventually self-destruct. When honest labor and the work ethic return to American business, cracks in the foundation will heal and the enormous amount of cash generated by a free enterprise system will eventually funnel back to the right channels.

These changes can't happen overnight. And they can't occur without conscious efforts to change the standards we live by. Self-gratification must be replaced with social consciousness. Rugged individualism must be tempered with moral conscience. Caring for others must be restored as a basic human responsibility. The frantic "living for today and tomorrow be damned" philosophy must give way to concern for future generations. We must begin listening to our hearts and feelings. We must learn to distinguish good from evil and then have the courage to follow the road we all know is right. And finally, we must band together to encourage these changes in the moral values of our leaders.

A good sailor, a great man, and a superb entrepreneur, the late C.S. Broadston, counseled those starting out in their own business to "look skyward, because if the stars can guide ships through the dark of night and bring a weary sailor to his final port, so can they guide you through the portals of life. They will give you strength to carry on when all seems hopeless. Have faith in God, in other people, and in yourself. Have the courage to dare to venture out beyond what you think you can do. In the end, by following your star, you will certainly achieve the happiness and satisfaction few others have mastered."

You, the entrepreneur, the small businessman or woman, the individual, can make a difference. You can throw out the harbingers of greed and fear. You can heal the system. It's too late for me, but there are plenty of young, aggressive, morally strong entrepreneurs and would-be entrepreneurs out there who can save private enterprise.

When the going gets tough, and it always does, remember this little jingle:

> "Be all you can be and never look back,
> Take the risk, be yourself, you'll go far,
> But remember the source of the power you feel
> And continue to follow a star."
> —Anonymous

Appendix A

Make Money Filter Corp.
Comparative Balance Sheets

As of December 31, Years 1, 2 and 3
($000)

Assets	Year 1	Year 2	Year 3
Cash	50	97	45
Short Term Investments	200	165	0
Accounts Receivable	3,780	3,918	4,205
Inventory	3,950	4,190	4,850
Prepaid Expenses	10	10	10
Total Current Assets	7,990	8,380	9,110
Land & Building	1,200	1,200	1,200
Machinery & Equipment	6,285	6,885	7,625
Vehicles	122	122	122
Total Fixed Assets	7,607	8,207	8,947
Accumulated Depreciation	(4,391)	(5,091)	(5,791)
Net Fixed Assets	3,216	3,116	3,256
Other Assets	44	46	45
Total Assets	11,250	11,542	12,311

Liabilities

Short Term Bank Notes	1,300	550	250
Accounts Payable	1,350	1,312	1,006
Accrued Expenses	1,412	1,226	1,025
Total Current Liabilities	4,062	3,088	2,281
Long Term Mortgage Payable	500	450	400
Long Term Note Payable	3,990	3,790	3,590
Total Liabilities	8,552	7,328	6,271

Net Worth

Common Stock	500	1,500	2,852
Retained Earnings, Begin/Year	1,721	2,198	2,714
Profit	977	1,016	1,224
Dividends	(500)	(500)	(750)
Retained Earnings, End/Year	2,198	2,714	3,188
Total Net Worth	2,698	4,214	6,040
Total Liabilities and Net Worth	11,250	11,542	12,311

Appendix B

Make Money Filter Corp.
Comparative Statements of Income

For the Years Ended December 31, Years 1, 2, and 3
($000)

	Year 1	Year 2	Year 3
Sales	17,950	19,500	20,120
Cost of Sales	13,200	14,300	15,025
Gross Profit	4,750	5,200	5,095
% to Sales	26.5%	26.7%	25.3%
Operating Expenses			
Selling	525	577	600
General & Administrative	1,210	1,500	1,300
Depreciation	700	700	700
Other	5	20	10
Interest Expense	525	502	480
Bonuses	100	150	150
Total Operating Expenses	3,065	3,449	3,240
Profit Before Taxes	1,685	1,751	1,855
Income Taxes	708	735	631
Net Profit	977	1,016	1,224
% to Sales	5.4%	5.2%	6.0%

Appendix C
Make Money Filter Corp.
Pro Forma Statements of Income

For the Years Ended December 31, Years 1, 2, and 3 (Actual)
and Years 4, 5, and 6 (Forecast)
($000)

	Year 1	Year 2	Year 3	Year 4	Year 5	Year 6
Sales	17,950	19,500	20,120	20,000	21,000	21,500
Cost of Sales	13,200	14,300	15,025	14,940	15,687	16,060
Gross Profit	4,750	5,200	5,095	5,060	5,313	5,440
% to Sales	26.5%	26.7%	25.3%	25.3%	25.3%	25.3%
Expenses						
Selling	525	577	600	650	750	850
General & Admin	1,210	1,500	1,300	1,436	1,473	1,471
Depreciation	700	700	700	700	700	700
Other	5	20	10	10	10	10
Interest Exp	525	502	480	458	436	414
Bonuses	100	150	150	100	150	150
Total	3,065	3,449	3,240	3,354	3,519	3,595
Profit Before Tax	1,685	1,751	1,855	1,706	1,794	1,845
ADD BACK:						
Depreciation	700	700	700	700	700	700
Bonuses & Owner's Draw	300	350	350	300	350	500
Interest Expense	525	502	480	458	436	414
Cash Profit Bef. Tax	3,210	3,303	3,635	3,164	3,280	3,459
Taxes	(1,476)	(1,519)	(1,672)	(1,455)	(1,508)	(1,591)
Cash Profit	1,734	1,784	1,963	1,709	1,772	1,868
Add:						
Decrease in Working Capital	1,061			1,389		
Less:						
Increase in Working Capital		(1,364)	(1,547)		(150)	(600)
Dividends	(500)	(500)	(750)	(500)	(500)	(500)
Purchase of Fixed Assets		(600)	(740)			(500)
Net Cash Flow	2,295	(680)	(1,040)	2,598	1,122	268

Appendix D
Investment Banks and Venture Capital Firms

ACQUIVEST GROUP, INC.
1 Newtown Executive Park
Suite 204
Newton, MA 01262

ADVEST INCORPORATED
6 Central Row
Hartford, CT 06103

ALLIED CAPITAL CORPORATION
1625 I Street, NW., Suite 603
Washington, DC 20006

ALLSTATE INSURANCE CO.
Allstate Plaza E-2
Northbrook, IL 60062

AMERVEST CORPORATION
10 Commercial Wharf West
Boston, MA 02110

AMEV CAPITAL CORP.
1 World Trade Center, 50th Floor
New York, NY 10048

ATLANTIC AMERICAN CAPITAL, LTD.
Lincoln Center. Suite 851
5401 W. Kennedy Blvd.
Tampa, FL 33609

ATLANTIC VENTURE PARTNERS
P.O.Box 1493
Richmond, VA 23212

BANCBOSTON CAPITAL CORP.
100 Federal Street
Boston, MA 02110

BANKAMERICA CAPITAL CORPORATION
555 California Street, 42nd Floor
San Francisco, CA 94104

BEAR STERNS & COMPANY
Investment Banking Division
55 Water St.
New York, NY 10041

BLAKE INVESTMENT GROUP
1101-30th Street, NW, Suite 101
Washington, DC 20007

BNE ASSOCIATES
Bank of New England
60 State Street,
Boston, MA 02109

BRADFORD ASSOCIATES
22 Chambers Street
Princeton, NJ 08540

BUTLER CAPITAL CORP.
767 Fifth Avenue, Sixth Floor
New York, NY 10153

CAPITAL CORPORATION OF AMERICA
225 So. 15th Street, Suite 920
Philadelphia, PA 19102

CARL MARKS & CO., INC.
77 Water Street
New York, NY 10005

CHARLES DeTHAN GROUP
51 E. 67th Street
New York, NY 10021

CHARTERHOUSE GROUP INTERNATIONAL
535 Madison Avenue,
New York, NY 10022

CHASE MANHATTAN CAPITAL MARKETS
1 Chase Manhattan Plaza—3rd Flr
New York, NY 10081

CITICORP VENTURE CAPITAL, LTD.
Citicorp Center
153 E. 53rd Street, 28th Floor
New York, NY 10043

CONNECTICUT NATIONAL BANK
Investment Banking Division
1604 Walnut Street
Philadelphia, PA 19103

CONTINENTAL ILLINOIS VENTURE
CORP.
231 So. LaSalle Street,
Chicago, IL 60697

DAIN BOSWORTH, INC.
100 Dain Tower
Minneapolis, MN 55402

DILLON REED & COMPANY, INC.
535 Madison Avenue
New York, NY 10022

DJS GROUP
745 Park Avenue, 21st Floor
New York, NY 10155

DREXEL BURNHAM LAMBERT, INC.
55 Broad Street
New York, NY 10004

E.F.HUTTON LBO, INC.
1 Battery Park Plaza
New York, NY 10004

EAB VENTURE CORPORATION
90 Park Avenue
New York, NY 10016

FIDELITY BANK
Investment Banking Division
Broad & Walnut, Sixth Floor
Philadelphia, PA 19109

FIRST CHICAGO VENTURE CAPITAL
1 First National Plaza
Suite 2628
Chicago, IL 60670

FIRST CONNECTICUT SBIC
177 State Street
Bridgeport, CT 06604

FIRST INTERSTATE CAPITAL CORP.
515 So. Figueroa Street,
Los Angeles, CA 90071

FLEET GROWTH INDUSTRIES, INC.
111 Westminster St.
Providence, RI 02903

FOOTHIL CAPITAL CORPORATION
2049 Century Park East
Los Angeles, CA 90067

FOUNDERS VENTURES, INC.
477 Madison Avenue
New York, NY 10022

FRONTENAC CAPITAL CORP.
208 So. LaSalle Street
Suite 1900
Chicago, IL 60604

GENERAL ELECTRIC VENTURE CAPITAL
3135 Easton Turnpike
Fairfield, CT 06431

GOLDER, THOMA & CRESSEY
120 So. LaSalle Street
Chicago, IL 60603

HAMBRECHT & QUIST
235 Montgomery Street
San Francisco, CA 94104

HAMBRO INTERNATIONAL VENTURE
FUND
17 E. 71st Street
New York, NY 10021

HILLMAN VENTURES, INC.
2000 Grant Bldg.
Pittsburgh, PA 15219

HOWARD, LAWSON & CO., INC.
2 Penn Center Plaza
Philadelphia, PA, 19102

INTERFIRST VENTURE CORPORATION
P.O.Box 83644
Dallas, TX 75283

ITC CAPITAL CORPORATION
1290 Avenue of the Americas
New York, NY 10104

JAMES RIVER CAPITAL ASSOCIATES
9 So. 12th Street
Richmond, VA 23219

JOHN HANCOCK VENTURE CAPITAL
MANAGEMENT, INC.
John Hancock Place, 57th Floor
Boston, MA 02117

KEELEY MANAGEMENT COMPANY
2 Radnor Corporate Center
Radnor, PA 19087

KIDDER PEABODY & COMPANY
Investment Banking Division
Mellon Bank Center
Philadelphia, PA 19102

LEPERQ de NEUFLIZE & COMPANY
345 Park Avenue
New York, NY 10154

MANUFACTURERS HANOVER VENTURE
CAPITAL CORP.
140 E. 45th Street
New York, NY 10017

MARYLAND NATIONAL BANK
Investment Banking Group
P.O.Box 987
Baltimore, MD 21203

MELLON BANK
Corporate Finance Group
Mellon Bank Center
Philadelphia, PA 19102

MENLO VENTURE
3000 Sand Hill Road
Menlo Park, CA 94025

MIDLAND CAPITAL CORPORATION
950 Third Avenue
New York, NY 10022

NARRAGANSETT CAPITAL
40 Westminster Street
Providence, RI 02903

NORWEST VENTURE CAPITAL MANAGEMENT
1730 Midwest Plaza Bldg.
801 Nicollet Mall
Minneapolis, MN 55402

OXFORD PARTNERS
Soundview Plaza
1266 Main Street
Stamford, CT 06902

PAINE WEBBER VENTURE MANAGEMENT
100 Federal Street
Boston, MA 02110

PENNWOOD CAPITAL CORPORATION
645 Madison Avenue
New York, NY 10022

PHILADELPHIA CAPITAL ADVISORS
Philadelphia National Bank Bldg.
Broad & Chestnut Streets
Philadelphia, PA 19107

PNC VENTURE CAPITAL GROUP
Fifth Avenue & Woods Streets
Pittsburgh, PA 15222

PRU CAPITAL, INCORPORATED
1 Seaport Plaza, 31st Floor
199 Water Street
New York, NY 10292

QUINCY PARTNERS
P.O.Box 154
Glen Head, NY 11545

ROSENFELD & COMPANY
625 SW Washington Street
Portland, OR 97205

ROTHSCHILD, INCORPORATED
Rockefeller Plaza
New York, NY 10020

RUST VENTURES LP
114 W. Seventh Street
Suite 1300
Austin, TX 78701

SALOMON BROTHERS, INC.
1 New York Plaza
New York, NY 10004

SECURITY PACIFIC CAPITAL CORP.
4000 MacArthur Blvd., Suite 950
Newport Beach, CA 92660

SEIDLER AMDEC SECURITES, INC.
515 So. Figueroa Street
Los Angeles, CA 90071

SMITH, BARNEY, HARRIS, UPHAM
1345 Avenue of the Americas
New York, NY 10105

SPROUT CAPITAL GROUP
140 Broadway
New York, NY 10025

SUMMIT VENTURES
1 Boston Place
Boston, MA 02108

TA ASSOCIATES
45 Milk Street
Boston, MA 02109

TDH CAPITAL
259 Radnor-Chester Rd
Radnor, PA 19087

TUCKER ANTHONY AND RL DAY, INC.
120 Broadway
New York, NY 10271

UNION VENTURE CORPORATION
445 So.Figueroa Street
Los Angeles, CA 90071

WARBURG, PINCUS VENTURES, INC.
466 Lexington Avenue
New York, NY 10017

WELLS FARGO EQUITY CORPORATION
1 Embarcadero Center
San Francisco, CA 94111

WELSH,CARSON,ANDERSON & STOWE
45 Wall Street, 16th Floor
New York, NY 10005

WILLIAM BLAIR VENTURE PARTNERS
135 So. LaSalle Street, 29th Floor
Chicago, IL 60603

WISSAHICKON PARTNERS
19 Vandeventer Avenue
Princeton, NJ 08542

Appendix E
Asset-Based Lenders

CONGRESS FINANCIAL CORPORATION
American City Bldg.
Columbia, MD 21044

GENERAL ELECTRIC CREDIT CORPORATION
Eastern Corporate Finance Dept.
3003 Summer Street
Stamford, CT 06905

GLENFED CAPITAL CORPORATION
Carnegie Center
Princeton, NJ 08540

ITT CAPITAL CORPORATION
1400 North Central Life Tower
St. Paul, MN 55101

SECURITY PACIFIC BUSINESS CREDIT, INC.
45 So. Hudson Avenue
Pasadena, CA 91101

FIDELITY CAPITAL
Fidelity Bank Bldg.
Broad & Walnut Streets
Philadelphia, PA 19109

Appendix F
Merger and Acquisition Consultants and Larger Business Brokers

A.H. GRUETZMACHER AND COMPANY
39 South LaSalle Street
Chicago, IL 60603

ALBERT L. EMMONS
580 Jackson Avenue
Westwood, NJ 07675

ARNOLD S. COHEN COMPANY
1290 Avenue of the Americas
Suite 1614
New York, NY 10104

BOLLINGER/WELLS
230 Park Avenue
New York, NY 10169

CHARLES K. MURRAY ASSOCIATES, INC.
P.O. Box 1406
Greenwich, CT 06836

CORPORATE DEVELOPMENT, INC.
2235 Park Towne Circle
Suite 100
Sacramento, CA 95825

DAVID A. FARIES & ASSOCIATES
67 Central Avenue
Los Gatos, CA 95030

DUFF & PHELPS, INC.
55 East Monroe Street
Chicago, IL 60603

FIRST CORPORATE GROUP
100 Northcreek—Suite 108
Atlanta, GA 30327

FIRST MANHATTAN GROUP
77 Water Street
New York, NY 10005

FIRSTMAIN ASSOCIATES, INC.
8235 Douglas Avenue, LB 58
Dallas, TX 75225

GENEVA BUSINESS SERVICES, INC.
2923 Pullman
Santa Ana, CA 92705

GROWTH DYNAMICS, INC.
595 Madison Avenue
New York, NY 10022

HAMMOND, KENNEDY & COMPANY, INC.
230 Park Avenue
New York, NY 10169

HOWARD M. SINGER, INC.
280 Madison Avenue
New York, NY 10016

HRK ASSOCIATES, INC.
690 Island Way—Suite 206
Clearwater, FL 33515

IRVING B. GRUBER
2409 Marbury Road
Pittsburgh, PA 15221

JAMES BROWN, INC.
31 North Porchuck Rd.
Greenwich, CT 06830

JOHN DeELORZA ASSOCIATES
1640 Vaux Hall Rd.
Union, NJ 07083

JOSEPH W. PRANE CO.
213 Church Rd.
Elkins Park, PA 19117

KENROY ASSOCIATES, INC.
20 West Ridgewood Avenue
Ridgewood, NJ 07450

KYLE & HAYES-MORRISON
234 Fountainville Center
Fountainville, PA 18923

M + A INTERNATIONAL, INC.
600 Cherry St., Suite 1125
Denver, CO 80222

M. MICHAEL CANTOR
2150 Ibis Isle Rd., Apt. 14
Palm Beach, FL 33480

MACKENZIE ASSOCIATES, INC.
111 Presidential Blvd.
Bala Cynwyd, PA 19004

MANAGEMENT SERVICES WORLDWIDE
2201 Route 38
The Executive Bldg.
Cherry Hill, NJ 08002

MANHATTAN VENTURE COMPANY
340 East 57th Street
New York, NY 10022

MERGE MASTER COMPANY
26 Linden Avenue
Springfield, NJ 07081

MORGAN MERRITT, INC.
4000 Town Center—Suite 190
Southfield, MI 48075

NORTON STUART CONSULTANTS
P.O. Box 250
Lansdowne, PA 19050

PERREAULT & CO., INC.
5656 Stetson Ct.
Anaheim Hills, CA 92807

PIERCE INTERNATIONAL, LTD.
1910 K Street NW
Washington, DC 20006

RALPH K. HEYMAN
230 Park Avenue—Suite 1518
New York, NY 10169

RICHARD H. RABNER & ASSOCIATES
151 So. Warner Rd.
Wayne, PA 19087

ROBERT H. PERRY & ASSOCIATES
Greensboro, NC 27402

ROY BONWICK ASSOCIATES, INC.
5 South Main Street
Suite 522
Branford, CT 06405

SIGMA COMPANIES, INC.
410 North Michigan Avenue
Chicago, IL 60611

THRONE & COMPANY
205 East Joppa Rd.—Suite 108
Baltimore, MD 21204

WILLIAM H. HILL ASSOCIATES, INC.
3100 University Blvd. South
Suite 210
Jacksonville, FL 32216

WRIGHT-WYMAN, INC.
211 Congress Street
Boston, MA 02110

ZUNDER COMPANY
1100 Alma St.—Suite 204
Menlo Park, CA 94025

Appendix G

Sample
Buy/Sell Agreement For
A Stock Purchase

This Agreement is made and entered into as of the_____ day of_____, 19XX, between (name of Buyer), hereinafter referred to as the "Buyer", and (name of Seller), hereinafter referred to as the "Seller".

Recitals

1. Seller owns all of the issued and outstanding shares of common stock of (name of the company being sold), a Delaware corporation, hereinafter referred to as the "Company."

2. The Company is engaged in the business of (whatever business it is in), in the State of (State of residence of Company).

3. Seller desires to sell and Buyer desires to purchase all of the subject shares on the terms set forth herein.

NOW THEREFORE, in consideration of the sale and purchase of the subject shares and of the premises and the mutual promises, covenants and conditions hereinafter set forth, the parties hereby agree as follows:

ARTICLE I

DEFINITIONS

1.1 "Closing Date" shall mean the date on which the Closing hereunder is held. The Closing shall be at _____AM in the offices of (name of Seller or Buyer lawyer).

1.2 "Intellectual Property" shall mean any patent, copyright, trademark, service mark, brand name or trade name, any registration of the same, and any other proprietary rights, inventions, trade secrets, know-how or processes, and any rights in or to the foregoing.

ARTICLE II

PURCHASE AND SALE

2.1 Purchase Price. On the Closing Date, subject to the terms and conditions set forth in this Agreement, Seller agrees to sell and convey to Buyer, and Buyer agrees to purchase the subject shares, for an amount equal to $_____.

2.2 Payment. Payment of the purchase price shall be made as follows:

a. Buyer shall deliver to Seller a Promissory Note (the "Note") substantially in the form of Exhibit_____ attached hereto in the original principle amount of $_____.

b. The balance of the Purchase Price shall be paid to Seller in the form of a wire transfer to a bank account designated by Seller, or by cashier's check.

All payments hereunder are subject to the terms and conditions herein set forth, and will be made by Buyer in reliance upon the representations, warranties, covenants and agreements contained herein.

2.3 Note, Guaranty and Security Interest. The Note shall be personally guaranteed by the Buyer. In addition, the Note shall be secured by a security interest in the assets of the Company. Additionally, the Note shall be secured by all of the common stock issued or to be issued of the Company. These Guaranties and Security Interests are pursuant to a Guaranty and Security Agreement substantially in the form of Exhibit_____ attached hereto. Seller agrees that the security interest in the assets of the Company shall be subordinated to the interest of the Lender.

2.4 Leases. At the Closing, Buyer shall personally guarantee to Seller the payment of any obligations under any leases which arise from and after the Closing Date.

ARTICLE III

DELIVERIES

3.1 Seller's Deliveries. On the Closing Date, subject to the terms and conditions set forth in this Agreement, Seller shall make the following deliveries:

(a) Stock certificates representing Subject Shares, endorsed in blank;

(b) Stock record books, minute books, and corporate seals of the Company;

(c) Resignations of the officers and directors of the Company;

(d) All files, records and correspondence of the Company;

(e) All other items or documents necessary or reasonably appropriate hereunder.

3.2 Buyer's Deliveries. On the Closing Date, subject to the terms and conditions set forth in this Agreement, Purchaser shall make the following deliveries:

(a) Payment of the Purchase Price as heretofore provided;

(b) All other items or documents necessary or reasonably appropriate hereunder;

(c) The Note, duly executed by Buyer, together with a Guaranty thereof by Buyer's shareholders;

(d) The Guaranty and Security Agreement, duly executed by the parties thereto, together with the deliveries required thereunder.

ARTICLE IV

CLOSING

The Closing hereunder shall take place at the offices of Able, Baker and Grey, counsel for Buyer, on the Closing Date, or at such other place as may be mutually agreed upon in writing by the Buyer and the Seller.

ARTICLE V

REPRESENTATIONS AND WARRANTIES OF SELLER

Seller represents and warrants to Buyer that, except as specifically set forth in Exhibit_____ annexed herein, the following statements are true and correct as of the Closing Date:

5.1 Seller. Seller has full power and authority to sell the Subject Shares and to enter into this Agreement and to carry out the transactions contemplated hereby. This Agreement constitutes a valid and binding obligation of Seller enforceable in accordance with its terms.

5.2 Ownership. Seller is the owner of the Subject Shares, free and clear of all claims, liens and encumbrances whatsoever. Seller will convey to Buyer, at the Closing Date, good and marketable title to the Subject Shares free and clear of all claims, liens and encumbrances whatsoever, and upon said conveyance, Buyer will have good and marketable title to the Subject Shares free and clear of all liens, claims and encumbrances whatsoever.

5.3 Organization and Standing. The Company (i) is a corporation duly organized and existing and in good standing under the laws of its state of incorporation, (ii) is entitled to own or lease its properties and to carry on its business as and in the places where such properties are now owned, leased or operated, or such business is now conducted, and (iii) is duly qualified as a foreign corporation in good standing in each jurisdiction in which the nature of the business or character of its properties makes qualification necessary and the failure to qualify would have a material adverse effect on such corporation or would permanently preclude such corporation from enforcing its rights with respect to any material asset. The copies of the Articles of Incorporation, Bylaws, Minute Book, and stock records of the Company, as in effect on the date hereof and previously delivered by the Seller to the Buyer, are true, correct, current and complete.

5.4 Capitalization. The authorized capital stock of the Company consists of 1,000 shares of capital stock, of no par value per share. The Subject Shares have been validly issued, are now outstanding, are fully paid and nonassessable and constitute all of the issued and outstanding shares of capital stock of the Company.

5.5 No Options or Warrants. There are no outstanding options, warrants, rights or privileges, pre-emptive or contractual, to acquire any shares of the capital stock of the Company.

5.6 Financial Statements. The Financial Statements and the Interim Financial Statements which have been presented by Seller to Buyer are true, complete and correct and have been prepared in accordance with generally accepted accounting principles consistently followed throughout the periods indicated. These Statements present fairly the financial position of the Company as of the dates indicated and the results of operations for the periods then ended.

5.7 Liabilities. To the best of Seller's knowledge, except as and to the extent reflected or reserved against in the Company statements, or otherwise disclosed herein, (i) the Company had no material Liabilities or Obligations, and (ii) as of the date of Closing, the Company will not be subject to, and will not have, any Liabilities or Obligations which in the aggregate are material, except as either disclosed in the Interim Statements or as may have arisen in the ordinary course of business of the Company since the date of said Balance Sheet, none of which newly arisen Liabilities or Obligations shall have a material adverse effect upon the Company or its organization, business, properties or financial condition.

5.8 No Violation. Neither the execution and delivery of this Agreement nor compliance with the terms and provisions of this Agreement by Seller or the Company, will: (i) conflict with or result in a breach or violation of any of the terms, conditions or provisions of the articles of incorporation or bylaws of the Company or of the terms and provisions of any indenture or other agreement to which Seller or the Company may be a party or to which any of them may be bound or to which any of the may be subject, or any judgment, order, decree, ruling of any court or governmental authority or any injunction to which either of them is subject.

5.9 Contracts. As used herein "contracts" means any contract, agreement, or understanding, including but not limited to instruments or evidences of indebtedness, leases and licenses. Except as listed in Exhibit _____, the Company is not a party to any written or oral contracts:

(a) for the employment of any officer, director, consultant, or employee;

(b) with any labor union;

(c) for the purchase of any materials or supplies or for the sale of any product or service;

(d) relating to any licenses, distributorships, representatives or leases;

(e) relating to any bonus, pension or profit sharing plan;

(f) if not referenced above which are material to the Company.

5.10 Insurance. As of the Closing Date, The Company will carry the appropriate insurance against loss by fire casualty and other such losses as may be customary for the type of business operated and such insurance policies will be turned over to Buyer at Closing Date.

5.11 Litigation. There are no claims, actions, suits, proceedings or investigations pending or threatened against or affecting the Seller or the Company, at law or in equity or admiralty or before or by and federal, state, municipal or other governmental department, commission, board, agency or instrumentality, nor has any such action been pending during the 12 month period preceding the date of this Agreement; and Seller or the Company are not operating under or subject to, or in default with respect to any order, writ, injunction or decree of any court or federal or other governmental department or other instrumentality.

5.12 Compliance With Laws. To the best of Seller's knowledge the company has complied with all laws, regulations and orders including, but not limited to, OSHA, EEOA, and EPA or any similar or equivalent state legislation or rule applicable to its business in any material aspect. All permits, licenses and authorizations required by such regulatory bodies have been obtained and are in effect for the Company.

5.13 No Conflict Of Interest. Except for the normal rights of a stockholder, officer or director, as the case may be, (a) no stockholder, director, officer or employee of the Company has any interest in any property, real or personal, tangible or intangible necessary for or used in the business of the Company; and (b) no stockholder, director, officer or employee has an interest, direct or indirect, in any person or entity which (i) competes with the Company, or, (ii) is a party to any contract, oral or written, with the Company.

5.14 Accounts Receivable. The Company's financial statements and interim statements accurately and fairly reflect the amount of the trade receivables of the Company as of the date of such statements, in accordance with generally accepted accounting principles consistently applied. All trade accounts receivable arise out of sales occurring in the ordinary course of business and Seller has no reason to believe that any person obligated upon such accounts has any right of offset to payment thereof.

5.15 Inventory. The inventory of the Company as reflected on the most recent Interim Statements consists of items of a quality and quantity usable or salable in the normal course of business and which are not obsolete or unusable. Such inventory is valued at the lower of cost or market in accordance with generally accepted accounting principles.

5.16 Intellectual Property. All licenses, trademarks, copyrights, patents, etc. and all other such Intellectual property belonging to or used by the Company in its ordinary course of business are listed in Exhibit _____ attached hereto.

5.17 Labor Controversies. There are no controversies pending or threatened between the Company and any union or any employee. The Company is not subject to any threatened strikes or work stoppages or any organizational efforts by any union or collective bargaining unit not currently representing the employees of the Company.

5.18 Pension and Profit Sharing Plans. The Seller has delivered to Buyer copies of all pension and profit sharing plans or programs and has included in such delivery the most recent Internal Revenue Service determination letter issued in respect of each such plan or program together with all pertinent trustee reports and tax returns for such plans or programs.

5.19 Certain Tax Matters. No election has been made under Section 341 (f) of the Internal Revenue Code to treat the Company as a "consenting corporation" nor is the Company a "personal holding company" as defined under Section 542 of the Code.

5.20 Securities Matters. The shares of the Company are not required to be registered under provisions of Section 5 of the Securities Act of 1933 or any applicable state securities law.

5.21 Conduct of Business. Since the last Interim Statements and until the Closing Date the Company has not undertaken to enact any transactions not in the ordinary course of business other than those transactions which have been listed on Exhibit_____.

5.22 Material Change. Since the date of the last Interim Statement, there have been no adverse changes of a material nature in the condition of the Company, financial or otherwise that is not disclosed in Exhibit_____.

5.23 Tax Returns. The Company has made timely filings of all required Federal and State tax returns. There are no claims pending against the Company for unpaid or disputed tax liabilities and the last year which has been audited by the Internal Revenue Service is 19XX and by the State 19XX.

5.24 Disclosure. No representation or warranty made by the Seller herein contains any untrue statement of a material fact or omits to state a material fact necessary to make such representation or warranty not misleading.

ARTICLE VI

REPRESENTATIONS AND WARRANTIES BY BUYER

Buyer represents and warrants to Seller that the following statements are true and correct on the Closing Date:

6.1 Organization and Standing. Buyer is a corporation duly organized, existing and in good standing under the laws of the State of _____.

6.2 Breach of Statute or Contract: Required Consents. Neither the execution and delivery of this Agreement nor compliance with the terms and provisions of this Agreement by Buyer will: (i) conflict with or result in a breach or violation of any of the terms, conditions or provisions of the articles of incorporation or bylaws of the Buyer or any judgment, order, decree or ruling or any court or governmental authority or of any contract or commitment of which Buyer is a party which is material to the operations or conduct of business of the Buyer; or (ii) require the affirmative consent or approval of any nongovernmental third party (except Buyer's shareholders).

Buyer is not in violation of any applicable law, order, rule or regulation promulgated or judgment entered by any federal or state court or governmental authority relating to the operation or conduct of the business of Buyer which might impair the consummation or the transaction contemplated hereby.

6.3 Litigation. Buyer is not a party to or subject to any legal, administrative, arbitration, investigation proceeding or controversy nor are any such actions threatened which might materially affect the financial condition of Buyer.

6.4 Authority. Buyer has full power and authority to enter into this Agreement and to carry out the transactions contemplated hereby, and all corporate and other proceedings required to be taken by Buyer in connection with this Agreement have been duly and validly taken. This Agreement constitutes a valid and binding obligation of Buyer and is enforceable in accordance with its terms.

ARTICLE VII

CONDITIONS PRECEDENT OF BUYER

The obligations of Buyer hereunder are subject to the conditions that:

7.1 Representations and Warranties True. The representations and warranties of Seller contained in this Agreement shall be true on the Closing Date.

7.2 Compliance With The Agreement. Seller shall have performed and complied with all agreements and conditions required by this Agreement to be performed or complied with by him prior to or on Closing Date.

7.3 Opinion of Company's Counsel. Buyer shall have received an opinion of counsel to the Company and Seller, dated the Closing Date in the form of Exhibit
_____ .

7.4 Injunction. On the Closing Date there shall be no effective injunction, writ, restraining order or any order of any kind issued by a court or competent jurisdiction directing that the transaction contemplated herein shall not be consummated as herein provided.

7.5 Casualty. Neither the business of the Company nor any of its property shall have been affected in any material way, prior to Closing Date, by any flood, fire, accident or other casualty or act of God or the public enemy.

7.6 Adverse Development. Between the date of the last Interim Statements and the Closing Date there shall have been no material adverse developments which materially affect the value of the business or the assets or the goodwill of the Company.

7.7 Deliveries. On or before the Closing Date Seller shall have delivered to Buyer all of the materials specified herein.

7.8 Financing. Buyer shall have obtained financing for the transaction from his own sources satisfactory to the Buyer.

ARTICLE VIII

CONDITIONS PRECEDENT OF THE SELLER

The obligations of Seller hereunder are subject to the conditions that:

8.1 Representations and Warranties True. The representations and warranties of Buyer contained in this Agreement shall be true on the Closing Date.

8.2 Compliance With The Agreement. Buyer shall have performed and complied with all agreements and conditions required by this Agreement to be performed or complied with by him prior to or on Closing Date.

8.3 Opinion of Company's Counsel. Seller shall have received an opinion of counsel to the Buyer, dated the Closing Date in the form of Exhibit
_____ .

8.4 Injunction. On the Closing Date there shall be no effective injunction, writ, restraining order or any order of any kind issued by a court or competent jurisdiction directing that the transaction contemplated herein shall not be consummated as herein provided.

8.5 Payment. Payment shall be made as provided herein.

8.6 Deliveries. On or before the Closing Date Buyer shall have delivered to Seller all of the following documents: (i) Certified Articles of Incorporation of Buyer; (ii) Copies of Buyer's Bylaws certified by Buyer's Secretary; (iii) Certificate of Good Standing; (iv) all other deliveries required hereunder.

ARTICLE IX

INDEMNIFICATION

9.1 By Seller. Seller hereby agrees, notwithstanding the Closing, the delivery of instruments of conveyance, and regardless of any investigation at any time made by or on behalf of any party hereto or of any information any party hereto may have in respect thereof, he will save and hold Buyer and the Company harmless from and against any damage, liability, loss or deficiency arising out of or resulting from and will pay to Buyer and the Company the amount of damages suffered thereby together with any amount which they or any of them may pay or become obligated to pay on account of:

(a) the breach of any warranty or representation by Seller herein or any misstatement of a fact or facts herein made by the Seller;

(b) the failure by Seller to state or disclose a material fact herein necessary to make the facts herein stated or disclosed not misleading;

(c) any failure of the Seller, the Company or its officers or directors to perform or observe any term, provision, covenant or condition hereunder on the part of any of them to be performed or observed, or;

(d) any act performed, transaction entered into, or state of facts suffered to exist by Seller or the Company or its officers or directors in violation of the terms of this Agreement.

9.2 By Buyer. Buyer hereby agrees, notwithstanding the Closing, the delivery of instruments of conveyance, and regardless of any investigation at any time made by or on behalf of any party hereto or of any information any party hereto may have in respect thereof, he will save and hold Seller harmless from and against any damage, liability, loss or deficiency arising out of or resulting from and will pay to Seller the amount of damages suffered thereby together with any amount which he may pay or become obligated to pay on account of:

(a) the breach of any warranty or representation by Buyer herein or any misstatement of a fact or facts herein made by the Buyer;

(b) the failure by Buyer to state or disclose a material fact herein necessary to make the facts herein stated or disclosed not misleading;

(c) any failure of the Buyer, to perform or observe any term, provision, covenant or condition hereunder to be performed or observed, or;

(d) any act performed, transaction entered into, or state of facts suffered to exist by Buyer in violation of the terms of this Agreement.

ARTICLE X

NATURE AND SURVIVAL OF REPRESENTATIONS

All statements contained in any certificate delivered by or on behalf of Seller or Buyer pursuant to this Agreement or in connection with the transactions contemplated hereby shall be deemed representations and warranties by Seller and Buyer hereunder. All representations and warranties and agreements made by Seller or Buyer in this Agreement or pursuant hereto shall survive the Closing hereunder.

ARTICLE XI

NOTICES

All notices, requests, demands, and other communications hereunder shall be in writing and shall be deemed to have been duly given if delivered or mailed first class postage prepaid to the following addresses:

(a) To Seller:

(Seller's address)

(b) To Buyer:

(Buyer's address)

or to such other address or to such other person as Buyer and Seller shall have last designated by notice to the other.

ARTICLE XII

MODIFICATION

The Agreement contains the entire agreement between the parties hereto with respect to the transactions contemplated herein and shall not be modified or amended except by an instrument in writing signed by or on behalf of all of the parties hereto.

ARTICLE XIII

EXPENSES

Each of the parties hereto shall pay their own expenses in connection herewith including but not limited to fees for legal, accounting, consulting and other services.

ARTICLE XIV

ASSIGNMENT

This Agreement shall not be assignable by either party hereto without the prior written consent of the other party.

ARTICLE XV

LAW TO GOVERN

This Agreement shall be governed by and construed and enforced in accordance with the laws of the State of _____.

IN WITNESS WHEREOF, the parties hereto have duly executed this Agreement as of the date first above written.

SELLER   BUYER
_____   By_____
                                          Its_____

Appendix H

Sample
Buy-Back Agreement Between
Partners or Shareholders
In a Close Corporation

THIS AGREEMENT, entered into this _____day of _____, 19XX, between (name of shareholder) ("Jones") and (name of second shareholder) ("Smith"), hereinafter referred to as Shareholder or collectively as Shareholders;

WITNESSETH:

WHEREAS, XYZ Corp., a Delaware corporation ("Corporation") has authorized and outstanding shares of no par value Common Stock ("Stock"); and,

WHEREAS, the Shareholders are interested in the management of the business of the Corporation and are respectively the owners of the Stock set forth below in Section 1.1; and,

WHEREAS, the parties hereto mutually desire to make provision for the purchase and sale of the Stock upon the occurrence of certain significant events; and to make provision for other significant events involving the transfer and ownership of the Stock;

NOW THEREFORE, the Shareholders mutually hereby agree:

ARTICLE I
STOCK SUBJECT TO AGREEMENT

1.1 Stock Subject To This Agreement. The following number of shares of Stock are presently held by the Shareholders:

Shareholder	Shares
Jones	100
Smith	100

The terms of this agreement shall apply to all Stock presently held by the Share-holders and any additional Stock acquired by a Shareholder during his lifetime in his own behalf, or by his estate after his death, whether by purchase, Stock dividend or otherwise. It is contemplated that any such additional Stock will be endorsed in accordance with Section 1.2 hereof and identified by a written memorandum executed by the parties and attached hereto, but failure so to endorse and include the additional Stock in a memorandum shall not remove such Stock from the terms of this Agreement.

1.2 Endorsement of Stock Certificates. Each Stock certificate representing shares of Stock now held or hereafter acquired by the Shareholders shall be endorsed substantially as follows:

> "The shares represented by this certificate are subject to the provisions of the Agreement to Purchase Corporate Stock, dated _____, which Agreement is available for inspection at the principal office of the Corporation."

Provided, however, that failure so to endorse any of the Shareholders' Stock certificates shall not invalidate this Agreement. The Corporation shall keep a copy of this Agreement available for inspection by all properly interested parties at the principal office.

1.3 Use of Stock as Collateral. The Shareholders have the right to pledge Stock owned by them as Collateral security for personal indebtedness, even though the certificate of such Stock is endorsed as provided in Section 1.2, but any Stock so pledged shall remain subject to the terms of this Agreement. The mere pledge of Stock shall not be an event which provides the Shareholder the option to purchase or sell Stock pursuant to Article 2 of this Agreement.

1.4 Rights of the Shareholders. The Stock owned by the respective Shareholders subject to this Agreement shall be voted by them, and upon the death of a Shareholder by the legal representative of his estate, until purchase of his Stock pursuant to this Agreement or other permitted transfer or disposition, as the case may be. Any dividends payable on the Stock shall be paid to the respective Shareholders or their respective legal representatives, as the case may be.

ARTICLE II

PURCHASE AND SALE OF STOCK

2.1 Restrictions of Lifetime Transfers of Stock. (a) A Shareholder shall not, during his lifetime, sell, assign, give, or otherwise transfer or dispose of any shares of Stock without first giving written notice to the non-transferring Shareholder of such intention to sell or make disposition thereof, which notice shall state the Stock proposed to be disposed of, the amount of the consideration offered, if any, and the name of the prospective purchaser or assignee. The date the non-transferring Shareholder receives such notice shall be the Transfer Notice Date. The nontransferring Shareholder may, at his option, purchase all, but not part, of the shares of Stock offered in such notice for a purchase price which is the lower of (i) the price offered as contained in such notice, or (ii) $XXX,XXX, which amount shall be payable within 90 days of the Transfer Notice Date.

2.2 Upon Death. Upon the death of a Shareholder, the Corporation shall purchase all of the shares of Stock owned by the deceased Shareholder on the date of his death for $1,000,000, payable within 30 days of receipt of the proceeds of a $1,000,000 life insurance policy on the life of the deceased Shareholder.

ARTICLE III

INDEMNIFICATION

3.1 Indemnity. In the event the Stock of a Shareholder is purchase and the Shareholder no longer owns the Stock, the Purchasing Shareholder agrees to assume all obligations of the Selling Shareholder relating to the Selling Shareholder's personal guarantee of certain debt of the Corporation ("Guarantee") and to indemnify and save the Selling Shareholder harmless from any liability on account of the Guarantee. This Section 3.1 is not intended, however, to require the purchasing Shareholder to cause the release of the selling Shareholder from his commitment under the Guarantee.

ARTICLE IV

AMENDMENT AND TERMINATION

4.1 Amendment. This Agreement may be amended at any time by written instrument executed by the Shareholders.

4.2 Termination. Notwithstanding any other terms or provisions of this Agreement, this Agreement shall terminate:

(a) Upon the written agreement of the Shareholders.

(b) With respect to any particular Shareholder, upon the disposition by the Shareholder, in accordance with this Agreement, or all of his Stock.

(c) With respect to any Stock transferred as permitted pursuant to Section 2.1, but only with respect to the Stock so transferred.

Provided, however, that regardless of the termination of the Agreement, the rights and obligations of the parties and their successors and assigns shall continue beyond the termination.

ARTICLE V

MISCELLANEOUS PROVISIONS

5.1 Scope of Agreement. This Agreement shall be binding upon and be enforceable by the parties hereto and their respective heirs, legal representatives, successors and assigns, who are obligated to take any action which may be necessary or proper to carry out the purpose and intent hereof; provided, however, that the rights of the Shareholders hereunder are personal to them, their families and representatives and, without the written consent of the parties hereto, or as specifically provided herein, may not be assigned to or be enforceable by any assignee, transferee or other present or future Shareholder of the Corporation.

5.2 Severability. Any provision of this Agreement which is prohibited or held unenforceable by final order of any court or competent jurisdiction shall, within such jurisdiction, be ineffective to the extent of such order without invalidating the remaining provisions of this Agreement or affecting the validity or enforceability of such provision in any other jurisdiction.

5.3 Effective Date. This Agreement is effective as of the day and year first above written.

5.4 Articles and Bylaws of the Corporation. All provisions of the Articles of Incorporation and Bylaws of the Corporation shall remain in full force and effect as to the Shareholders' Stock except to the extent inconsistent with the express provisions of this Agreement, in which event the provisions of this Agreement shall control. The Shareholders agree to cause the Corporation to waive its rights, relating to its "first refusal" option under the Eighth Article of the Corporation's Certificate of Incorporation in the event of an event giving rise to the conditions under Section 2.1 hereof.

5.5 Arbitration. Any dispute arising out of or relating to this Agreement or the breach thereof shall be discussed between the parties hereto in good faith effort to arrive at a mutual settlement of any such controversy. If, notwithstanding, such dispute cannot be thus resolved within a period of 30 days, any party may submit the same for arbitration in the City of Wilmington, State of Delaware, to an arbitrator selected from the panel of the American Arbitration Association in accordance with its rules and regulations. The award shall be made by the decision of the arbitrator and judgment upon the award rendered by the arbitrator may be entered in any court having jurisdiction thereof.

5.6 Notices. All notice herein provided for, if mailed rather than delivered, shall be mailed by certified or registered mail with return receipt requested, addressed to the addressee at his or its last know address.

5.7 Governing Law. This Agreement shall be governed by and construed and enforced in accordance with the laws of the State of Delaware.

IN WITNESS WHEREOF, the Shareholders have executed this Agreement in the manner appropriate to each, the day and year first written above.

_____

Shareholder "Jones"

_____

Shareholder "Smith"

Bibliography

A Checklist Guide to Successful Acquisitions, Victor Harold, Pilot Books, 1983

Acquisitions, Mergers, Sales, Buyouts & Takeovers: A Handbook With Forms, Charles A. Sharf, et.al., Prentice-Hall, 1985

An Insider's Guide to the Merger & Acquisitions Business, George R. Hornig, Ballinger Publications, 1988

Buying and Selling a Business, Robert F. Klueger, Wiley & Sons, 1988

Buying and Selling a Small Business, Verne A. Bunn, Arno Press, 1979

Buying and Selling a Small Business, Michael M. Coltman, ISC Press, 1983

Buying, Selling & Merging Businesses, Jere D. McGaffey, American Law Institute, 1979

Buying, Selling, Starting a Business, Ray L. Gustafson, GHC Press, 1982

Everything You Always Wanted to Know About Mergers, Acquisitions and Divestitures But Didn't Know Whom to Ask, Roger Kuppinger, R. Kuppinger, 1986

Guide to International Venture Capital, The Editors of Venture Magazine, Simon & Schuster, 1985

How to Buy a Business with Someone Else's Money: The ABC's of Leveraged Buyouts, Lionel Harris, Times Books, 1987

How to Buy a Small Business, Maxwell J. Margold, Pilot Books, 1986

How to Profitably Sell or Buy a Company or Business, F.Gordon Douglas, Van Nostrand Reinhold Co., 1981

Leveraged Buyouts, Stephen C. Diamond, Dow Jones-Irwin, 1985

Make It Yours: How to Own Your Own Business, Louis Mucciolo, Wiley & Sons, 1987

Mergers & Acquisitions, Terrence E. Cooke, Basil Blackwell Press, 1986

Mergers & Acquisitions: Will You Overpay?, Joseph H. Marren, Dow Jones-Irwin, 1985

Negotiating the Purchase or Sale of a Business, James C. Comisky, PSI Research, 1986

Profitable Acquisitions: Guidelines for Buying and Selling Companies for Businessmen and Financiers, Thomas H. Hopkins, McTaggart Press, 1984

Starting on a Shoestring: Building a Business Without a Bankroll, Arnold S. Goldstein, Wiley & Sons, 1984

The Arthur Young Management Guide to Acquisitions and Mergers, Robert M. Feerick, Wiley & Sons, 1988

The Complete Guide to a Successful Leveraged Buyout, Allen Michel & Israel Shaked, Dow Jones-Irwin, 1987

The Complete Guide to Buying and Selling a Business, Arnold S. Goldstein, New American Library, 1986

The Mergers and Acquisitions Handbook, M. Rock, McGraw-Hill, 1987

Valuation of Privately Owned Business, Steven M. Reisinger, Acquisition Planning, Inc., 1981

What You Should Know About Acquisitions & Mergers, Milton B. Burnstein, Oceana Press, 1973

When You Buy or Sell a Company, Paul B. Baron, Center for Business Information, 1986

Also by Lawrence W. Tuller:

Getting Out: A Step By Step Guide to Selling a Business or Professional Practice, Lawrence W. Tuller, TAB Books, 1990

The Battle-Weary Executive: A Blueprint for New Beginnings, Lawrence W. Tuller, Dow Jones-Irwin, 1990

Index